Proving the Value of Meetings and Events: How and Why to Measure ROI

Jack J. Phillips
Monica Myhill
James B. McDonough

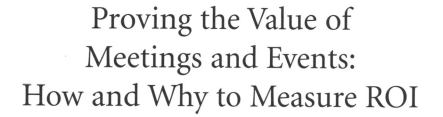

ROI Institute, Inc.
P.O. Box 380673
Birmingham, AL 35238-0673

www.roiinstitute.net

MEETING PROFESSIONALS INTERNATIONAL

Meeting Professionals International
3030 Lyndon B. Johnson Freeway,
Suite 1700
Dallas, TX 75234-2759
www.mpiweb.org

ROI INSTITUTE™

MEETING PROFESSIONALS INTERNATIONAL

Special thanks go to these sponsors.

ROI INSTITUTE™

Contents

Preface

No publication is the work of the authors or editors alone, and this book is no exception. The ROI Methodology described in detail throughout the book is the reflection of the efforts of many individuals who have worked with this process to make it useable, successful, and sustainable. For more than a decade—through the ROI Institute—hundreds of clients have used this methodology and refined it. To these clients, we owe a tremendous debt of gratitude.

We offer a special thanks to those individuals who provided case studies for this book. Each case represents much work and extra effort on the part of these professionals. They fully recognize their obligation to show the value of the meetings and events to their team and clients. They also recognize an obligation to help this industry have more accountability. The case authors approached this challenge with much responsiveness and enthusiasm. Thank you very much for such first-rate contributions.

While these are excellent case studies, the most surprising feedback that we received from dozens of other individuals is that they are currently working on projects they would like to submit to us later. There are many works in progress within this industry. We look forward to publishing case studies from these individuals in the future.

The first part of each chapter provides information about evaluation at a particular level. This is followed by a case study indicating how that particular issue was addressed by at least one organization. Presenting both perspectives has made this book much longer than we initially envisioned, but we hope it becomes a great reference guide as it shows how to bring more accountability to your meetings with more examples for each level of data.

Most of these case authors have attended one or more MPI-sponsored educational opportunities to learn about ROI. These individuals are eager to help this industry learn more about proving the value of meetings and events. They recognize that this is the only way to show their organizations' senior leadership that meetings and events do make a difference and, ultimately, earn a seat at the table.

Acknowledgements

From Jack Phillips...

I particularly appreciate the support from MPI for implementing the ROI Methodology in the meetings and events industry. This is a bold, but necessary, step to increase accountability for meetings and events. The entire MPI staff, as well as its board, has been supportive of this effort. Much appreciation goes to Susan Magee, Director, Professional Development; Sandra Riggins, Chief of Staff; and Mark Andrew, Chairman of the Board. They all see the vital need for having this publication. The Marketing Team of Edjuan Bailey and Paula Norse has created an excellent promotion plan for ROI and this book.

Much appreciation goes to Gaylord and its team for providing funding for many of the ROI projects and part of the funding for this book. Mike Mason, Vice President of Sales for Gaylord, is an advocate for this methodology and sees the need for it in our industry. Thanks, Mike, for all your great support.

At the ROI Institute special thanks goes to Lori Ditoro, Managing Editor, for her efforts to edit this case book. She went beyond the call of duty to make this book a reality. She was joined late in the project by Michelle Segrest, Publications Manager, and together they made an outstanding editorial team. Jaime Beard, Crystal Langford, and Katherine Horton also provided input, assistance, support, and sacrifices to complete this book on time. As always, I owe much support and a special thanks to Patti Phillips, co-founder and CEO of the ROI Institute. Although Patti's name does not appear on this book cover, she helped develop much of its content and also helped with the editing processes. She is truly a professional who understands this methodology and how it can help this industry.

From Monica Myhill...

I feel honored to have been given the opportunity to work with the many exemplary meeting industry professionals who submitted case studies for this book. If it weren't for them and their willingness to share their experiences, this book would not be possible. I must also thank Jack Phillips for his continued support and guidance. Jack has been a mentor to me and many others in their pursuit of evaluation and measurement. Last, but definitely not least, I need to thank Stuart, Morgan, and Max for their smiles, hugs, laughter, and willingness to eat yet another frozen pizza for dinner.

About the Editors

Jack J. Phillips, Ph.D.

As a world-renowned expert on accountability, measurement, and evaluation, Dr. Phillips provides consulting services for Fortune 500 companies and major global organizations. The author or editor of more than fifty books, Dr. Phillips conducts workshops and conference presentations throughout the world.

Books most recently authored by Dr. Phillips include *Show Me the Money*, Berrett-Koehler, 2007; *How to Build a Successful Consulting Practice*, McGraw-Hill, 2006; *Investing in Your Company's Human Capital: Strategies to Avoid Spending Too Much or Too Little*, Amacom 2005; *Proving the Value of HR: How and Why to Measure ROI*, SHRM 2005.

He is Chairman of the ROI Institute, Inc., and can be reached at 205.678.8101, or by e-mail at jack@roiinstitute.net.

Monica Myhill, CMP

Monica Myhill, CMP, serves as President of Meeting Returns, an organization partnering with the ROI Institute, Inc., to provide return on investment (ROI) impact and evaluation studies for meetings and events through the use of the ROI Methodology developed by Dr. Jack J. Phillips. She is well-known as a meeting industry ROI and evaluation expert, consultant, industry speaker, and author. Ms. Myhill has more than twelve years of experience in developing, marketing, managing and evaluating education programs, conferences, and special events in North America and Europe. She can be contacted by phone at 303.220.1920 or by email at Monica@meetingreturms.com.

James B. McDonough

During his twenty years with Fusion, Jamie McDonough has designed and produced numerous meetings, conferences, and instructional experiences. His clients include Price Waterhouse Coopers, Bausch & Lomb, American Society for Training and Development (ASTD), Eastman Kodak, and the Project Management Institute. He also produced the White House Conference on Travel & Tourism.

A member of Meeting Professionals International (MPI) since 1992, Mr. McDonough has had the honor of producing the Opening General Session at MPI's World Education Congresses and Professional Education Conferences since 1993. In addition, he has produced two Opening General Sessions at MPI's Professional Education Congress-Europe programs.

Mr. McDonough has also produced the MPI Foundation/Marriott Program

"Maximizing Your ROI," the first ROI Summit at the 2004 MPI World Education Congress, the 2005 ROI Platinum program. He is currently chair of the MPI International Chapter Leaders Committee.

A Message from the CEO

This book is the result of many hours, days, weeks and, quite literally, years of work. It is a tribute to those in the meeting and event profession who have a passion for making a positive change, securing a "seat at the table," and demonstrating the strategic value of meetings.

Special thanks go to all those who saw that this industry could be a profession—from the volunteers and staff at the MPI Foundation, MPI, and our colleagues at Fusion Productions who have championed the cause since 1994—to the MPI chapters, the "first ROI Certification class," The ROI Institute and, of course, the valued sponsors over the years.

The ROI effort is another fine example of returning value to our members. MPI is pleased to play a continuing part in making our members successful business partners within their organizations.

Bruce MacMillan, CA
President & CEO
Meeting Professionals International

Foreward

John Caparella
Gaylord Hotels

By definition, the word 'value' is described as *a fair return or equivalent in goods, services, or money for something exchanged*. In the meetings and events industry, proving this value has been an elusive task. And as the industry becomes more expensive at almost $150 billion per year in the United States, determining a way to do this has become increasingly important.

The demand for basic ROI measurement systems in our industry became more apparent after 9/11, when meeting and events were among the first massive cutbacks to be made. Although it was widely assumed that meetings and events delivered value when properly designed and conducted, there was no definitive way to prove or measure this. And decision-makers have even been questioning if there is any value to having formal meetings and events. Now, more than ever, it is imperative that there be a method by which planners can demonstrate the value of their efforts.

At Gaylord Hotels, we strive to achieve a level of service that demonstrates our commitment to the customer. We design facilities specific to the needs of meeting, convention and event groups, and we custom-tailor programs every day to make the experience for the planner seamless. But our clients needed more, in the form of a concrete way to show that their dollars were well-spent so they could provide the justification to keep doing what they do.

Faced with this challenge, we embarked on a mission to find a way to equip this group with a methodology and a set of guidelines by which they could monitor and thereby calculate the value of their meetings and events. Our solution was to fund a three-year effort by MPI to develop an ROI measurement strategy, which is fully described in this book, *Proving the Value of Meetings and Events*. It is a source of cutting-edge information that professional meeting planners and event organizers can use to address the critical ROI issue.

Determining increased accountability for meetings and events can be a long and tedious process. Until now, professional planners have not been equipped with this capability. We are very proud to have contributed to this book, which shows how a disciplined, rigorous approach can be applied, yet managed in a way that it does not drain the resources or consume the precious time of the meetings and events staff.

We hope that you will enjoy the information here and learn from these case studies. We are pleased to be a part of bringing this to you. Should you have any questions or concerns, please direct them to MPI, the ROI Institute, or me here at Gaylord Hotels.

John Caparella
Executive Vice President and
Chief Operating Officer
Gaylord Hotels

Introduction

MPI and ROI—A Brief History

In 1994, "Friends" debuted on TV and the Internet became accessible to millions in North America. The economy was good. Technology "dot.coms" were just beginning their rise.

The meeting industry was growing, with major suppliers recognizing the power and influence of their meeting planning colleagues. Forward-thinking leaders at MPI lobbied for a major change in the organization. Meeting Planners International would become Meeting Professionals International, reflecting the partnership of planners and suppliers as well as the idea that the meeting industry can be a profession.

Although the name change was a historic moment, a name does not make a profession. There were still many perceptions to overcome. The perception that meeting planners were logistics experts or just "party planners" and "coffee cup counters" was still prevalent.

The meetings business was strong—seemingly unstoppable. Meetings were "feelgood" events—a time to cheer on new products or participate in extravagant awards dinners with open bars and elaborate menus. The economy was healthy. For a planner, as long as the budget was met, there were no worries.

The visionaries at the MPI Foundation had another view. . . change for the industry was imminent and would be dramatic. The MPI Foundation, working with Fusion Productions, identified a "Business Case for Change," which included change drivers and areas where these changes would impact the meetings industry:

- Technology will change the way we do business and impact our social fabric. People will be able to do things faster using technology. They will be able to produce products more cost effectively, with less labor and improved quality.
- Response time will decrease and functions will change or be removed. The future will hold new education delivery methods with programs distributed on the Web. Online conference registration, hotel/airline reservations, and RFPs will be the norm.
- Global competition will be opened through technology. People will not need years of experience, costly infrastructure, and local experience to get a foothold and sell.
- Outsourcing will become a real threat.

- Faster, Better, Cheaper: All our organizations will need to increase production speed for new products and services, and give better value and at a higher level of quality—or someone else will.
- Demands for time and productivity will increase exponentially.
- Mergers and Acquisitions: To get faster, better and cheaper, an organization may develop a better product or service, a cheaper process, or open a new global market. But the research and development cycle is long. The alternatives are to either merge or acquire. In all practicality, a merger is always an acquisition.
- Organizational changes will occur at a constant pace. Since mergers and acquisitions are all about leveraging costs, duplicative functions will be eliminated.
- Practically speaking, the elimination of functions means long-standing relationships and support mechanisms may be gone and functions that do not have data to support their contributions will be eliminated, as well.
- Reengineering: In the accelerated marketplace, organizations are going to look at all processes, supply chains, inventories, etc., and identify ways to streamline, reduce costs, and increase efficiencies. They are also going to scrutinize functions that do not directly add value for their customers, such as meetings, travel, training, printing, etc.
- Maximize all resources, do more with less, eliminate functions that do not add value to the customer, downsizing/rightsizing.
- Focus on Measurement: Given the focus on process analysis, measurement will become critical to evaluating the value of all operations within an organization.
- Demonstrating value to the organization's goals.

In the future, planners, once considered strictly logistics experts, will be held accountable for much more, such as education delivery, finance, marketing, and measurement. Planners will not necessarily be the "doers" but the facilitators of the process. Although not articulated as such, they will need to position themselves as a strategic resource able to facilitate the processes needed to implement strategies and reach global goals across an enterprise. They will need to be regarded as a member of the management team.

Maximizing Your ROI: Return on Investment

The MPI Foundation proposed a project to create a training program for meeting professionals to learn how to illustrate the value of meetings to their customers/employers. The logic followed that if senior executives understood the value of the meeting or conference to the organization's goals, then they would continue to fund meetings, and the planner would become more of a strategic team member.

Working with Fusion Productions, in 1995 the MPI Foundation launched the first videotape training program for the meetings industry on the topic of the value of meetings at the Professional Education Conference-North America in Vancouver, British Columbia, and Canada. Designed to be an "awareness" program, it incorporated interviews with planners who were successful at measuring the results of meetings and demonstrating to stakeholders the value that the meeting provided their organization. Also included were study guides and forms to begin the process.

At the heart of this program is the "your ROI" concept. You, the planner, are critical to the entire process. You drive the communication process. You facilitate the stakeholder discussions. You bring together the experts necessary to gain the data you need to analyze the results.

Sounds like a lot of work. However, it's really not much different than bringing together the hotel team to provide a quality experience, coordinating 600 individual air schedules, or ensuring that all the specific dietary needs are properly and/safely addressed.

Where does one start?

Know your organization, know how the meeting supports the organization, and know how you and your meeting will be measured.

- **Environmental scan**: What are your organization's strategic goals? Not just the vision or mission statement, but what are the goals as defined by the board and/or senior leadership?
- **Purpose**: How will this meeting support the achievement of these goals?
- **Success**: What does "it" look like, and how will it be measured?

During a pre-conference planning meeting and after (lengthy) discussion of these three areas, a Fusion client's CEO said, "This has been the single best exercise I've been a part of for the last six months. This discussion has got me thinking in new ways about our organization." The credit went to the planner who facilitated the discussion, which involved the CEO and several global region presidents . . . and the credibility of that planner went "through the roof."

The process outlined in the program was tested with an expert panel of planners from NEC Germany, Microsoft, Tandem Computers, National Black MBA Association, and the International Society for Optical Engineering.

The Basic Process

1. Identify the meeting stakeholders, their needs/wants and desired meeting outcomes.
2. Establish measurable objectives based on the outcomes desired by the stakeholders.
3. Design measurement tools based on the objectives.
4. Design, develop, and deliver content and a meeting experience that supports the objectives.
5. Demonstrate "your ROI" by analyzing the data and reporting results back to all stakeholders.

Over the next few years, the ROI discussion began to ramp up. Education sessions were held at MPI chapters and global conferences. The trade magazines began to run articles on ROI and the ROI program. The term quickly became the "buzz-word" for the industry.

The message was clear: As you validate the time and expense for the meeting, you also validate your role in facilitating that process. Change impacts everything we do. If we resist, we only become frustrated and obsolete. Accept a philosophy that embraces life-long learning… open up to new experiences, and the results will be overpowering.

Additional workshop sessions were developed by Fusion such as "ROI Two," "Strategic ROI," and the MPI ROI E-Learning program.

At every session given, an informal poll was taken. While more than ninety percent of all planners stated that ROI was their number one issue, only sixty percent of meeting professionals were measuring anything. And only fifty percent of that group shared their findings with anyone outside their planning team. Everyone was in agreement that measurement was important, but the questions were still out there: "What do we measure?" and, even more important, "How do we measure?"

Measurement sounds like a job for the accountants, not planners A great deal of apprehension surrounded the process. Meeting professionals wanted tools, examples of measurement forms, etc.

Looking at the data, MPI Foundation discovered that although our initial objectives of awareness had been achieved and the need for ROI was high, without the tools the application was low. Again, working with Fusion, and with sponsorship by Gaylord Hotels, the MPI Foundation "Measurement Systems" project was born. The project was comprised of several steps.

1. Research and gather various measurement "tools" (i.e., surveys, evaluations, questionnaires) being used by MPI membership.

2. Identify meeting industry leaders to review the documents.
3. Identify measurement experts to review the documents.
4. Bring both groups together for a measurement conclave to debate and discuss the various tools and techniques.

Fusion brought in Jack Phillips, Ph.D., chairman of the ROI Institute, Inc., an organization with more than twenty years' experience in ROI Methodology for a variety of industries including the meeting-related industry of training and development.

Phillips electrified the group with his presentation and description of the ROI Methodology™. During the conclave, the group discussion evolved into several areas to be explored:

- Books (such as this one) on ROI for the meetings industry
- An MPI platinum program for the chapters
- An MPI ROI Summit—a standalone conference for meeting professionals

On behalf of MPI and with funding from Gaylord Hotels, in 2004 Fusion designed and produced the first-ever ROI Summit Conference held within the 2004 World Education Congress in Denver, Colorado. The Summit featured Jack Phillips, Ph.D., Marvin Lackey, and Christine Duffy. Presentations, recordings, transcripts, tools, and related articles were posted on a Summit Web site to serve as an ongoing resource for those who attended the Summit.

From the presentations and discussions at the Summit, an MPI Platinum program was created, and the MPI Foundation funded an ROI Methodology for Meeting Professionals program for all chapters in 2005.

Meetings and Events Industry— Why ROI Now: Gaining a Seat at the Table

Is meeting planning a business?

Consider other popular industries. The motion picture industry reports the worldwide box office at $23.24 billion in 2005. Major League Baseball teams gross just under $2 billion, and the National Football League teams just under $2.5 billion.

The meetings and events industry accounts for $122.3 billion in North America alone. You bet it's a business.

> "I need my people to think like business people and focus on the 'business of meetings'—not the meeting business."
>
> *CEO during the association CEO focus group 1993*

Focus on the business of meetings...

The impact and the effect of a changing business climate provided opportunities for meeting professionals to demonstrate the effectiveness and value for their meetings.

Recent trends include:
- Results oriented
- Program/process improvement
- Budget justification

Job security

Today it is critical for you as a meeting professional to not let the trends pass you by, but to take advantage of them.

How can you gain C-level access and a seat at the table? By being recognized for your relevance given the value you provide toward the goals of the organization.

When you sit with the executive team, you become instrumental to the strategic decision making and are able influence change. Our organizations are changing. The economy slump brought a new focus to the "bottom line." Technology has increased various meeting opportunities. CEOs want their planners to think in terms of the business of the meeting—NOT the meetings business.

Your role will change from an ancillary employee to a more active decision maker. The skills you use to manage your meeting supply chain are the same skills you will use to facilitate the communication process within your organization. As a meeting professional, you bring a unique competency to the table that the other executives do not possess. They don't have the fundamental understanding of human learning and performance and the importance of creating an environment that fosters human growth.

Speaking the language of business and focusing on business objectives is critical. ROI is a term our CEOs and CFOs understand. Not ROO, Return on Involvement, Return on Events, Return on Learning, Return on Meetings, etc.

Ask the tough questions: Does the meeting purpose directly relate to the goals and objectives of our organization? How does the meeting affect employee and organizational productivity? How is our meeting tied to our business strategies? How is it helping to achieve the organization's goals? The question we now have to ask is: "What is the problem you want to solve?" not, "What do you want to have for the awards dinner?"

Remember, you and your department are in competition for the attention and budgets of all the other departments within your organization, such as marketing, training, and sales.

So how can ROI measurement support your department's goals and ultimately the organization's goals?

- Show business contributions of selected meetings, events, training
- Earn respect of senior management
- Gain the confidence of clients
- Improve meeting processes
- Identify inefficient meetings that need to be redesigned or eliminated and
- Identify successful meetings, events, training

Certainly the benefits to implementing an ROI strategy for your meetings outweigh the barriers. This book addresses all of them.

The ROI Methodology™ can help demonstrate the strategic value of meetings with senior decision-making executives at corporations, associations and organizations. This methodology will assist us as we get to that C-level.

What are the CEOs telling us? CEOs are telling us that your work must be strategic, measurable, and linked to business goals.

CEOs are looking for improvements in the business—they are expecting better business performance—better results. They may express it differently, but it's there: employee engagement, shareholder value, stakeholder satisfaction, innovation, sales growth.

1. Deeply understand your organization's key strategies. If you think you already know them, be sure your understanding is the same as your senior leadership's understanding.
2. Measure the results. Those measures must be done in ways that are meaningful, outcome-based—not activity based—supporting the key performance indicators of your senior leadership. You must be connected to those indicators if you want to make a real difference. (And I know you do.)
3. Communicate those results. This is very effectively done through your newsletter or on the Intranet.

ROI: Why It Is Important Today?

There is little doubt that the initial premises for ROI have come to pass and the need to implement a formal model is more important than ever. Today we all readily accept the role of technology, global competition, and the resulting need for companies to reduce cost and downsize all functions (including meeting departments) to be competitive. Equally important today is the then-unforeseen role of government (read Sarbanes Oxley) which in large companies has created the need to document objectives, costs, and value using a consistent acceptable methodology.

In our profession this has translated into the need to show our value and ROI at two levels. The first level is the challenge to demonstrate how we as meeting professionals strategically manage "the business of meetings." This is more of a big picture or macro view. Are we good managers/guardians of the human and capital investment made by our organizations in our departments? This has led to a great deal of discussion around leveraging such strategies as the consolidation and leveraging of out total spend, supply chain management, partnering with other departments such as procurement, travel and finance, and/or outsourcing.

The second level (and purpose of this book) focuses much more on the micro level or that of the individual meeting or event. This has resulted in the MPI Foundation ROI project where a comprehensive model that illustrates from the simplest "I am measured by their satisfaction," and "What is the return on their objectives (ROO)?" to the highest level of justification being ROI.

It is important to understand that just like in other areas of our organizations—such as sales, marketing, finance or production functions—not every one uses all the macro strategies to run their departments. Nor do they justify a complete ROI impact study at the micro level, on every individual project or task that they implement. However, all successful businesses today collect the data, focus on the end objectives and value, and know where and when to apply the above concepts.

As you will see, in today's world you will not be able to calculate the ROI for every meeting or event. Nor would that be an appropriate allocation of your time and resources. However, you will need to have a business "acceptable model" and a process that allows you to communicate the value of your efforts, and in the appropriate cases, demonstrate in business terms the ROI of the meetings.

Thinking back to those initial discussions of 1994, it is hard to believe that the MPI Foundation, like many seminal events, was completely aware of what was to come from their efforts. The trend study and resulting discussion from the Maximizing Your ROI project uncovered just where we were as "professionals" vs. "planners" and where we may be falling short. The project set forth sweeping change in the way we view our profession. The discussion of what business skills were required in order to be considered a professional led to a discussion of identifying the gap between where we are today as planners and where we need to go as professionals. This ultimately led to the question of career paths and competencies. The initial ROI seminars led to ROI Two and Three and three seminars which focused more on topics such as our role in strategically managing the department and supply chains and the role of technology. These in turn led to further discussions on the different needs of senior meeting professionals vs. tactical needs of planning a function.

Each discussion and each new element are not only healthy debates and additions but are also critical to the advancement of our meeting profession.

Fundamental to it all is having a common business acceptable model to start measuring the most fundamental task in which we all participate and that is meetings. Today with the ROI Methodology™ we have that fundamental starting point. Just as technology and globalism are no longer theory, we have a process that helps us capture and frame all elements of a meeting from satisfaction to ROI.

Fusion Productions is proud of our partnership with MPI and the MPI Foundation and to play such a critical role in bringing the ROI concept to the meeting industry. We are proud of the role played since 1994 in the development of the Maximizing Your ROI: Return on Investment, ROI Two, Strategic ROI, The Foundation Measurement Systems Project, the ROI Summit, and the MPI Platinum Program: ROI Methodology™ for Meeting Professionals. We plan to continue to support meeting professionals with their quest for strategic meeting management content.

Hugh K. Lee
President, Fusion Productions

MPI Chairman 2004-2005

Jamie McDonough
Director, Training and Meetings,
Fusion Productions

Chair MPI International Chapter
Leadership Committee 2006-2007

Chapter 1
ROI Process: Issues and Trends

The debate about the issue of measuring the return on investment (ROI) in meetings and events is rampant. Rarely does a topic stir up emotions to the degree that the ROI issue does. Some individuals characterize any ROI measurement as seriously flawed and inappropriate for this industry. Others passionately characterize ROI as the answer to their accountability concerns. The truth probably lies somewhere in between these extreme viewpoints. The important point is to understand the reasons for ROI and its inherent weaknesses and advantages. Then taking a rational approach to the issue and implementing an appropriate mix of evaluation strategies, including the ROI, are possible. This chapter presents the basic issues concerning ROI and its use in the meetings and events industry.

Key ROI Issues

ROI Will Not Go Away

One thing is certain: ROI is not a fad. It is here to stay. As long as the need for accountability of meetings, events, and trade show expenditures exists and the concept of an investment payoff is desired, ROI will be measured to evaluate major investments in this industry. A fad is a new idea or approach or a new spin on an old approach. The concept of ROI has been used for centuries.

The 75th anniversary issue of *Harvard Business Review* (*HBR*) traced the tools used to measure results in organizations. (Sibbet, 1997) In early issues of *HBR*, during the 1920s, ROI was an emerging tool to place a value on the payoff of investments. In recent years, the application of the concept has been expanded to all types of investments including training, change initiatives, technology, quality, and meetings. With increased adoption and use, it appears that ROI is not going away. Today, hundreds of organizations routinely develop ROI calculations for education, training, communication, leadership development, and human resources programs. In the last three years, it has been used to show the value of meetings and events.

The Ultimate Level of Evaluation: ROI

The ROI Methodology collects and processes up to five levels of evaluation results plus another level for input. The concept of different levels of evaluation is both helpful and instructive in understanding how the return on investment is calculated. Table 1-1 shows the six-level framework used in this book. The table also shows the current status and goals for the industry.

Table 1-1. Measurement in the Meetings and Events Field

Level	Measurement Category	Current Status ▼ Coverage (Now)	Goal in 5 Years ▼ Coverage (Goal)	Comments About Status
0	**Inputs/Indicators** Measures inputs into meetings and events including the number of meetings, attendees, audience, costs, and efficiencies.	100%	100%	This is being accomplished now.
1	**Reaction and Perceived Value** Measure reaction to, and satisfaction with, the experience, ambiance, content, and value of the meeting.	100%	100%	Need more focus on content and perceived value.
2	**Learning** Measures what participants learned in the meeting – information, knowledge, skills, and contacts (take-aways from the meeting).	10 – 20%	80 – 90%	Must use simple learning measures.
3	**Application and Implementation** Measures progress after the meeting – the use of information, knowledge, skills, and contacts.	5%	15 – 25%	Need more follow-up.
4	**Impact and Consequences** Measures changes in business impact variables such as output, quality, time, and cost linked to the meeting.	< 2%	10%	This is the connection to business impact.
5	**ROI** Compares the monetary benefits of the business impact measures to the costs of the meeting.	< 1%	5%	The ultimate evaluation.

At Level 0, Input and Indicators, the various inputs of the meeting or event are captured in all meetings now (100%). These include costs, efficiencies, duration (in hours or days), participant profiles, locations, and agendas. This is only input and does not speak to the results.

At Level 1, Reaction and Perceived Value, the reaction from meeting participants is measured along with the perceived value. Almost all organizations evaluate at Level 1, usually with a generic, end-of-meeting questionnaire. While this level of evaluation is important as a customer satisfaction measure, a favorable reaction does not ensure that participants have learned new skills or knowledge.

At Level 2, Learning, measurements focus on what participants learned during the meeting using self assessments, checklists, role plays, simulations, group evaluations, and other assessment tools. A learning check is helpful to ensure that participants have absorbed the meeting material or messages and know how to use or apply them properly. Also, this level measures the number of new professional contacts and the extent to which existing contacts were strengthened. The industry is behind the target at this level. However, a positive learning measure is no guarantee that what was learned or the contacts acquired will actually be used.

At Level 3, Application and Implementation, a variety of follow-up methods are used to determine if participants applied what they learned or explored the contacts acquired. The completion of action items, the use of skills, and the follow up with contacts are important measures at Level 3. While Level 3 evaluations are important to gauge the success of the application after the meeting, they still do not guarantee that a positive impact will occur with the individual or the organization.

At Level 4, Impact and Consequences, the measurement focuses on the actual results achieved by meeting participants as they successfully apply the meeting material, messages, or contacts. Typical Level 4 measures include output, sales, quality, costs, time, and customer satisfaction. Although the meeting may produce a measurable business impact, a concern may still exist that the meeting cost too much.

At Level 5, Return on Investment—the ultimate level of evaluation—the meeting's monetary benefits are compared with the meeting's costs. Although ROI can be expressed in several ways, it is usually presented as a percent or benefits/costs ratio. The evaluation chain is not complete until the Level 5 evaluation is conducted.

The ROI Methodology has received much attention in the meetings and events press. Dozens of articles have been written and many interviews conducted. The following excerpt captures the issues, concerns, and opportunities for the use of ROI, as reported in one publication.

SPEAKING THE LANGUAGE

ROI is not a new concept to the meetings industry, but it is an elusive one. For years, the term has been used so loosely, and in so many contexts, that it's thought to refer to everything from the ergonomics of chairs to the relevance of the keynote address. And while many factors affect ROI, none singularly define it; rather, return on investment measurements must include all the aspects of a meeting to arrive at an explicit and definitive value.

The good news: After years of searching in vain for a reliable method with which to calculate ROI, the meetings industry finally seems poised to adopt an effective methodology that could finally clearly reveal the value of the meeting professional as a strategic member of any organization's executive team.

"The term ROI has been bandied about and misunderstood in this industry for years," says Doug McPhee, national account manager for Conferon in San Diego. Although the concept of ROI always carries with it a sense of significance and urgency, it's remained largely ill-defined. As a result, the very mention of this topic frustrates some planners. "I'm so sick of hearing ROI, ROI, ROI!" complains Loretta Lowe, an independent planner based in San Francisco. "Many meeting industry associates pay lip service to the discussion but don't really give us tangible samples of reports to manage this," Lowe says.

"Most of the talk I've heard about this has been vague," agrees Neil Schwartz, who plans meetings for the California Credit Union League in Rancho Cucamonga, California. "Most people really don't know how to proceed with the topic."

Indeed, many efforts to measure ROI in the meetings industry have dealt with what are called "intangibles"—such as whether the attendees and organizers felt the meeting was a success, and whether it improved employee morale, communication, and satisfaction. And while these benefits, far from being exact measurements, are part of a meeting's return on investment—in terms of both time and money—they are only part of a much larger whole.

To promote a more complete understanding of that whole, Meeting Professionals International (MPI) has recently partnered with the ROI Institute (based in Birmingham, Alabama), an organization that has been refining the measurement of ROI in various industries for some twenty-five years. "We initially developed our ROI Methodology for development and training, and it quickly grew to include the area of human resources," says Jack Phillips, ROI Institute chairman. "Since then, the methodology has migrated into the areas of quality control, technology, organizational development, and consulting. The meetings industry is a fairly new application." And while several firms currently offer services to help planners measure ROI, Phillips' Methodology appears to have achieved the most traction in the meetings industry, where he says it enjoys a particular relevance.

"The meeting industry has escaped this level of accountability for a long time, and we've seen budgets come and go with the economic changes. In good times, there are lots of meetings; in tough times, budgets are cut because executives don't know for sure that they're bringing value," he observes. "There's been a disconnect between the logistical planners and the content and strategy developers. How do you bridge that gap? ROI." In other words, when planners employ a methodical approach to measuring ROI, they will inevitably be involved in planning not only the meeting logistics but also the meeting content.

Phillips' Methodology introduces a concrete, systematic approach to ROI measurement in place of what has, in the meeting industry, traditionally been more of a touchy-feely proposition.

"This takes it to a completely different level than we've been used to," says McPhee. Indeed, Phillips' Methodology enables planners to calculate a precise dollar figure to apply to a meeting's bottom line.

"One of my favorite sayings is that bean-counters need beans to count," says Julia Rutherford Silvers, an author and event planning expert based in Las Vegas. "So when planners talk about having difficulty communicating with their procurement departments, the answer is we've got to show them the beans. We've got to put the numbers before them." And that's exactly what Phillips' Methodology is designed to do. "The idea is to take the analysis all the way through to the end result, which is an actual ROI calculation, and that allows us to speak the language of the CFO."

Taken from "The Fifth Element" by Susie Amer,
Successful Meetings, April 2005

A Practical Approach for Calculating ROI

The calculation of the return on investment in meetings, events, trade shows, and sponsorships begins with the basic model shown in Figure 1-1, where a potentially complicated process can be simplified with sequential steps. The ROI process model provides a systematic approach to ROI calculations. (Phillips and Phillips, 2005) A step-by-step approach helps keep the process manageable so users can address one issue at a time. The model also emphasizes that the methodology is a logical, systematic process that flows from one step to another. Applying the model provides consistency from one ROI calculation to another. Each step is briefly described in this section.

Evaluation Planning

Several parts of the evaluation process must be explained when developing the evaluation plan for an ROI calculation. The purpose of evaluation should be considered prior to developing the evaluation plan because the purpose will often determine the scope of the evaluation, the types of instruments used, and the type of data collected. A variety of tools are used to collect data and should be considered in the plan along with the timing of the data collection.

For most meetings and events, a follow-up is usually conducted one to six months after the meeting. The specific analysis anticipated should be included. The output of this phase is a data collection plan and an ROI analysis plan.

Figure 1-1. The ROI Process Model

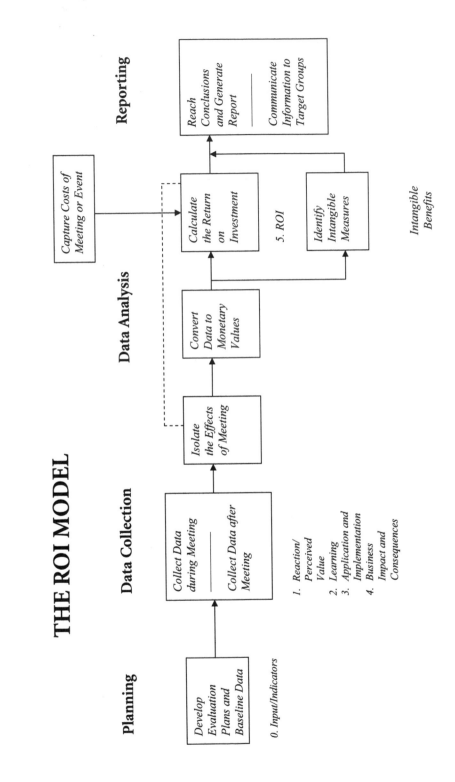

THE ROI MODEL

| Planning | Data Collection | Data Analysis | Reporting |

Develop Evaluation Plans and Baseline Data

0. Input/Indicators

Collect Data during Meeting
___
Collect Data after Meeting

1. Reaction/ Perceived Value
2. Learning
3. Application and Implementation
4. Business Impact and Consequences

Isolate the Effects of Meeting

Convert Data to Monetary Values

Capture Costs of Meeting or Event

Calculate the Return on Investment

5. ROI

Identify Intangible Measures

Intangible Benefits

Reach Conclusions and Generate Report
___
Communicate Information to Target Groups

Collecting Data

Data collection is central to the meeting evaluation. For ROI analysis, both hard data (representing sales, productivity, quality, cost, and time) and soft data (including work habits, job satisfaction, and customer satisfaction) are collected. Data are collected using a variety of methods including surveys, questionnaires, interviews, focus groups, and monitoring impact data in the organization. These techniques are described in this book. The important challenge in this step is to select the data collection method or methods most appropriate for the setting and the specific meeting, within the time and budget constraints for the meeting and the planner.

Isolating the Effects of the Meeting

An often overlooked issue in most evaluations is the process of isolating the effects of the meeting or event. This step is essential because many factors may influence performance data after the meeting has been conducted. In this step, specific techniques are explored to determine the amount of impact directly related to the meeting. The result is increased accuracy and credibility of the ROI calculation. A variety of strategies have been used to address this important issue ranging from a comparison group analysis to the use of estimates. Collectively, the strategies presented in this book provide a comprehensive set of tools to address this important issue.

Converting Data to Monetary Values

To calculate the return on investment, the impact data collected are converted to monetary values and then compared to the meeting costs. This requires that a value be placed on each unit of data connected with the meeting. Several techniques are available to convert data to monetary values including the use of experts, records, external databases, and estimates. The specific technique selected usually depends on the type of data and the situation. Fortunately, standard values have been developed in most organizations. The process is challenging, particularly with soft data, but can be methodically accomplished using one or more of the techniques in this book.

Identifying Intangible Benefits

In addition to tangible, monetary benefits, most meetings and events will have intangible, non-monetary benefits. The ROI calculation is based on converting both hard and soft data to monetary values. However, when measures are identified that cannot be converted to monetary values, credibly and with minimum resources, these measures are considered intangible benefits and include items such as: increased customer satisfaction, increased employee engagement, improved teamwork, improved image, reduced complaints, and reduced conflicts.

During data analysis, every attempt is made to convert all data to monetary values. All hard data—such as output, quality, and time—are converted to monetary values. The conversion of soft data is attempted for each data item. However, if the process used for conversion is too subjective (or requires too much time) and the resulting values lose credibility when converted, then the data are listed as intangible benefits with an appropriate explanation. For some meetings, intangible, non-monetary benefits are extremely valuable, often carrying as much influence as hard data items.

Tabulating Meeting and Event Costs

The other part of the equation on a benefits/costs analysis is the costs of the meeting. Tabulating the costs involves monitoring or developing all the related costs of the meeting targeted for the ROI calculation. The cost components that may be included, depending upon the ROI perspective, are:

- The cost to analyze the need for the meeting, if applicable
- The cost to design and develop the meeting/event
- The cost of marketing or promotion
- The cost of all meeting materials—such as participant handouts, signage, and decorations
- The cost of the speakers, and/or facilitators, including travel and delivery time
- The cost of the facilities for the meeting
- Travel, housing, and food/beverage costs for the participants and others
- Other destination costs, such as tour services, transportation, and destination management companies
- Salaries plus employee benefits of the participants and staff for the time to attend the meeting
- Administrative and overhead costs of the meeting planning function allocated in some convenient way to the meeting or event
- Costs of evaluating the meeting

In addition, other direct and indirect costs related to the meeting or event should be included. The conservative approach is to include all these costs so that the total is fully-loaded.

Calculating the ROI

The return on investment is calculated using the meeting benefits in monetary values and the meeting costs. The benefits/costs ratio (BCR) is the meeting benefits divided by the meeting costs. In formula form, it is:

$$BCR = \frac{Meeting\ Benefits}{Meeting\ Costs}$$

The return on investment uses the net benefits divided by meeting costs. The net benefits are the meeting monetary benefits minus the costs. In formula form, the ROI becomes:

$$ROI\ (\%) = \frac{Net\ Meeting\ Benefits}{Meeting\ Costs}\ x\ 100$$

This is the same basic formula used in evaluating other investments where ROI is traditionally reported as earnings divided by investment.

Standards

Every process needs standards, and the ROI Methodology is no exception. The standards shown in Table 1-2 represent adjustments and refinement of the ROI Methodology over the time of its use within a variety of fields and industries. These Guiding Principles are adjusted to this particular industry, representing the necessary standards for a credible, conservative approach to evaluation through the different levels.

Table 1-2. ROI Standards

Guiding Principles

1. When a higher-level evaluation is conducted, data must be collected at lower levels.
2. When an evaluation is planned for a higher level, the previous level of evaluation does not have to be comprehensive.
3. When collecting and analyzing data, use only the most credible sources.
4. When analyzing data, select the most conservative alternative for calculations.
5. At least one method must be used to isolate the effects of the meeting.
6. If no improvement data are available for a population or from a specific source, it is assumed that little or no improvement has occurred.
7. Estimates of improvements should be adjusted for the potential error of the estimate.
8. Extreme data items and unsupported claims should not be used in ROI calculations.
9. Only the first year of benefits (annual) should be used in the ROI analysis of short-term meetings.
10. Costs of the meeting should be fully-loaded for ROI analysis.
11. Intangible measures are defined as measures that are purposely not converted to monetary values.
12. The results from the ROI Methodology must be communicated to all key stakeholders.

Taking a Sensible Approach

Obviously, meeting planners and event organizers must take a sensible approach with this analysis, deciding which meetings and events should be evaluated and to which level. By far, the majority of events will be evaluated at the first level. Smaller numbers will be evaluated at Level 2, an even smaller number at Level 3, and even smaller numbers at Levels 4 and 5. Table 1-1 shows the recommended evaluations (as a goal) when many different meetings are involved.

Consider this: for corporate planners developing a hundred meetings each year, only five percent of those meetings should be evaluated at the ROI level. Taking a selective approach for the meetings evaluated at those levels is important. Typically, the meetings evaluated for impact and ROI are those that are expensive, strategic, and critical to success—those that attempt to resolve a major issue or problem. For the most part, the remainder of the meetings should be evaluated at the lower levels described in the table.

For an association that conducts only one major meeting, that meeting should be evaluated to the ROI level, but only if data is needed to show the actual value from the attendee or exhibitor perspective.

Final Thoughts

ROI calculations are being developed by organizations to meet the demands of a variety of influential stakeholders. The result is a process that shows the value of meetings and events in a format desired by many senior administrators, executives, attendees, and sponsors. This chapter has demonstrated that the ROI process represents a significant and challenging dilemma for most organizations. While many factors drive an interest in, and the need for, the ROI process, some question its appropriateness and necessity. However, ROI calculations can be developed reliably and accurately for almost any type of meeting or event. To accomplish this, the process must be approached with careful planning, methodical procedures, and logical and practical analyses. Above all, the steps, techniques, assumptions, and issues must follow a conservative approach to ensure the credibility needed for acceptance of the process.

Notes

Amer, S. "The Fifth Element," *Successful Meetings* (New York, NY: VNU Business Media, April 2005).

Phillips, P. and J. Phillips. ROI Basics (Alexandria, VA: ASTD Press, 2005).

Sibbet, D. "75 Years of Management Ideas and Practice 1922-1997," *Harvard Business Review* (Boston, MA: Harvard Business Review, 1997).

Chapter 2
Defining Needs and Objectives

This chapter presents the first step of a comprehensive ROI methodology: defining the initial needs for the meeting and the corresponding objectives. If needs are not clearly defined early in the process, a less than optimal meeting may be the result, creating inefficiencies and uncertainties. This chapter explores the different levels of needs assessments to ensure that the meeting or event is necessary and is linked to important organizational and individual needs.

Levels of Needs

Meetings and events are sometimes ineffective because of undefined needs. Another problem stems from a misalignment between the meeting and specific business needs. Because this issue is so serious, some planners take appropriate steps to ensure alignment, particularly if the proposed meeting is expensive.

When business impact is desired, meetings and events must begin with a clear focus on the outcome. The end result must be defined in terms of business needs and business measures so that the outcome—the actual improvement in the measures—and the resulting ROI are clear. Knowing the desired outcome provides a necessary focus on the needs through every step in the process. Beginning with the end in mind also involves pinpointing all the details throughout the meeting to ensure that it is properly planned and executed.

Proper analysis requires discipline and determination. A structured, standardized approach is needed, an approach that adds credibility and allows for consistent application. While the process described in this book is comprehensive, not every meeting or event should be subjected to this type of analysis. Some needs are obvious and require little analysis other than the work needed to develop the meeting or event. Additional analysis may be needed to ensure that the meeting is right for the audience. The amount of analysis undertaken often depends on the stakes involved.

Before beginning the needs analysis, the relationship presented in Figure 2-1, may be helpful. This shows the link between needs, objectives, and evaluation. This chapter explores the needs at the five levels described in the figure, beginning with payoff needs and progressing to preference needs. The objectives derived from these needs are clearly defined and serve as the drivers for the meeting. The right side of the model is essentially the evaluation levels presented in the previous chapter.

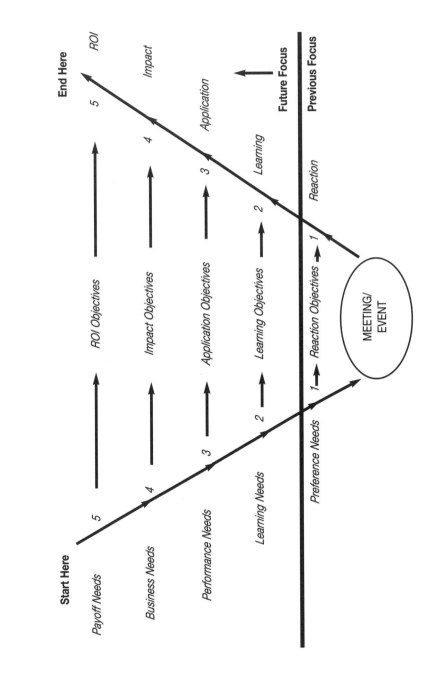

Figure 2-1. Linking Needs with Evaluation

Although it may seem confusing, this figure is helpful for planners. For example, the line between Level 1 and Level 2 shows what has happened to the industry. Most meetings are developed at Level 1. The basis for a meeting is often centered on preference needs, in terms of timing, location, budgets, and costs. The objectives focus on a favorable reaction to the meeting, in terms of location, timing, facilities, and the experience. The measurement is often obtained through a questionnaire to capture reactions. Little effort has been placed on the other levels—even Level 2. At Level 2, the content is more clearly defined in terms of what participants should know or learn, and specific learning objectives are set—what attendees should take away from the meeting. Then the learning measurements would be self-assessments regarding the amount of learning. For many meetings, this may be all that is necessary. However, these days, because of clients and others who demand accountability, moving to higher levels of the evaluation chain is needed, which means that objectives need to be set and the needs assessments must include higher levels of analysis.

The Payoff Needs

For meetings and events that address significant problems or opportunities with potentially high rewards, the potential payoff may be obvious. For lower-profile meetings with a vague purpose, the possible payoff is less apparent. Figure 2-2 shows the potential payoff in monetary terms. A meeting's payoff will essentially be in either profit increases or in cost savings.

Profit increases are generated by meetings that improve sales, increase market share, introduce new products, open new markets, enhance customer service, or increase customer loyalty. These should pay off with increases in sales revenue. Other revenue-generating measures include: increasing memberships, increasing donations, obtaining grants, and generating tuition from new and returning students—all of which, after subtracting the cost of doing business, leave a profitable benefit.

Figure 2-2. The Payoff Opportunity

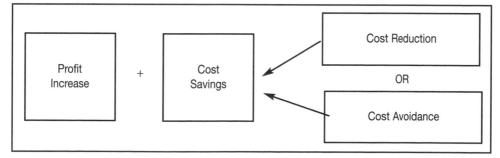

However, most meetings will pay off with cost savings. Cost savings may be generated through cost reductions or cost avoidances. For example, a meeting that improves quality, reduces cycle time, lowers downtime, decreases complaints, avoids employee turnover, or minimizes delays will generate cost reductions. When the goal is solving a problem, monetary value is often based on cost reduction.

Cost-avoidance pay offs come from meetings implemented to reduce risks, avoid problems, or prevent unwanted events. Some may view cost avoidance as an inappropriate measure for developing monetary benefits and calculating ROI. However, if the assumptions are correct, an avoided cost (e.g., compliance fines) can be more rewarding than reducing an actual cost. Preventing a problem is more cost effective than waiting for it to occur and then fixing it.

Determining the potential payoff is the first step in the needs analysis process. This step is closely related to the next step, determining the business need, since the potential payoff is often based on a consideration of the business measures that need to change. Determining the payoff involves two factors: the potential monetary value derived from the business measure's improvement and the approximate cost of the meeting. Knowing these monetary values in detail can yield a more credible forecast of what can be expected from the meeting. However, this step may be omitted in situations when the issue (business need) must be resolved regardless of the cost or if it is obviously a high-payoff activity.

To begin the analysis, several questions should be answered. Below are some appropriate questions to ask about the proposed meeting:

- Why is this an issue?
- Is this issue critical?
- Is this a problem?
- Is it feasible to improve it?
- Who will support the meeting?
- How much will the meeting cost?
- Are there some important intangibles involved?
- Is a forecast needed?

- What happens if we do nothing?
- Is this issue linked to strategy?
- Is it possible to correct the problem?
- How much does the problem cost?
- Who will not support the meeting?
- How can we fund the meeting?
- Is there a potential payoff (positive ROI)?

The answers to these questions may make the case for proceeding without analysis or indicate that additional analysis is needed. They may also show that the meeting is not needed. Understanding the implications of whether to move forward can show the legitimacy of the proposed meeting. For many potential meetings, answers to these questions may be readily available. The need may have already been realized and the consequences might be validated.

Seeking and placing value on a meeting opportunity leads to an important decision: to forecast or not to forecast ROI. If the stakes are high and the support for the meeting is not in place, a detailed forecast may be the only way to gain needed support and funding for the meeting. When a forecast is pursued, how thorough the analysis should be becomes an issue. In some cases, an informal forecast is provided, giving certain assumptions about alternative outcome scenarios. In others, a detailed forecast is needed and may involve collecting data from a variety of experts, using previous studies from another meeting, or perhaps more sophisticated analysis, which is beyond the scope of this book.

Business Needs

Determining specific business needs is linked to the previous step in the needs analysis, developing the potential payoff. A business need is represented by a business measure. Any process, item, or perception can be measured, and this measurement is critical to this level of analysis. If the meeting focuses on solving a problem—something clearly in the mind of the client—the measures are often obvious. If the meeting prevents a problem, the measures may also be obvious. If it takes advantage of a potential opportunity, the measures are usually still there. Otherwise, how will the opportunity be described? The important point is that measures are usually in the system, where the meeting participant resides, ready to be captured for this level of analysis. The challenge is to define the measures and find them economically and swiftly.

To help focus on the desired measures, clarification between hard data and soft data is needed. Hard data are primary measures of improvement presented in rational, undisputed facts that are usually accumulated. They are the most desired type of data because they are easy to measure and quantify and are relatively easy to convert to monetary values. The ultimate criteria for measuring the effectiveness of an organization rests on hard data items—such as sales, productivity, profitability, cost control, and quality assurance.

Hard data are objectively based and represent very common and credible measures of an organization's performance. Hard data can usually be grouped into four categories, as shown in Table 2-1. These categories—output, quality, cost, and time—are typical performance measures in every organization.

Table 2-1. Examples of Hard Data

OUTPUT	**TIME**
Sales	Cycle time
Units produced	Equipment downtime
Tons manufactured	Overtime
Items assembled	On time shipments
Money collected	Time to project completion
New accounts generated	Processing time
Forms processed	Supervisory time
Loans approved	Time to proficiency
Inventory turnover	Learning time
Patients visited	Meeting schedules
Applications processed	Repair time
Students graduated	Efficiency
Output per hour	Work stoppages
Productivity	Order response
Work backlog	Late reporting
Incentive bonus	Lost time days
Shipments	
	QUALITY
COSTS	Scrap
Unit costs	Waste
Costs by account	Rejects
Variable costs	Error rates
Shelter costs	Failure rates
Treatment costs	Dropout rates
Budget variances	Rework
Fixed costs	Shortages
Overhead cost	Product defects
Operating costs	Deviation from standard
Project cost savings	Product failures
Accident costs	Inventory adjustments
Meetings costs	Timecard corrections
Sales expense	Incidents
Participant costs	Compliance discrepancies
	Agency fines

Hard data may lag behind changes and conditions in the human organization by many months. Therefore, supplementing hard data with soft data—such as attitude, motivation, and satisfaction—may be useful. Often more difficult to collect and analyze, soft data are used when hard data are not available or to supplement hard data. Soft data are also more difficult to convert to monetary values and are usually subjective. They are less credible as a performance measurement and are often behavior oriented. Table 2-2 shows common examples and types of soft data.

Table 2-2. Examples of Soft Data

WORK HABITS	CUSTOMER SERVICE
Tardiness	Customer complaints
Presenteeism	Customer satisfaction
Violations of safety rules	Customer dissatisfaction
Communication break-downs	Customer impressions
Excessive breaks	Customer loyalty
	Customer retention
WORK CLIMATE/SATISFACTION	Customer value
Grievances	
Discrimination charges	**EMPLOYEE DEVELOPMENT/**
Employee complaints	**ADVANCEMENT**
Job satisfaction	Promotions
Organization commitment	Capability
Employee engagement	Intellectual capital
Employee loyalty	Programs completed
Intent to leave	Requests for transfer
Stress	Performance appraisal ratings
	Readiness
INITIATIVE/INNOVATION	Networking
Creativity	
Innovation	**IMAGE**
New ideas	Brand awareness
Suggestions	Reputation
New products and services	Leadership
Trademarks	Social responsibility
Copyrights and patents	Environmental friendliness
Process improvements	Social consciousness
Partnerships	Diversity
Alliances	External awards

The important issue with soft-data categories is the difficulty of converting them to monetary values. While some of the measures listed in Table 2-2 could be converted to money, most soft-data items are more realistic and practical. This issue defines an intangible benefit based on the standards of the ROI Methodology. If a soft-data measure can be converted to money, it becomes tangible and is reported as a monetary value or placed in an ROI calculation. If a data item cannot be converted to money credibly with minimum resources, it is listed as an intangible measure. To avoid debates over what should be considered soft or hard data, the terms *tangible* and *intangible* will be used more often in this book.

The sources of impact data, whether hard or soft, are plentiful. They come from routine reporting systems in the organization and individual work units. In many situations, these items have led to the need for the meeting or event. A vast array of possible documents, systems, databases, and reports can be used to select the specific measure or measures to monitor throughout the meeting.

Some planners and participants believe that data sources are scarce because the data are not readily available to them near their workplace or within easy reach through database systems. With a little determination and searching, the data can usually be identified. In our experience, more than ninety percent of the measures that matter to a specific meeting or event have already been developed and are readily available in databases or systems. Rarely do new data collection systems or processes need to be developed.

Performance Needs

The next step in the needs analysis is understanding what caused the business measure to miss its mark and not be where it is desired. This step determines the specific performance of the participant that is not in place. It answers this question: What is the participant doing or not doing to inhibit the business measure (e.g., sales associates do not show the features and benefits of a product; managers do not use project management tools; engineers do not use the latest technology)?

If the proposed meeting addresses a problem, this step focuses on the cause of the problem, from an individual perspective. If the meeting takes advantage of an opportunity, this step focuses on what inhibits the organization from taking advantage of that opportunity.

This step may require using a variety of analytical techniques to uncover the causes of the performance problem or inhibitors to success. Examples include focus groups, probing interviews, surveys, problem analysis, and brainstorming. It is important to relate the issue to the organizational setting, to the behavior of the individuals involved, and to the functioning of various systems.

Learning Needs

The performance needs uncovered in the previous step often require a learning component to address them—such as when participants must learn how to perform a task differently, to use a process or a system, or to seek new ideas. For many meetings, learning is a minor solution and often involves simply understanding the process, procedure, policy, or new contacts. For example, when implementing a new ethics policy at a meeting, the learning component requires understanding how the policy works and the participant's role in policy implementation.

One of the most important approaches to determine learning needs is to ask the individuals who understand the process. They can best determine what information, skills, and knowledge are necessary to address the defined performance problems. At this time, determining how much of the knowledge and skills already exist is necessary. Other techniques are available to determine learning needs, such as job and task analyses, observations, demonstrations, testing, and management assessment. These are more involved than necessary for planners. Determining the specific learning needs can be very time consuming for major meetings where new procedures, technologies, and processes are presented. As in the previous step, it is important to avoid spending excessive time analyzing at this early stage in the process and to collect as much data as possible with minimum resources. Where the learning component is minor, as in most meetings, learning needs are simple.

Preference Needs

The final level of needs analysis is based on preferences, which drive meeting requirements and specifications. Essentially, participants prefer certain locations, schedules, or activities for the structure of the meeting or event. Preferences define how, where, and when a meeting will be conducted. Although everyone involved will have certain needs or preferences, the decision is based on the input of several stakeholders rather than the preferences of one individual. For example, the client will have a preference for location, timing, and facilities—all within a defined budget. Participants attending the meeting may have particular preferences, but their preferences could exceed resources, time, and budget requirements. The participants' immediate managers may have other preferences, such as minimizing the amount of disruption and costs. However, the budget almost always constrain the parameters of a meeting. The urgency for implementation constrains the preferences as well. Those who support or own the meeting often have preferences in terms of timing, budget, and the use of technology.

Levels of Objectives for Meetings and Events

Meetings and events are driven by objectives. In some situations, the meeting is aimed at creating a positive reaction to the experience, and that may be all that is needed. At some meetings, objectives define what must be learned or acquired at the meeting, requiring learning objectives. For other meetings, there is a need to understand more precisely what individual participants will do or should do as a result of the meeting. Therefore, application and implementation objectives are needed. In still other situations, understanding what impact the meeting has had on the individual or the organization is necessary. In these cases, specific impact objectives must define the ultimate consequences. Finally, in a few circumstances, a comparison of the costs of the meeting to the monetary benefits is needed and ROI objectives are necessary.

Regardless of the type of meeting or event, multiple levels of objectives are desired. These levels of objectives, ranging from qualitative to quantitative, define more precisely what will occur as a meeting or event is implemented. Table 2-3 shows the different levels of objectives briefly discussed in this chapter. These objectives are so critical that they need special attention in their development and use.

Table 2-3. Multiple Levels of Objectives

Levels of Objectives	Focus of Objectives
Level 1 Reaction and Perceived Value	Defines a specific, desired level of reaction to the meeting or event as it is revealed and communicated to stakeholders
Level 2 Learning	Defines specific skills, knowledge, information, and contacts that will be acquired during the meeting
Level 3 Application and Implementation	Defines the successful application of the meeting's content
Level 4 Impact and Consequences	Defines the specific business measures that will change or improve as a result of the meeting or event
Level 5 ROI	Defines the acceptable return on investment from the meeting or event, comparing the meeting's monetary benefits to the meeting's costs

Reaction Objectives

For any meeting or event to be successful, various stakeholders must react favorably—or at least not negatively—to the event. Ideally, the participants should be satisfied with the meeting and see its value. This creates a win-win relationship. Reaction data must be obtained routinely during and at the end of the meeting so that feedback can be used to make adjustments and perhaps even redesign certain parts of the meeting.

Developing reaction objectives should be straightforward and relatively easy. The objectives reflect immediate and long-term satisfaction with issues important to a meeting's success. They also form the basis for evaluating the chain of impact and emphasizing planned action, when feasible and useful.

Typical reaction objectives are listed below:

After this meeting, participants should have positive ratings on the following issues:
- Relevance of the meeting to my work
- Importance of the meeting to my success
- Effectiveness of speakers

- Appropriateness of meeting topics
- Amount of new information
- Motivational aspect of the meeting
- Planned use of the concepts/advice
- Recommend the meeting to others
- Value of the meeting to me
- Location of the meeting
- Facilities
- Service of the staff

Learning Objectives

Every meeting or event involves at least one learning objective and usually more. With major events, the learning component is incredibly important. In other situations, such as the implementation of a new policy, the learning component is minor but necessary. To ensure that participants learn what they need to know to make the meeting successful, learning objectives are developed.

Learning objectives are critical to measuring learning because they communicate the expected takeaways and define the desired information, knowledge, or skills necessary for meeting success. Learning objectives provide a focus for participants, indicating what they must learn and do. Developing learning objectives is straightforward.

Learning objectives can be stated in this way:

After completing the meeting, participants will be able to:
- Name the six pillars of the division's new strategy
- Identify five new technology trends explained at the conference
- Identify the six features of the new ethics policy
- Demonstrate the use of each software routine in the standard time
- Use problem solving skills when faced with a problem
- Know if they are eligible for the early retirement program
- Score 75 or better on the new-product quiz
- Demonstrate success with all five customer interaction skills
- Explain the value of diversity in a work group
- Document and submit suggestions and ideas for award consideration
- Score at least 9 out of 10 on a sexual harassment policy quiz

Application and Implementation Objectives

As the meeting is conducted, application and implementation objectives clearly define what is expected from participants after the meeting and sometimes to what level of performance. Application objectives are similar to learning objectives but reflect actual use in the participant's work or life situation. They also involve specific milestones, indicating when part or all of the process is implemented.

Application objectives are critical because they describe the expected outcomes in the intermediate area—the time between the learning and the impact that the learning will deliver. Application and implementation objectives describe how things should change or the state of the workplace after the content is implemented. They provide a basis for the evaluation of on-the-job changes and individual performance.

Application objectives are often stated in the following way:

When the meeting content is implemented:

- 50% of conference attendees follow up with at least one contact from the conference
- Pharmaceutical sales reps have communicated adverse effects of a specific prescription drug to all physicians in their territories
- Sales and customer service representatives use all five interaction skills with at least half the customers
- At least 99.1 percent of software users will follow the correct sequences after three weeks of use
- Within one year, ten percent of employees will submit documented suggestions for saving costs
- The average 360-degree leadership assessment score will improve from 3.4 to 4.1 on a five-point scale
- 95 percent of high-potential employees will complete individual development plans within two years
- Employees will routinely use problem-solving skills
- Sexual harassment activity will cease within three months after the zero-tolerance policy is implemented
- 80 percent of employees will use one or more of the three cost-containment features of the health-care plan

Impact Objectives

Meetings and events should drive one or more business impact measures. Impact objectives represent key business measures that should be improved as the application and implementation objectives are achieved. Impact objectives are critical to measuring business performance because they define the ultimate expected outcomes of the meeting. They describe business-unit performance that should be connected to it. Above all, impact objectives emphasize achieving bottom-line results that key client groups expect and demand.

Impact objectives may be based on output, quality, cost, and time. Impact objectives involving soft data may be based on customer service, work climate, and job satisfaction.

Impact objectives can be stated in the following ways:

After completion of actions from the meeting, the following conditions should be met:

- Pharmaceuticals, Inc., brand awareness should increase ten percent among physicians during the next two years
- The average number of new accounts opened at Great Western Bank should increase from 300 to 350 per month
- Tardiness at the Newbury foundry should decrease by 20 percent within the next calendar year
- An across-the-board reduction in overtime should occur for front-of-house managers at Tasty Time restaurants in the third quarter of this year
- Employee complaints should be reduced from an average of three per month to an average of one per month at Guarantee Insurance headquarters
- The company-wide job satisfaction index should rise by two percentage points during the next calendar year
- Sales expenses for all titles at Proof Publishing Company should decrease by ten percent in the fourth quarter

ROI Objectives

The fifth level of objectives for meetings and events is the acceptable return on investment (ROI)—the financial impact. These objectives define the expected payoff from the meeting, and compare the cost of the meeting to the monetary benefits. An ROI objective is typically expressed as an acceptable return on investment percentage that compares the annual monetary benefits minus the cost, divided by the actual cost, and is multiplied by one hundred. A zero percent ROI indicates a break-even meeting. A fifty percent ROI indicates that the cost of the meeting is recaptured, and an additional fifty percent "earnings" (fifty cents for every dollar invested) is achieved.

The Importance of Specific Objectives

Developing specific objectives at different levels for meetings and events provides important benefits. First, they provide direction to the participants involved in making the meeting successful—to help keep them on track. Objectives define exactly what is expected at different timeframes and show the anticipated outcomes of the meeting. Objectives provide guidance for the speakers so that they understand the goals and intended impact of the meeting. They also provide information and motivation for the planners and developers as they see the implementation and impact outcomes. In most meetings, multiple stakeholders are involved and will influence the results. Specific objectives provide goals and motivation for the stakeholders so that they see the gains that should be achieved. Objectives provide important information to help the key sponsor groups clearly understand how the landscape will look when the meeting is successful. Finally, from an evaluation perspective, objectives provide a basis for measuring the success of the meeting.

Final Thoughts

This chapter outlines the beginning point in the ROI Methodology. It shows how meetings and events can be structured from the beginning, with detailed needs identified, ultimately leading to developing meeting objectives at five levels. This kind of detail ensures that the meeting is aligned with individual and business needs and is results-focused throughout the process. Without this analysis, the meeting runs the risk of failing to deliver the value that it should, or not aligning with one or more business objectives. These steps take time but are essential for success. They are systematic and structured. When followed in a disciplined and determined way, they can make a meeting highly successful.

A case study describing a real needs assessment for a successful incentive program follows.

Case Study
Needs Assessment for a Successful Incentive Program
Cingular Wireless

By Chris Gaia, Vice President of Marketing, Maritz Travel

This case was prepared to serve as a basis for discussion rather than an illustration of either effective or ineffective administrative and management practices. Names, dates, places, and data may have been disguised at the request of the author or organization.

Abstract

A recent merger resulted in the Cingular Wireless employee base becoming a more diverse group with many ages, sexes, cultures, and backgrounds represented. However, Cingular's annual employee incentive and recognition event remained the same. To determine if the motivational program was still effective, Cingular asked Maritz Travel to conduct a program analysis. Maritz Travel found that the potential event ROI could significantly increase with changes in location, communications, and structure.

Background

Domestic and international incentive meetings and events remain a popular experience for a majority of employees. For those in charge of employee incentive and recognition programs, raising the bar each year while maintaining the desired program effect—motivating the work force—is challenging.

But the challenge extends beyond merely finding new event locations and accommodations each year. As the American work force becomes more diversified, event and meeting managers must consider the disparate ages, sexes, cultures, backgrounds, and preferences of its employee base or channel partners. What motivates a 25-year-old African-American female from New York can be different than the motivation required for a 50-year-old Caucasian male from Phoenix. This was the challenge facing Cingular Wireless, the largest wireless carrier in the United States.

Cingular Summit

The company held an annual national sales recognition event, Cingular Summit, which rewarded employees generating the top five percent of sales. The event was a four-day sales meeting and fun travel experience to a luxury resort in an exotic location. During past events, Cingular had solicited feedback through post-event participant surveys. However, a holistic, total assessment of the program had never been completed. Cingular wanted to know if the program was effective. Did it align with business objectives? Did the program engage and motivate employees? Cingular turned to Maritz Travel, a meetings, events, and incentive travel management company, to determine how to boost event ROI.

In the past, sales incentive and recognition event decisions regarding destination, length of trip, and activities were often made with little participant insight or understanding of how motivation programs could be improved.

Evaluation Methodology and Analysis

To ensure that Cingular's event decisions were on target, Maritz Travel analyzed the Cingular Summit to the next level with its own survey and analysis tool, Maritz Travel Insight. Instead of relying on instinct, past experience, managerial judgment, and general beliefs, this tool helps companies determine the optimal incentive travel rewards to motivate its large, unique work forces using the voice of the end customer, the incentive program participant.

Maritz Travel Insight polls employees online to measure which activities and interests are most motivational, based on a three part survey. Cingular asked all employees competing for participation in the Cingular Summit to take the survey, not just past winners. The survey parts were as follows:

- *Part One – Program Attributes.* This portion of the survey asked participants about their preferences on program attributes such as trip length, hotel type, destination choice, use of free time, opportunities to interact with senior management, etc. It also included choice evaluation questions to identify which programs respondents would work harder to earn.
- *Part Two – Trip Activities.* This section analyzed participants' preferences and priorities for travel-related activities. Respondents were asked to select activities they would most and least enjoy.
- *Part Three – Participant Details.* The last part of the survey uncovered respondent profile types using demographics, past reward travel experiences, and "firmagraphics," such as past trip earners, non-earners, and up to ten additional sub-groups.

In addition, program participants were shown two different trips, Trip A and Trip B, and were asked to choose the one they would work harder to earn.

- Trip A offered ten different destination choices at a large, luxury hotel for a four-night trip. Employees could choose between four travel dates and could bring a guest, but no children.

- Trip B offered only one destination, at a large, luxury hotel for five nights. This trip was offered on only one date and also allowed participants to bring a guest, but no children.

The respondents repeated this choice exercise several times with systematically different trip options and attributes to consider.

The survey also asked participants about activity choices. For example, out of the four trip activities listed below, participants had to choose one activity they would like to do most and one they would like to do the least. The respondents did this repeatedly with different subsets of activities. Examples included: local dining and restaurants; cultural experiences, such as cooking classes, art lessons, etc.; scenic and nature tours; and hunting and fishing.

The resulting data was compiled into an easy-to-use decision support tool that Cingular used to separate and quantify the value and impact of program attributes. For example, Cingular was able to review the trade-offs associated with different combinations of program elements, such as the benefit of offering a number of destinations versus the specific length of the trip versus offering a choice in travel dates.

The tool also enabled Cingular to carve out employee groups by age, sex, and other demographic features to determine which trips and activities would best motivate these sub-groups. For example, Cingular could view how a four-day trip would motivate parents with children at home, compared to a seven-day trip, or how Generation X employees respond to having a choice of two dates for a trip rather than one.

Results

The Cingular survey obtained a 25% response rate. Employee feedback indicated that local field representatives felt the program was national in scope and, therefore, dismissed it because they thought it didn't apply to them. Respondents preferred regional events over a national one (three to one), because they were more interested in celebrating success with direct managers and colleagues versus spending time with the national representatives.

Managers felt rules structures were focused on rewarding front-line sellers, and two-thirds of them felt they did not have a chance to win. Feeling disengaged, managers were unmotivated and did not promote the program. Sellers and managers wanted more timely performance feedback. Shorter stays at sun/fun destinations were preferred over longer stays elsewhere.

Recommendations and Use of Results

Based on the survey results, Maritz presented a total strategic solution. The company recommended that the Cingular Summit be changed to focus on six regional events held in two sunny locations—JW Marriott Grande Lakes in Orlando, Florida, and the Montage Resort in Laguna Beach, California.

A full communication strategy and solution to support the program was created, including more timely and enhanced messages. For example, participants were provided with information targeted to their specific region's trip and qualifying criteria. A Web site was created to provide employees with bimonthly updates on their rankings within their market and region, as well as to feature various winners and share best sales practices. In addition, monthly updates were provided on their progress toward the Cingular Summit qualifying goals.

Maritz also recommended changes in the program's design and rules structure to make it more relevant and appealing to a broader group. For example, store managers, who would be measured based on the sales generated by their stores, would make up 60% of the Cingular Summit winners. Cingular also expanded the criteria to attend the Cingular Summit to include customer service scores.

Questions for Discussion

1. How can companies best determine the motivational needs of diverse employees?
2. How could the needs assessment data collected in this case study impact the ultimate business results of the program?
3. The detailed survey Maritz conducted on Cingular's employee base revealed great information about each individual's preferences. Besides identifying travel incentive preferences, how can the company use this information to its advantage?
4. Would this be an appropriate program for a business impact or ROI evaluation? Why or why not?

Acknowledgements

Maritz would like to thank Karen Bennett, vice president of sales, Cingular Wireless, for her assistance in the creation of this case study.

About the Author

As vice president of marketing for Maritz Travel, Chris Gaia is responsible for product management, events strategy, and industry relations. With twenty-five years of marketing experience, Mr. Gaia has spoken on topics such as strategic planning, marketing strategy, and using technology to achieve competitive advantages to organizations such as American Bankers Association and the American Marketing Association. He has a Bachelor of Science degree and master's degree in business from the University of Missouri.

Editor's Notes

The Maritz Travel Insight tool helped Cingular identify the preferences and desires of incentive program participants as they related to the program and its rewards. The goal of the survey was to collect needs assessment data that would lead to the design of a more appealing and motivating incentive program. This enhanced and improved incentive program would then produce increased sales. Once the winners were selected for the Cingular Summit and the incentive travel portion was held, further evaluation to determine the business impact and ROI of the total program could be pursued to determine its success.

Chapter 3
Measuring Inputs and Indicators

The first of the seven types of data presented in this book, briefly described in Chapter 1, is presented in this chapter. Inputs and indicators are the first step in capturing data for meetings and events evaluations. For some meeting and event planners, this is the principal source of data collected. For example, reports published by various magazines and associations in the industry, including MPI, are dominated with this type of data. This chapter highlights some of the more common measures, including monitoring the types of events held and the number of meetings, events, exhibitors, people, hours, topics, and requests. It also explores the importance of tracking the costs in a variety of ways and presents how meetings and events have been managed.

The Importance of Measuring Inputs and Indicators

While debate exists regarding the importance of this level of data, few would suggest that it is not needed. Inputs and indicators are an important first step in the analysis, and this data shows insight, commitment, support, and the scope for the meeting or event. This is particularly helpful for companies, organizations, and associations where the commitment is low. Often, executives in these organizations boast about the amount of commitment to meetings, indicating statistics—such as the total number of participants, the number of days or hours, and the cost per participant—to show the amount of resources allocated to this effort.

This level of data represents the most common benchmarking data—they are easy to count. In some organizations and associations, they must be counted because they are part of the budget and cost control processes. Tracking inputs provides an opportunity to show who participates by location, organization, occupation, area, topic, and a variety of other areas. This helps clients understand who attends, identify gaps, and make adjustments as needed.

Another consideration is the way that investments in meetings and events are managed and used. A variety of efficiencies can be captured, indicating the extent to which processes are streamlined, deadlines and cycle times are met, and the planning function is operated on a lean basis, with a constant focus on improving efficiencies and effectiveness. This responsiveness to clients is often an important measure of customer service.

Planners and organizers must know how much money is spent on meetings and events. Many organizations calculate this expenditure and make comparisons with those of other organizations, although comparisons may be difficult due to the different basis for cost calculations. The cost per participant for one meeting could be compared with the cost per participant for a similar meeting. Huge differences may signal a problem. Also, costs associated with marketing or registration could be compared with those of other meetings to develop cost standards.

Input Categories

Several major input categories are needed to show the costs and efficiencies of meetings. Some overlap with the different categories may occur, but for the most part, they stand alone.

Tracking Meetings and Events—Topics and Themes

One of the most basic measures is tracking the number of meetings and events that have been organized—often by types. Different topics and themes can be tracked—for example, business development conferences, compliance meetings, and management retreats. Tracking can also be maintained with categories for business types, such as corporate or association meetings, professional or educational conferences. Tracking in this way shows the full scope of what types of meetings and events meeting professionals are conducting using logical categories.

Tracking People

The most obvious place to start with input is tracking the people involved in meetings and events. Several measures may be important to show the variety of the audience. The first measure, total number attending, is the actual number of people participating in a meeting or event, sometimes expressed as a percent of some target group. The number of people can be divided into different categories, as well. For example, showing participants involved in meetings and events by job, industry, age, gender, race, and other categories may be helpful in marketing and coverage issues.

Tracking Duration

Consistent with tracking people would be the hours or days involved in meetings and events, a common measure for benchmarking. Some organizations may track the total hours of meetings and events to create an impressive figure of how much time is consumed by participants' involvement in these activities. Breaking down the number of hours into job, job groups, and even functional areas may be more meaningful. Still others track the number of hours involved in the meeting or event by various groups including age, gender, and race.

Tracking Coverage

Another important way to track people and hours is to track the coverage by jobs, job groups, functional areas, or types of customers. For example, tracking coverage may involve tracking the number of individuals from a critical target category and the amount of time they spent in the meeting. Still another way is to show the breakdown of coverage by people and hours according to the different functions of the organization, beginning with research and development and continuing through sales, marketing, and customer support. Association planners may track attendance by type of member.

Since meetings are often aligned with particular strategic objectives, coverage can focus on them. The total number of hours consumed and the number of people attending the meeting can show current alignment with strategy. When particular strategic objectives have little or no coverage, immediate action may be needed to devote resources to them.

Finally, another way to show coverage by people and hours is to focus on particular operational problems. For example, one organization experienced serious customer service problems. Several meetings were held, with a focus on improving customer service. The number of people and the number of hours involved in the meetings were presented as a measure of commitment to customer satisfaction.

Tracking Requests

An often overlooked tracking issue is to indicate the percent of the meetings that are requested for various reasons. As discussed in Chapter 2, some meetings are implemented for the wrong reasons, or at least questionable ones. By coding each meeting based on how it originated, some insight can be gained about why meetings are conducted. With this tracking over time, the meetings and events staff and executives can see this critical input information and how it is changing or should change in the future.

Tracking Technology Use

Another area that should be tracked is the extent to which the internet and technology are used in the meetings and events industry. Although significant progress is being made in moving from traditional meeting delivery to more technology-based delivery, progress has been slower than most experts had forecasted. For planners attempting to make dramatic shifts in delivery, this becomes an important area to monitor.

Tracking Costs

The cost of conducting meetings and events is increasing—creating more pressure to know how and why money is spent. The total cost is required, which means that the cost profile goes beyond the direct costs, including all indirect costs. Fully-loaded cost information is used to manage resources, develop standards, measure efficiencies, and examine alternative delivery methods.

Tabulating meeting costs is an essential step in developing the ROI calculation, and these costs are used as the denominator in the ROI formula. Focusing on costs is just as important as focusing on benefits. In practice, however, costs are often more easily captured than benefits.

Communicating the costs without presenting the benefits is dangerous. Unfortunately, many planners have fallen into this trap for years. Costs are presented to management in many ingenious ways, such as the cost of the program, cost per participant, and cost per hour of meeting time. While these may be helpful for efficiency comparisons, presenting them without the benefits (or at least some plan to capture them) can cause problems. When most executives review meeting and event costs, a logical question comes to mind: What benefit was received from the meeting? This is a typical management reaction, particularly when costs are perceived to be excessive. Because of this, some planners have developed a policy of not communicating cost data for a specific meeting unless the benefits can be captured and presented along with the costs, even if the benefit data is subjective and intangible. This helps maintain a balance between the two issues.

The most important task is to define which specific costs are included in a tabulation of the meeting costs. This task involves decisions made by the meetings and events staff and usually approved by management. If appropriate, the finance and accounting staff may need to approve the list.

Tracking Efficiencies

Efficiency is an extremely important issue for meetings and events, particularly the larger ones. Efficiency is measured in different ways and from different viewpoints. One of the first measures is the efficiency of using the meetings and events staff, such as the number of meetings per planner. This data can also be misleading because outsourcing could make a big difference. The use of part-time planners changes the number as well, but it still represents a gross efficiency measure at the function level. While the goal is to have the number of meetings per planner as large as possible, a smaller number sometimes demonstrates a commitment to quality.

Efficiency data include the meeting hours provided per staff member. The hours provided is a reflection of how much content per staff member is contributed. Another efficiency measure is the average cost per hour provided. Still, other efficiency measures include the average time to conduct the needs assessment, the average time to design an hour of content, the average time to plan the meeting, and the time from a request to a launch of a new meeting.

Tracking Outsourcing

More companies, organizations, and associations are moving to outsourcing part of, and in some cases almost all, their meetings and events functions. If that is the goal, tracking the extent to which outsourcing is used is helpful. The percent of a total meeting or event that is outsourced to external contractors compared to the percent conducted by the internal staff is one way to measure outsourcing. The percentage of meetings organized internally and externally must be determined to see if the goals are being met. These percentages vary significantly based on the philosophy of the organization and the particular success achieved in outsourcing.

Key Issues

It is fitting to end this chapter with several key issues that have been briefly discussed. Input and indicator data are the largest data set, but the least valuable to executives. Input data do not represent results. They only show what goes into the process and do not reflect outcomes that data at the higher levels show.

Executives care little about this level of data. In a broad sense, they are curious about certain measures that represent volumes and efficiencies, but essentially, they want to see data that represent application, impact, and ROI. Therefore, the challenge is to pick those input and indicator data sets that would attract management attention, or those that emphasize key areas that are under consideration or need attention. Above all, this data set should be minimized in the overall report in terms of the space and time used to present it.

The most important value for this level of data is from the operational management perspective. These data represent costs, inputs, efficiencies, and other issues that are necessary to plan, organize, and manage the process. Ideally, these data are used by the operations part of the meetings and events team and used in a way that drives maximum effectiveness and efficiency.

Final Thoughts

This chapter is the first of six that describe the different levels and types of data. At Level 0, inputs and indicators describe what goes into the process of conducting a meeting or event. An abundant amount of information is available that can be captured, analyzed, and reported to key stakeholders. These include data about the number of meetings, events, people, days, audiences, topics, and requests. In addition, tracking costs, efficiencies, and outsourcing are also important, as they help the meetings and events staff manage their resources carefully, consistently, and efficiently.

Next is a case study that measures the key inputs and indicators—attendance numbers, detailed demographics, and attendee characteristics—at a conference and expo.

Case Study
An Event Audit
LinuxWorld Conference & Expo 2006

By John Mikstay, Manager, Events Audit, BPA Worldwide

This case was prepared to serve as a basis for discussion rather than an illustration of either effective or ineffective administrative and management practices. Names, dates, places, and data may have been disguised at the request of the author or organization.

Abstract

The creation and use of accurate measurement tools has always been a challenge in the exhibition and event industry. In the case of the LinuxWorld Show, management at IDG World Expo was interested in producing, for its sales staff and clients, one report with the most accurate information possible relating to show performance, including verified attendance numbers, detailed demographics, and attendee characteristics. The solution was the Event Insights Report, a joint offering by BPA Worldwide and Exhibit Surveys, Inc., that combines event audits and survey data.

Background

LinuxWorld Conference & Expo is an event exclusively focused on Linux and open source solutions. LinuxWorld provides corporate decision-makers with information and resources needed to implement Linux and open source solutions into business infrastructure and enterprise networks.

IDG World Expo produces technology-focused tradeshows, conferences, and events for professionals who seek world-class education, peer-to-peer networking, and one-stop comparison-shopping. IDG World Expo is a business unit of International Data Group (IDG), a leading technology media, research, and events company.

Event Insights

Founded in 1931 by a group of advertisers, publishers, and agencies, BPA Worldwide is an independent, not-for-profit, self-regulating organization governed by a tripartite Board of Directors. BPA Worldwide consumer and business media audits provide assurance, insight, and advantage to consumer and business-to-business media owners and media buyers in more than twenty countries. In

2004, after exhaustive research and consultative planning, BPA launched its Events Audit division and initiative to increase credibility, accountability, and transparency within the exhibitions industry.

To serve the exhibition industry more completely, a partnership was formed in January 2006 between BPA and Exhibit Surveys, Inc., a full-service research firm dedicated solely to providing market intelligence and measurement to the exhibition industry. The combined core competencies of audit and research was the basis for the formation of the joint offering, known as Event Insights, which was introduced in February 2006.

Rationale for Using Event Insights with LinuxWorld

Top management considers LinuxWorld Conference & Expo one of the most important events for IDG. To maintain itself as a leader in the IT industry and continue to grow and serve its clients effectively, conversations occurred between IDG, BPA Worldwide, and Exhibit Surveys, Inc., concerning what other metrics could be implemented to continue to achieve established successes and growth opportunities. It was agreed that LinuxWorld would be the first event to implement the use of the Event Insights' combined audit/research report as a measurement, analysis, and sales tool for both the show organizer and the exhibitors.

Evaluation Methodology

Measurement tools within the exhibition industry have experienced slow adoption. However, research has been widely used by show organizers and exhibitors throughout the industry to evaluate the show experience. Show organizers use research to determine the characteristics of attendees, their habits at the events, and how they might react to a show's changes, such as venue change and pavilions added/removed. Organizers also survey their exhibitors in a proactive effort with regard to exhibitor discontent with show decorators, inadequate participation, poor venue, etc. Show organizers and exhibitors often only use survey data internally. The data are closely guarded and the results considered proprietary information.

Audits have been accepted slowly because of the perception that they are meant only to uncover improper activities or to find something negative. However, show organizers are now more educated about audits and realize they provide a powerful selling tool for their staff. Since these audits can pinpoint the quality of an event audience, show organizers realize the use of this data can lower attrition rates, increase growth and revenue, and improve partnering with clients. Among exhibitors, the education process has created a dialogue in which exhibitors are empowered to demand third-party certification of a registration database from their event(s). They can then more effectively prove to their Chief Marketing Officers (CMOs) the rationale behind choosing one event over another, along with justifying the required participation investment.

The IT industry was hardest hit when the dot-com bubble burst and the economic downturn occurred at the beginning of the 21st century. However, the IT industry took an active leadership role within the exhibition industry in adopting audits as a standard accountability practice. Through major industry associations, discussions were raised about auditing events and making them industry standards. Post 9/11, other industry segments within the exhibition space also began to realize the opportunity to present accurate data to their clients. Today, more than seventy events are audited within the exhibition industry. Organizers understand the benefits that an independent, third-party audit report brings to their companies and clients.

Evaluation Planning

To better understand the desired impact of the Event Insights report, BPA Worldwide and Exhibit Surveys, Inc., facilitated a meeting with IDG to determine conference expectations and desired impact measures, including revenue, market share, efficiencies, and customer satisfaction. They explored the specific actions each party would be expected to take once the show was concluded, detailing as much as possible the steps, tasks, contacts, and follow-up expected and required. This included deadlines for when the registration data would be sent to BPA and when the final report results could be expected by IDG.

Based on the above criteria, BPA and Exhibit Surveys, Inc., then probed for specific processes that should take place, contacts that should be made, and desired takeaways from the meeting. These issues were resolved quickly since the steps necessary to provide the report analysis of both audit and survey data were comprehensive and already in place.

Although the LinuxWorld report contains audit and survey data, this study will primarily discuss the report's audit portion and the processes BPA used to produce the results.

Data Collection and Analysis

The methods of data collection pre-show, at-show, and post-show for both BPA and the LinuxWorld registration vendor are listed in this section.

Pre-Show Procedures

All contractual and financial obligations were initiated and concluded prior to any procedures occurring. Two months prior to the show, BPA sent a "parameter letter" to IDG, outlining the three stages of the process (pre-show, at-show, and post-show) and asking for show documentation relating to attending or exhibiting procedures. Next, to understand IDG's registration process, a questionnaire was sent to IDG asking for all event contact and logistical information. Copies of registration and fee forms were to be sent along with an electronic version of the show's logo (for identification of the brand on the report) and any documents of instruction for registering (these forms may already have been gathered through the "parameter letter" instructions). The registration portion asked:

- How do attendees pre-register?
- Are badges mailed to pre-registered attendees, and if so, how are they verified on-site?
- Is registration internal or outsourced? If outsourced, all contact information for the registration company is needed.
- Is on-site registration electronic or manual?
- How is payment collected (if applicable)?
- Are there separate on-site locations to credential (verify) pre-registered, on-site, other attendees, or exhibitors? If so, please explain.
- Are there satellite locations to credential (verify) attendees other than the main registration area? If so, please explain.

This rigorous information gathering was necessary to serve as a benchmark for registration verification on-site, while at least one BPA auditor observed. This also helped BPA fully understand the verification methodology in use by the client to determine if there were holes or flaws that could be exploited by attendees.

The results of the questionnaire revealed that IDG employed sound verification methodology for pre-show registrants and on-site attendees. It was also determined through several pre-show discussions with IDG (one month prior to the show) that a non-verified attendee audit would also occur. This would ensure post-show that all attendees, both verified and non-verified, would be contacted and act as a safety.

IDG was asked (as are all clients) if BPA could work directly with the outsourced registration vendor. This was agreed to as important to the data integrity and the process of directly transferring the database to BPA's Electronic Auditing department from the registration vendor, eliminating the show organizer from the equation. The LinuxWorld registration vendor was contacted pre-show and was sent a PowerPoint presentation prepared by BPA to show what was required for an auditable database. This included reviewing a test database for de-duplication, coding manuals for all registration codes, demographic fields complete and mirroring the registration form, and to clearly mark the attendees as verified or non-verified. All registration vendors have different methods of marking verified files, so it was important to know the preferred methodology.

The last portion of the questionnaire asked the organizer to list what type of demographic questions from his registration form he would like to report. This was an important aspect of the pre-show data gathering effort since this determined the structure of the audit report and the findings to be reported.

It was determined that IDG would report:

- "Primary business/industry type" to be cross-tabbed with "primary job function" for a clear picture of the attendees' demographic data
- "Company size by number of employees"
- "Classification of annual purchasing budget"

It was also determined, through pre-show discussions (one month prior to the show), that on the first page of information, referred to as "Audited Attendee Analysis," BPA would add another attendee breakout showing "special program attendees" to further break down the types of attendees. This is shown in Table 1. These attendees were registered through major exhibiting companies that were sponsoring events at the LinuxWorld Show.

Table 1. Audited Attendee Analysis (page 1 of LinuxWorld 2006 Event Insights Report)

3. AUDITED ATTENDEE ANALYSIS

Year which Event was Held	Event Location	Conference Attendees	Exhibit Only Attendees	Sub-Total: Conference & Exhibit Only Attendees	Speakers	Media	Special Program Attendees*	Exhibitors, Non-Exhibiting Sponsors & their Support Staff**	Total
2006	San Francisco, CA	969	5,481	6,450	132	175	406	2,526	9,689

* Includes verified special program attendees from HP and IBM. These attendees are not included in the audited demographic data.

** Verified and Non-Verified counts taken from the registration database provided by the registration company.

A jointly collaborated press release between Event Insights (representing both BPA Worldwide and Exhibit Surveys, Inc.) and IDG World Expo was sent (one week prior to the show) to announce the combined audit/research-style Event Insights report IDG planned to employ for the San Francisco event marketing strategy.

One week prior to the show, IDG sent a registration code to BPA for an observer to attend the event with full access and for the conference to review and document all observations of on-site procedures. BPA then "seeded" the registration file with pre-registered names of people not attending the event to test the verification methods employed on site.

At-Show Procedures

Just prior to the event, it was determined that the audit would not be confidential, as noted by the earlier press release. This is not always the case. BPA remains conscious that some organizers do not want this information made public before the process is completed and, therefore, attempt to keep a low profile while performing on-site evaluations.

A notes template was created for the on-site observer to systematically review all pre-show procedures and to begin making observations. This information was then condensed into a report filed post-show with the full audit and was made available to the show organizer. The evaluation process for LinuxWorld and for all events observed included:

- Meeting the registration vendor on-site (whether outsourced or internal)
- Observing registration procedures and verification methods of different registration types (based on what was benchmarked through the pre-show questionnaire records), including speakers, press, and exhibitors
- Determining how lead retrieval was handled (lead retrieval systems are sometimes employed as a secondary source of verification)
- Observing badge coding (i.e. different badge holder colors to differentiate attendee types, font size, and if the names and company information are easy to read, etc.)
- Observing security (how extensive is security for entering both exhibit halls and conference sessions)
- Noting general comments and observations of the Exhibition (special events, etc.)

The last on-site procedure BPA performed was to ask some prepared questions to random exhibitors and attendees. This gave the organizer more show feedback than might be obtained from an on-site, write-in survey or from questions asked by staff. The BPA observer will not reveal credentials to those being questioned if the organizer requests the audit to remain confidential through the pre- and at-show stages.

Since it is mandatory for BPA to review at least the first event audited with a new organizer client so benchmarks can be developed, an auditor was on-site at LinuxWorld. If, after the first event there are no changes for consecutive events (i.e., show personnel, registration, company, verification methodology,) it is unnecessary to attend that event again. Therefore, BPA requested a face-to-face meeting with the process contact, Brand Vice President Melinda Kendall. This was an important step since it is often the first time for contacts to meet. However, the auditor had an ongoing working relationship with the client.

As was the case with the pre-show questionnaire, it was determined that verification methods were sound and the on-site observations satisfactory for LinuxWorld. The report was then prepared to be available post-show for the audit file and IDG.

Post-Show Procedures

Post-show procedures for the attendance audit are employed identically for every event. LinuxWorld was no exception. As mentioned in the pre-show procedures, the questionnaire contained the contact information for the organizer's registration vendor, whether internal or outsourced.

Pre- and at-show discussions with the registration vendor determined the database procedures to be sound and viable to create auditable data leading to a more efficient analysis by BPA and Exhibit Surveys, Inc., (for their research analysis preparation) and better turnaround time for the report to the organizer.

Databases are received through BPA's Electronic Auditing department in a secured room. Clients and/or registration vendors are sent a password to a secured server where their database can maintain total security, especially with regard to the confidentiality and proprietary nature of the information. The registration vendor for LinuxWorld followed this process.

The database was received about ten days after the event concluded, and BPA began its post-show analysis. The procedures were as follows:

- Auditor check of the database with regard to all fields present, a three-stage de-duplication test, and confirmation of verified and non-verified data clearly marked.
- Database returned to electronic auditing to pull a sample of the **verified** data to be confirmed as having attended the event. This 429-record sample was considered large and was statistically valid for any size database.
- Confirmations department set up a test for the verified data where all records were contacted by phone and all demographic questions were tested, including a question simply asking the attendee if he did attend the event and in what capacity, based on the attendee breakdown segments. The analysis requires less than 2% error to pass and be accepted. This test took one week to complete, and it passed with less than 2% error.
- Confirmations department set up a test to be e-mailed to all non-verified records for verification to ensure that no one was missed. This was a special

request by the organizer as noted in the pre-show procedures. Job titles and company names were compared. The test took two to three weeks to complete allowing time for two to three email reminders. This is a "what you see is what you get" result, and the test resulted in a 15% response rate and the addition of more than 250 records to the verified files.

- The non-verified respondents were then put through a confirmations test to ensure the response validity. This also tested and passed with less than 2% error.

While the confirmations and non-verified tests were being completed, the auditor prepared the demographic data for analysis. IDG had requested that BPA provide them with the "Audited Attendance Analysis" (Table 1) as soon as possible for a post-show release of numbers for marketing and sales purposes. A preliminary analysis was sent without non-verified test results, and another sent immediately following the addition of those results.

As mentioned in the pre-show procedures, BPA was asked to present the "business/industry type" information as a cross-tab with "job function." The auditor provided this analysis along with a geographic breakout and other demographics previously requested.

An official Statement of Certification was provided at the end of the report, along with a copy of the LinuxWorld registration form and conference fee schedule (as is protocol with all reports). Once completed, the report and all of the supporting pre-show, at-show, and post-show reports were forwarded to the BPA Worldwide' Internal Auditing (IA) Department for an internal review of the process. This occurs on every audit completed at BPA, regardless of media type. Once the audit passes the checklist system of the IA department, it is sent to production and for final approval from the client. After final approval by IDG, BPA sent the printed report to the IDG offices in Framingham, Massachusetts.

Evaluation Results

At this point in the process, BPA had completed the audit portion of the Event Insights report and awaited the survey data portion of the report from Exhibit Surveys, Inc. This timetable depends on how many questions the client wishes to report in the survey portion and how difficult it is for Exhibit Surveys, Inc., to gather responses to attendee research. Exhibit Surveys, Inc., is skilled at implementing surveys with a two- to three-week timeframe. Research typically occurs simultaneously with the auditing process to prevent wasted time before final approval.

The report, once completed, was sent to IDG for review. Both BPA Worldwide and Exhibit Surveys, Inc., completed comparative analyses between the audit demographics and survey results to ensure only minor—if not non-existent—variance in percentages of responses among like demographic questions. This was an important exercise to ensure that sound methodology was used for respective portions of the report. The review results showed little or no variance in the response rates among like demographic questions.

Communication Strategies

IDG had several customers who anticipated the report. These clients used it extensively in internal event reporting and in planning for the next year. When exhibitors have specific questions about the audience demographics, (i.e., industry or titles), the entire report is scrutinized. Melinda Kendall, IDG Brand Vice President stated, "As we launch Next Generation Data Center to LinuxWorld, with a combined audience, it gives credibility to the launch to be able to authoritatively demonstrate the pre-existing LinuxWorld audience, taking away much of the perceived risk to the exhibitors."

Lessons Learned

The time required to prepare the audit and survey data is the key ingredient with regard to maintaining the report's relevance. The client expects tools, both existing and in new markets, they can use to promote to exhibitors immediately after the event. The responsibility of maintaining timely progress lies with BPA Worldwide and Exhibit Surveys, Inc. They also should examine the process to see where improvements can be made.

Recommendation

Following the completion of the second of two Event Insights reports, Ms. Kendall stated to BPA Worldwide, "We feel that auditing our events, and providing the additional research data, helps build much stronger and more trusting relationships with our customers. Not only do we provide credible, authoritative data after the event, but knowing that we will be telling the truth post-event opens up new opportunities to partner with customers pre-event as well." She also explained that this occurs by discussing pre-registration figures and expected attendance to allow exhibitors to better plan booth activities.

Resources

Exhibition & Event Industry Audit Commission (EEIAC) B-to-B Audit Standards
BPA Worldwide B-to-B Audit Standards

Questions for Discussion

1. Discuss the ways in which the Event Insights report was aligned to the specific needs of the show organizer.
2. Will this measurement and accountability trend in the area of trade show audits decline or increase in the coming years?
3. How can the demand for measurement and accountability be expanded more effectively within the event industry more effectively?
4. What types of trade shows and meetings would most benefit from an audit such as this?

About the Author

John Mikstay serves as Manager, Events Audit at BPA Worldwide, a not-for-profit self-regulating organization founded in 1931 and governed by a tripartite Board of Directors. BPA Worldwide is the global industry resource for verified audience data and media knowledge and delivers consumer and business media audits of unsurpassed rigor, objectivity, accuracy, transparency, and timeliness. Mr. Mikstay has more than ten years' experience in the trade show industry, where he worked in sales and show management with Reed Exhibitions, CMP Media, and Primedia Business Exhibitions (Prism). He currently sits on the ABM Events Council, the ISO Committee for Exhibition Terminology, and the CEIR Research Committee. He can be contacted by phone at 203.447.2881 or by email at jmikstay@bpaww.com.

Editor's Notes

When moving toward calculating an ROI, a meeting or event must first have the "right" attendees present for the meeting objectives to be fulfilled. In this case, the right attendees for a trade show exhibitor would be those in his target market and at the appropriate job level to make decisions about purchasing the exhibitor's product or service. If the right attendees are not present at the trade show, objectives at each level of evaluation will fail.

As this case demonstrates, it was essential for the trade show organizer to prove to the exhibitors the value of exhibiting at the trade show. IDG, the show organizer, chose to provide this value through a careful and detailed third-party documentation of exhibit attendees. The carefully collected audit results were then reviewed by exhibitors to determine if the "right" attendees were indeed present at the show.

Chapter 4
Measuring Reaction and Perceived Value

The next four chapters present ways to measure the results data collected when evaluating meetings and events. This chapter focuses on measuring reaction and perceived value. Collecting this level of data during and at the end of the meeting is the first operational phase of the ROI Methodology. Participant feedback may represent powerful data to use when making adjustments and measuring success. Although several methods may be used to capture reaction and perceived value data, this chapter outlines the most common approaches for data collection and explores ways to use the information for maximum value.

The Importance of Measuring Reaction and Perceived Value

It would be difficult to imagine a meeting being conducted without collecting feedback from those involved in it. Collecting this type of data involves several key issues and audiences, making this one of the most important data collection steps in the process. Attendee feedback is critical to understanding how the meeting is perceived. With the constant focus on customer service, measuring attendees' satisfaction with each meeting is important. For some planners, success is only measured with reaction data. However, other measures should be included for a more complete evaluation. As this book clearly shows, reaction data are only one of the seven types of data.

The concept of continuous process improvement suggests that a meeting must be adjusted and refined when it is repeated. An important link between obtaining feedback, making changes, and reporting changes to the groups providing the information is required for meeting success. This survey-feedback-action loop is critical for improvement.

A recent application of reaction data is using it to predict the future success of a meeting using analytical techniques. This involves asking participants to estimate the application and in some cases, the subsequent value of that application. In this situation, reaction data become a forecast.

Some planners collect reaction data using standard questions, and compare them with data from other meetings so that norms and standards can be developed. This is particularly helpful with completely new meetings. Some external firms even base part of the planning team's success on the level of client satisfaction, making reaction data very important.

Data Collection Issues

Several important issues can affect data collection and are discussed here. These issues represent the fundamentals and concerns that must be addressed along the way.

Sources of Data

When considering possible data sources for feedback on the success of a meeting, several categories can be used in all meetings. Participants are probably the most important customers. They are key stakeholders who must attend, participate, and learn new information, knowledge, skills, and people to make the meeting successful. Participant feedback is critical to making adjustments and changes in the meeting. The next key customer group is the speakers and facilitators, who also play a role in a successful meeting. They facilitate the different sessions and learning processes and influence the participants.

The third group of key customers is the sponsors and supporters, those who are not directly involved but have an interest in the meeting. Their perceptions of the meeting's success or potential success are important feedback because this group is in a position to influence the meeting's continuation. The fourth group of key customers is the client, who funds or approves the meeting. This individual, or group of individuals, requested the meeting, supports it, approves budgets, allocates resources, and ultimately lives with the meeting's success or failure. This individual or group must be completely satisfied with the meeting.

Content vs. Non-Content

Capturing reaction data about the content of the meeting is an important consideration. Too often, feedback data reflect aesthetic issues that may not include information about the substance of the meeting. For example, a planner needed to show the value of a marketing meeting, which focused on client development. The audience was relationship managers, who have direct contact with customers. This meeting was designed to discuss product development, marketing, and business development strategies. Table 4-1 shows the comparison of content vs. non-content issues that can be explored on a reaction questionnaire.

Table 4-1. Comparison of Content vs. Non-Content

Focus on Non-Content Issues	Focus on Content Issues
Demographics	Facilities
Location	Service
Transportation	Timing of meeting
Registration	Relevance of materials
Logistics	Importance of content to my success
Hotel service	Appropriate use of time
Media	Amount of new information
Food	Quality of speakers
Breaks and refreshments	Perceived value of meeting
Cocktail reception	Contacts made
Speaker	Planned use of material
Materials/topics	Forecast of impact
Overall satisfaction	Overall satisfaction

The traditional way to evaluate these activities is to focus on non-content issues. As the table shows, the column to the left indicates areas important to activity surrounding the session, but few measures reflect the value achieved from the meeting. The column on the right shows a focus on content with only minor input on issues such as the facilities and service provided. This does not imply that the quality of the service, the atmosphere of the event, and the location of the meeting are not important. It is assumed that these issues will be taken care of and addressed appropriately. A more important data set tracks the detailed information about the perceived value of the meeting, the importance of the content, and the planned use of material or a forecast of the impact—indicators that successful results did and will occur. This example underscores the tremendous shift occurring in the meetings and events industry: a move from measuring entertainment to measuring reaction, learning, and sometimes, application, impact, and ROI.

The Deceptive Feedback Cycle

Too much reliance is sometimes placed on overall reaction data, particularly when they are used as the principal tool for evaluating planners. It is easy to manipulate the overall satisfaction rating, which is often referred to as a "smile" or "enjoyment" rating. The objective is for the participants to enjoy the meeting, and the planner is the centerpiece of that enjoyment. As shown in Figure 4-1, if the participants enjoy the meeting, the overall satisfaction ratings are high. Therefore, planners are primarily rewarded on those ratings. When this is the case, they naturally focus their actions on enjoyment—making the meetings they plan enjoyable experiences. Certainly, nothing is wrong with enjoying the meeting. The problem lies in the excessive use of the measure, "Overall, how satisfied are you with the meeting?" This measure does not correlate with other important success measures. A certain level of enjoyment and satisfaction is an absolute must. However, planners risk focusing on entertainment only and short-changing the content. As some professional planners say, "We quickly migrate to the business of entertaining instead of the business of learning."

Figure 4-1. The Deceptive Feedback Cycle

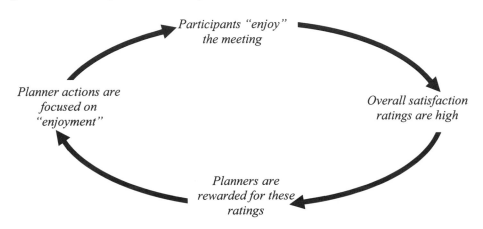

To avoid this, planner effectiveness should also be evaluated on learning measures and, occasionally, application and impact measures. This keeps a balanced perspective and prevents an over-reliance on just reaction data. Evaluations should focus more on content-related issues. The value of overall reaction data has to be constantly put into perspective. For the content developer, speakers, and participants, reaction data are important, but from the point of view of the client and sponsor, this data may not be very valuable.

Key Areas for Feedback

Many topics are targets for feedback because so many issues and processes are involved in a typical meeting. Feedback is needed for almost every major issue, step, or process to make sure outcomes are successful. Table 4-2 shows the typical areas of feedback for most meetings.

Table 4-2. Detailed Reaction Data

Adapted from Rapid Evaluation, Susan Barksdale and Teri Lund. Alexandria, VA: ASTD, 2001. Used with permission.

Reaction Data		
Type of Data	**Reason for Collecting**	**Data Components**
Participant demographics	Audience served versus needs Trends in attendance Future planning Diversity	Job title Department/division Education Experience Length of service Reason for participation
Logistics and service	Facility changes Facility complaints Customer satisfaction	Location Room Comfort Communication Access to food and refreshments
Readiness	Right participant Proper timing Ready to learn	Appropriate experience level Prerequisites Motivation to learn Opportunity to use the concepts Timing of meeting
Objectives	Proper objectives Progress with objectives	Clarity of objectives Appropriateness of objectives Success with objectives
Meeting materials	Adjustments Design changes Stimulate interest	Usefulness of materials Appearance of materials Amount of new information
Speakers	Speaker performance data Complaints with speakers	Experience level Knowledge and expertise Communication success Responsiveness to participants Involvement of participants Pacing of presentation
Media/delivery	New media Comparison of types of media Effectiveness of media	Delivery Media effectiveness
Value of content	Alignment with business Future planning Adjustments to content Design changes	Alignment with business need Why meeting was selected Relevance of content to job Importance to job success Motivational aspect Connection to business strategies Satisfaction with content

Networking	Networking success	Number of contacts
		Quality of contact
		Interaction with others
Special events	Effectiveness	Success of activity
		Importance to meeting
Social activities	Effectiveness	Applicability to meeting
Value of meeting	Marketing	Good investment in me
	Pricing	Good investment of my time
	Commitment	Fair price for meeting
	Support	Overall satisfaction
Planned use	Follow-up potential	Planned actions
	Adjust expectation	Intent to use
	Transfer of learning	Barriers to use
	Support of meetings	Enablers of use
		Recommend to others
		Willingness to provide data
Future needs	Planning meetings	Additional needs
		Other meetings
Marketing and registration	Source of enrollment	Source of enrollment
	Decision-making process	Decision-making process
	Pricing	Pricing
	Ease of registration	Registration process
Open comments	Opportunity to identify unknown issues	Other comments

For the most part, this table is self explanatory. It shows the data categories that are typical in collecting reaction data from meetings. Collecting data on all the categories would be too much because the survey or questionnaire would be too long. This provides a list for consideration of some of the basic issues. Other measures could be included, but Table 4-2 highlights some of the more important ones, particularly those closely related to the meeting's content.

Data Collection Timing

The timing of data collection revolves around particular events connected with the meeting. Any event or activity is an appropriate time to collect data, beginning with pre-meeting data collection and progressing to end-of-meeting collection.

Sometimes, collecting pre-assessment data is helpful. Although this may not be common, it is a way to solicit attitudes and perceptions toward topics or issues that will be discussed during the meeting. Also, pre-assessments may involve learning assessments that can be used to understand the degree to which participants currently understand the content. Therefore, pre-assessments may contain Level 1 and Level 2 questions.

Data collection during meetings that occur over multiple days is important. For example, if a meeting lasts three days, waiting until the end of the third day to collect feedback data may be inappropriate. By then, participants may not be able to judge some of the issues, events, and processes that occurred earlier. Capturing daily feedback is better. At the end of each day, feedback is collected about the material covered on that day, including the pace and flow of the session, the degree of involvement of the participants, and the content's value.

Another approach is to collect data immediately after each session, giving the participants the opportunity to judge key issues while the material is fresh in their minds. Still another approach is evaluating different events separately. For example, if a tour is connected to the meeting, the tour may need to be evaluated separately. Perhaps participants attend a separate networking event in the evening and are given an opportunity to provide quick feedback at the beginning of the next day. Even with daily or event-based feedback, capturing the end-of-meeting data is still important to evaluate the entire meeting experience.

Using Questionnaires and Surveys

Questionnaires and surveys are the most common data collection methods for measuring reaction. Questionnaires and surveys come in all sizes, ranging from short reaction forms to detailed, multi-paged instruments. They can be used to obtain subjective data about participants' reactions as well as to document data for future use in an ROI analysis. With their versatility and popularity, properly designing questionnaires and surveys is critical.

Several basic types of questions are available. Depending on the purpose of the evaluation, the questionnaire or survey may contain any or all of the types of questions shown in Figure 4-2.

Figure 4-2. Types of Questions or Statements

1. Open-Ended Questions:
   What problems will you encounter when attempting to use the knowledge or information in this meeting?

2. Checklists:
   For the following list, check all the business measures that may be influenced by this meeting.

☐ Revenue	☐ Cost Control
☐ Productivity	☐ Cycle Time
☐ Quality	☐ Customer Satisfaction
☐ Efficiency	☐ Job Satisfaction

3. Dichotomous Questions (Yes/No Responses)
   As a result of this meeting, I have a better understanding of my responsibilities for customer service.

   Yes ☐   No ☐

4. Numerical Scales

	Strongly Disagree			Strongly Agree	
	1	2	3	4	5
A. This meeting is relevant to my job.	☐	☐	☐	☐	☐
B. This meeting is important to my success.	☐	☐	☐	☐	☐

5. Multiple Choice Questions:

   Which of the following describes the networking in this meeting?
   a. Too little
   b. Too much
   c. Just right

6. Ranking Scales:
   The following list contains six important factors that will influence the success of this meeting. Place a one (1) by the item that is most influential, a two (2) by the item that is second most influential, and so on. The item ranked six (6) will be the least influential item on the list.

   Proper Tools _____ Technology _____
   My Teams' Culture _____ Management Support _____
   Communications _____ Technical Support _____

The key is to select the question or statement that is most appropriate for the information needed. A dichotomous question (yes/no) and the numerical scale (one to five) are typical reaction measurement types. Essentially, the individual indicates the extent of agreement with a particular statement, providing an opinion of a varying degree. Still, open-ended questions can be used, particularly when asking about specific problem areas. Checklists, multiple-choice questions, and ranking scales are more appropriate for measuring learning and application, which are described in later chapters. Surveys are a type of questionnaire but focus on participant's attitudes only.

Designing Questionnaires/Surveys

Survey and questionnaire design is a simple and logical process. Poorly designed questionnaires/surveys are confusing, frustrating, and potentially embarrassing. The following steps will help ensure that a valid, reliable, and effective instrument is developed:

1. Determine the information needed.

2. Select the type(s) of questions/statements.

3. Develop the questions/statements.

4. Keep questions/statements as simple as possible.

5. Test the questions.

6. Design for easy tabulation.

7. Prepare a data summary.

8. Finalize the questionnaire/survey.

9. Communicate the purpose.

10. Ensure that participant responses are anonymous.

Securing High Response Rates

For most reaction evaluations, questionnaires and surveys will be used. When an evaluation is planned, exploring a wide range of issues and details is tempting. However, asking for too much detail in the reaction questionnaire can negatively impact the response rate. The challenge, therefore, is to approach questionnaire and survey design and administration to attain maximum response rates. The following actions can be taken to ensure a successful response rate. Although the term questionnaire is used, the following also apply to surveys:

- Early in the process, let participants know that they will need to complete a questionnaire.
- Indicate how the data will be used and perhaps how it has been used in the past.
- Design for a quick response, usually not to exceed ten to twenty minutes.
- Make responding to the questionnaire easy, using forced-choice questions.
- Communicate the estimated amount of time required to complete the questionnaire.
- Ask participants if they would like to see a copy of the summary.
- Make it look professional.
- Collect the data anonymously.

Using Interviews and Focus Groups

Another method to capture reaction data is the interview, which is not used as frequently as questionnaires. Interviews may be conducted by the planner or a third party. While more expensive than questionnaires, they are more versatile. They are focused, allow for clarification, and provide an opportunity for probing.

The focus group may also be helpful when in-depth feedback is required. A focus group involves a small group discussion, including participants, and is facilitated by a person experienced with conducting focus groups.

Interviews and focus groups should be used only when in-depth feedback about reaction is required. They are only appropriate when significant consequences could result due to this feedback. For example, they would be used when a meeting is conducted on a pilot basis and serious adjustments may be needed to implement the process.

Uses of Reaction Data

Unfortunately, reaction data are often collected and disregarded. Too often, planners use the information to feed their egos and then let it quietly disappear into their files, forgetting the original purpose behind its collection. For successful evaluation, the information collected must be used to make adjustments or validate meeting success; otherwise, the exercise may be a waste of time. A few of the common uses for reaction and perceived value data are listed below:

1. Monitor customer satisfaction.
2. Identify strengths and weaknesses in the meetings.
3. Evaluate speakers.
4. Evaluate planned improvements.
5. Develop norms and standards.
6. Link with follow-up data.
7. Market future meetings.

Final Thoughts

This chapter discusses the second of seven measures of data reported in the ROI Methodology. Measuring reaction should be included in every meeting evaluation and is a critical part of success. Although data can be used in many ways, two important ones stand out. The first is making adjustments and changes. The second is reporting the level of satisfaction with the meetings and including this as one of the seven key types of data. Reaction data can be collected with questionnaires, surveys, interviews, and focus groups. By far, the questionnaire or survey is the most common instrument. Sometimes, a simple, one-page reaction questionnaire is appropriate. Whatever method is used, collecting data, reacting quickly, making adjustments, and summarizing the data for reporting to stakeholders is critical to a successful meeting.

Two case studies follow that illustrate how two organizations measured reaction and perceived value.

Notes

Barksdale, S. and T. Lund. *Rapid Evaluation*. (Alexandria, VA: ASTD, 2001).

Case Study
Measuring Perceptions and Safety Attitudes
General Mills Foodservice

By Mark A. Fite,
President of Option Technologies Interactive, a division of iDNA, Inc.,
and Wendi Friedman Tush, President of the Lexicomm Group

This case was prepared to serve as a basis for discussion rather than an illustration of either effective or ineffective administrative and management practices. Names, dates, places, and data may have been disguised at the request of the author or organization.

Abstract

An organization working to improve safety performance at manufacturing facilities initiated a series of meetings designed to change employee attitudes regarding safety. The meeting objectives were to inject a safety mindset into the corporate culture, to improve safe behavior, and ultimately to reduce financial and human capital losses due to safety issues. Meeting facilitators used wireless electronic keypads to gather data anonymously from meeting participants concerning their safety mindset.

Background

Located in Minneapolis, Minnesota, General Mills Bakeries and Foodservice, a division of General Mills, Inc., produces ready-to-eat breakfast cereals, refrigerated dough and other baking items, snack and convenience products, frozen vegetables, beverages, and yogurt. Some of the firm's better-known brands include Cheerios, Lucky Charms, Chex, Betty Crocker, Pillsbury, Gold Medal, Green Giant, and Yoplait. The division operates factories throughout the United States, producing frozen dough products and baking mixes. Safety is a core value.

CHAMPS Meeting

Bakery and Foodservices has been working to improve safety performance at its plants. Safety issues cost the company in a variety of ways, including employee pain and suffering, insurance losses, and loss of productivity. Many company locations instituted behavioral based safety programs, including one called CHAMPS (Changing Habits and Attitudes Make People Safe), to help with this effort. This program was a series of six-hour safety meetings offered at each facility and attended by all employees. The goal of the meeting was to increase safe behavior by improving safety attitudes and perceptions.

During the CHAMPS meeting, instructors placed three chairs in the front of the meeting room. These chairs matched three different attitudes representing "where people sit" with regard to their personal attitudes about safety:

- Chair 1: We need to be relentless about safety. It is ingrained in everything we do.
- Chair 2: Safety is important, but can sometimes conflict with key performance goals.
- Chair 3: Accidents happen. There is a gap between what we say and what we do.

Participants in the CHAMPS course were asked to identify the chair that best represents "where they sit" with regard to their personal attitude concerning safety at the beginning and end of the meeting. The objective was to move people from a "Chair 3" attitude, a more fatalistic attitude that accidents will happen, to a "Chair 1" attitude, a proactive attitude that accidents are preventable and safety must be pursued relentlessly.

Typically, managers find that employees start out with a "Chair 3" attitude. Individuals who have witnessed a serious accident become powerful advocates for a "Chair 1" attitude. The challenge for the CHAMPS meeting was to move a high percentage of employees along the hierarchy of understanding so that safety awareness would become even more effectively ingrained as an integral part of each facility's culture.

Evaluation Methodology

To assess the effectiveness of the CHAMPS meeting, facilitators asked participants a combination of questions on their reactions to the sessions and the changes in safety-practice attitudes, pre- and post-meeting.

These questions included:

1. Are the objectives of the meeting clear to you?
2. Did the presenters know the materials?
3. Did you find the interaction and hands-on participation helpful?
4. Can you apply what you are learning to your current job?
5. Overall, did the meeting meet your expectations?

Answers to these questions were collected using a wireless audience response system from iDNA Information Systems. The wireless keypads were perceived to be a critical tool at these meetings. Program leaders wanted to ensure that participants answered all the questions as honestly as possible. In their research, Draper and

Brown demonstrated that interactive keypad systems give participants high confidence in the anonymity of responses.

Each participant answered each question using the following three-point scale:

1. Not at all
2. Somewhat
3. Definitely

The facilitators also used the system to measure baseline and post-session attitudes regarding safety. They were particularly interested in assessing which attitude "Chair" each employee saw as representing his/her own perspective. The goal was to raise the percentage of employees with a "Chair 1" attitude and to empower workers with a greater willingness to work with others to achieve safety excellence.

Data Collection and Data Analysis

A total of 286 manufacturing employees participated in this study. Leaders used an interactive keypad system from iDNA Information Systems to assess participant reactions to the CHAMPS meeting. When using the keypad system, facilitators presented a brief description of the safety attitude that each empty chair at the front of the room represented. They then asked the following question at the outset of the six hour meeting: "Which chair are you in?"

Facilitators then gave participants at least fifteen seconds to consider the question and enter an answer. Following the session, facilitators again asked participants to assess their safety attitude. They reviewed the descriptions of the three chairs and asked: "Which chair are you in now that the meeting is over?" To ensure honesty, the facilitator asked participants to exchange handheld keypads with another participant twice during the meeting. In this way, the participants could be certain that responses were completely anonymous.

After data collection, the facilitators exported the results from the questionnaire to a spreadsheet file that combined data from all groups for the overall analysis. Instructors compared the data from the "chair" question to measure the change in attitudes regarding safety.

Evaluation Results

Table 1 shows participant reactions to the content, materials, and facilitator. Based on this data, 93.3% of participants gave the CHAMPS meeting a positive rating overall when the responses to "somewhat" and "definitely" were combined. Ninety-one percent indicated that they could apply the material they learned on the job, while 90.3% indicated the interactive aspects of the meeting were helpful.

Table 1. Participant Reactions to the Content, Materials, and Facilitator

Question	Not at all 1	Somewhat 2	Definitely 3
1. Are the objectives of the meeting clear to you?	3.1%	28.7%	68.2%
2. Did the facilitators know the materials?	0.7%	47.2%	52.1%
3. Did you find the interaction and hands-on participation helpful?	9.7%	43.4%	46.9%
4. Can you apply what you are learning to your current job?	9.1%	32.8%	58.2%
5. Overall, did the meeting meet your expectations?	6.7%	36.1%	57.2%

Table 2 shows reactions of participants to the question concerning safety attitudes. At the end of the meeting, 71.70% indicated that they felt the company should be relentless about safety. Between the meeting start and meeting end, 15.20% of participants had moved their opinion about safety from "Chair 2" to "Chair 1."

Table 2. Reactions of Participants to Question Concerning Safety Attitudes

"Which chair are you in now that the meeting is over?"	Session Start	Session End	CHANGE
Chair 1 = We need to be relentless about safety. It is ingrained in everything we do.	56.50%	71.70%	15.20%
Chair 2 = Safety is important, but can sometimes conflict with key performance goals.	34.80%	19.60%	-15.20%
Chair 3 = Accidents will happen. There is a gap between what we say and what we do.	8.70%	8.70%	0.00%
TOTALS	100.00%	100.00%	N/A

Participant performance, reaction ratings, and comments all indicate that the CHAMPS safety meeting was well received by participants. Traditionally, positive Level 1 data is a good predictor of application or behavioral changes. Since the meeting was mandatory, the meetings ran the risk of creating restlessness and fatigue. Participant reactions indicated that the content was well delivered and perceived as relevant in the workplace. The delivery methods used appear to have worked well at maintaining the interest of participants.

The results of the study suggest that employees attending CHAMPS found the meeting well executed. A significant majority exhibited the desired attitudes about safety at the conclusion of the meeting.

The facilitators shared a written report with safety managers describing the reactions and attitudes measured in the CHAMPS meetings along with recommendations for future course refinements.

Lessons Learned, Recommendations, and Use of Results

If the meeting is to have a long-term effect on the behavior of participants, follow-up communication and additional meetings may be useful. Based on attendee reactions and input, managers are regularly updating materials associated with the meeting. Over time, it will be important to determine whether attendees actually retain the information and attitudes developed during the meeting.

Resources

Draper, S. W., & Brown, M. I. (2004) Increasing Interactivity in Lectures Using an Electronic Voting System. *Journal of Computer Assisted Learning,* 20, 81-94.

Burnstein, R. A., & Lederman, L.M. (2001). Using Wireless Keypads In Lecture Classes. *Phys. Teach.,* 39, 41, 272-275.

Hake, R. (1998) Interactive-Engagement vs. Traditional Methods: A Six Thousand Student Study. *Am. J. Phys.,* 66, 64-74.

Horowitz, H.M. (1998). "Student Response Systems: Interactivity in a Classroom Environment." *Proceedings of Sixth Annual Conference on Interactive Instruction Delivery. Society for Applied Learning Technology,* 8-15.

Questions for Discussion

1. How could meeting objectives be made more measurable at each level of evaluation?
2. What other means of data collection could have been used to conduct this study?
3. What could be done to improve or enhance this study?
4. What are the pros and cons of using an interactive keypad system for measurement of participant reactions?
5. Is this meeting appropriate for a full ROI analysis? Why or why not?

Acknowledgements

The authors wish to thank Charles Kendall, Division Safety Manager, General Mills Bakeries and Foodservice, for his input and assistance with this case.

About the Authors

Mark A. Fite is President of Option Technologies Interactive, a division of iDNA, Inc. He has spent more than twenty years as a corporate manager and business development leader. Mr. Fite has been involved in founding and growing six companies focused on various aspects of meeting and classroom technology and has held senior leadership roles at firms involved with presentation software and hardware, survey systems, staging, video production, and satellite communications. Mr. Fite has been a leader in the student response business since 1991 when he helped to co-found MeetingNet Interactive Systems, Inc., a pioneer in offering wireless handheld group response systems. He can be reached at 407.872.3333 or mfite@optiontechnologies.com.

Wendi Friedman-Tush is President of the Lexicomm Group. She is finishing her certification in the Phillips ROI Methodology. The Lexicomm Group is a branding and strategic communications company creating campaigns that provide measurable results to help clients achieve their most important business objectives. She can be reached at 212.300.2142 or Wendi@lexicommgroup.com.

Editor's Notes

This is an excellent example of the use of technology to collect and process data. Because the meeting focused on changes in attitudes about safety, learning was a part of the measurement.

Case Study
Measuring Exhibit Performance
NetWorld+Interop Las Vegas

By Joel Federbush,
Director of Business Development and Marketing for Exhibit Surveys

This case was prepared to serve as a basis for discussion rather than an illustration of either effective or ineffective administrative and management practices. Names, dates, places, and data may have been disguised at the request of the author or organization.

Abstract

Trade show organizer Key3Media commissioned an independent, in-depth study of NetWorld+Interop Las Vegas 2003 attendees. An attendee survey provided Key3Media management with the overall characteristics presented, including the quality of these attendees in terms of product interest, buying plans, buying influences, and demographic data. To enhance the relationship between Key3Media and the trade show exhibitors, study results were shared with all involved.

Background

Held in Las Vegas since 1994, Networld+Interop (N+I) 2003 is a three-day spring convention with more than 40,000 attendees and 270 exhibitors. It serves as an information technology showcase for industry titans such as Microsoft Corporation, Cisco Systems, Hewlett-Packard, and Intel Corporation. The Las Vegas Convention and Visitors Authority pegged the show's non-gaming economic impact at $54.5 million.

Rationale for Study

The Exhibit Performance Report, as outlined in this case study, was designed for Key3Media to provide a quantitative measure of the performance of selected exhibiting companies. Key3Media's objective was to use the study as a management tool for making strategic and tactical decisions about future shows, and as a learning tool for identifying strengths and weaknesses that could lead to increased ROI in the future, not only for themselves, but also for exhibitors, maximizing the value of the event received by attendees.

More specifically, it provided:

- Key3Media the opportunity to meet face-to-face with its exhibitors to talk about the show, with sound data about the ROI/ROO delivered from the show.
- Current and prospective exhibitors with factual third-party-generated data needed to justify exhibiting in the show.
- Exhibitors with data to help them plan more effective exhibits to attract and reach specific prospects at the show.

Evaluation Methodology

With the focus of corporate management on measuring ROI, companies often think of measurement as only measuring bottom line results from exhibiting (i.e., message conveyance, brand enhancement, awareness building, lead generation, sales from leads, or PR achieved). Measuring bottom-line results is important, but measurement should do more than only measure ROI. If the ROI is not good, what are the reasons? Is it the fault of the show, the exhibit, or the personnel working the exhibit?

Ideally, performance analysis should include (1) analyzing the show audience to define potential audience, (2) measure exhibit attraction, (3) measure exhibit efficiency, and (4) measure results. This information is critical for making decisions about the future participation in the show and for identifying areas of strength and weakness that will lead to improved ROI in the future.

Potential Audience

The size and value of a potential exhibit audience (regardless of the criteria used to define potential audience) is the primary basis for measuring exhibit performance. Potential audience is also the basis for determining whether an exhibitor attends a show, and if so, the level of investment justified. Exhibit Surveys, Inc., has found that rarely is a company able to reach all its "Total Prospects," and hence, it was necessary to have a more realistic estimate of potential audience. Product interest is the best predictor for an exhibitor's audience level and subsequent success at a show. The size of an exhibitor's potential audience then becomes an important factor in determining participation in the show.

Exhibit Attraction

The next step is to attract these attendees to the exhibit. Several factors impact attraction. The larger the exhibit, the easier it is to attract a higher percentage of a potential audience. The use of pre-show and at-show promotion will help drive traffic to the exhibit. On average, about 65% to70% of high-tech audiences attend a show with a pre-planned agenda. It becomes imperative for exhibitors to promote to these attendees in advance so their booth becomes part of the attendee's show agenda. Show management also has a key role to provide access to the attendee list so that these promotions can reach the exhibitor's target audience.

Exhibitors with smaller exhibits and exhibitors not well-known to the show audience may need to use special attention-getting techniques to attract visitors. While promotion, advertising, and other materials will help raise awareness, they do not immediately help a lesser-known company attract visitors.

Product interest is a natural drawing card. If attendees have a high interest in an exhibitor's products, they will visit the exhibit. Companies with a small portion of the audience interested in their products need to be more conscious about "selectively" attracting visitors. Exhibitors also need to match the products they are exhibiting with those categories that have a high interest. An attractive exhibit draws visitors. Attendees use graphics as a road map to the exhibit. Therefore, the graphics should boldly and clearly identify products. Exhibitors should not assume that attendees are aware of their brand or trade names and should stay away from acronyms in their main graphics (unless there is an explanation).

Exhibit Efficiency

Exhibit Efficiency is a critical step toward measuring results. Often, exhibitors are successful in attracting their potential audience but fail to make adequate face-to-face contact with prospects. In general, the level of face-to-face contact has declined at exhibits, despite the attendees' desire for more personal contact. Attendees who want to move themselves along the purchasing path do so through personal contact with exhibit personnel. Factors impacting exhibit efficiency are:

1. Having an appropriate number of staff on duty.
2. Optimizing staff performance.
3. Understanding attendee profile.
4. Preparing the staff with special training.

Results

The last step of the model measures the results. Measuring bottom line results is important, but measurement should include all the steps of the model. If the results are inadequate, what are the reasons? Is it the fault of the show (the potential audience size and value), the exhibit (exhibit attraction factors), or the staff working the exhibit (exhibit efficiency factors)? Using this model as a guide ensures that you get a complete picture of a company's performance leading to actionable recommendations for improvement.

Data Collection

An online, post-show attendee survey was sent to a random sample of 3,842 attendees (a copy of this post-show questionnaire can be viewed at http://www.exhibitsurveys.com/roinilv03). A reminder was sent to non-respondents three days later. To increase the response sample, an additional 3,940 attendees were sent this same post-show questionnaire two weeks later. All respondents were entered into a drawing for a $300 cash prize, and two winners were selected. A total of 588 questionnaires were returned by the cut-off date for a net return of 8% (after correcting for undeliverable emails). The maximum statistical error due to this sample size is ±4% at a 95% confidence level.

Results

The following results, based on a series of questions within the post-show attendee survey, are taken from respondents that indicated they visited specific N+I Las Vegas exhibits. In the actual study, thirty-three exhibiting companies were measured. However, for illustrative purposes, data for only Company X and four of their competitors are included in this case study. Additionally, noted throughout this case study, individual company scores are compared against Exhibit Surveys' high-tech tradeshow (a) averages and against N+I (b) averages. These averages are provided as a benchmark for comparison when analyzing results.

(a) High-tech show averages are comprised over thirty individual high-tech tradeshows in the U.S. that Exhibit Surveys measured the previous year.

(b) N+I averages are comprised of averaging the scores to each question from the thirty-three exhibits measured in the actual study. The thirty-three companies are representative of large- and medium-size exhibits (based on square footage) across all major product categories.

Potential Audience

Potential Audience, as shown in Table 1, is calculated by taking the "Total Prospects" and multiplying it by the show's Audience Interest Factor (AIF), the percentage of show attendees visiting at least two out of every ten exhibits included in the survey. To determine AIF and other relative exhibit performance data, thirty-three exhibiting companies were listed on the questionnaire.

Table 1. Total Prospects and Potential Audience for Five Companies

Company	Total Prospects	Potential Audience
Company X	15,200	14,000
Company A	15,000	7,800
Company B	14,800	7,700
Company C	14,700	7,700
Company D	14,500	7,500
Show Average	10,300	5,700

Buying Plans

Buying Plans, as shown in Table 2, are the percentage of respondents planning to purchase the type of products exhibited by each company and can be projected to the net attendance. These figures do not in any way indicate the number of units of a product to be potentially purchased. Net Buying Influences (NBI) is the net percentage of attendees who have one or more roles (final say, specify supplier, and/or recommend) in purchasing the types of products exhibited at the show. For example, 85% of the audience has a buying role influencing the purchase of Company X-type products. More specifically, 30% have the final say, 27% specify the supplier, and 59% recommend products for purchase.

Table 2. Buying Plans and Buying Influences for Five Companies

Company	Buying Plans, % of Respndents	Buying Influences, % of Respndents			
		Final Say	Specify Supplier	Recommend	Net Buying Influences
Company X	46	30	27	59	85
Company B	44	30	26	57	83
Company C	43	30	26	57	83
Company A	43	24	21	48	74
Company D	41	27	24	55	81
Show Average	24	26	19	43	66

Personal Contact

Table 3 gives the percentage of all respondents and the exhibit's visitors who have had some previous contact with that company in the past twelve months. These results indicate that, for most exhibitors, this is the only opportunity during the year that their exhibit booth staff have the opportunity to talk to many of their prospects. For example, 14% of Company X visitors have had some personal contact with Company X in the previous twelve months. Therefore, 86% represent potential for new or renewed personal contacts (100% of total audience minus

14% that visited). The lower the percentage of previous personal contact, the more valuable the show becomes in providing opportunity for that exhibitor to reach new prospects.

Table 3. Previous Personal Contact for Five Companies

Company	Previous Personal Contact, %	
	All Respondents	Visitors to Each Exhibit
Company B	1	8
Company A	2	8
Company X	2	14
Company D	4	19
Company C	4	22
Show Average	10	22

Booth Traffic

The scores in Table 4 represent the traffic to and activity within the Company X's exhibit and each of the competitors exhibits. Generally, well-known exhibits and those with products of higher interest have a better chance of achieving the highest total traffic.

Attendees had the choice of checking whether they looked at the exhibit, saw a theater presentation, talked to a representative, saw/participated in a product demonstration, and/or requested further follow-up. The Net Face-to-Face percentage is the portion of the attendees who had some meaningful interaction in the exhibit with booth personnel (talked to a representative, saw/participated in a demonstration, and/or requested follow-up). The Total Traffic figure is the percentage of attendees who had at least some exposure to the exhibit (i.e., checked at least one of the five choices).

Table 4. Booth Traffic Scores for Five Company's Exhibits

Company	Booth Traffic %						
				Face-to-Face			
	Total Traffic	Looked	Saw Theater	Talked to Rep	Saw Demo	Requested Follow-Up	Net Face-to-Face
Company X	83	54	26	47	27	13	55
Company C	68	46	14	42	23	11	47
Company A	57	40	12	23	12	6	29
Company B	56	42	6	22	8	5	26
Company D	55	38	14	22	12	5	28
Show Average	35	25	5	15	7	4	18

Staff Interaction Rate (SIR)

Scores in Table 5 take Table 4 to the next level. The Staff Interaction Rate (SIR) is simply the percentage of all visitors to the exhibit (Total Traffic) who had face-to-face interaction in the exhibit. It measures the success of exhibit staff in achieving face-to-face contact with visitors at the booth. The goal is to achieve face-to-face contact with as high a percentage as possible.

Table 5. Staff Interaction Rate (SIR) for Five Company's Exhibits

Company	% of Attendees		
	Total Traffic	Net Face-to-Face	Staff Interaction Ratio (SIR)
Company X	83	61	73
Company C	68	49	72
Company A	57	33	58
Company D	56	28	50
Company B	55	34	62
Show Average	35	18	51

Exhibit Attraction and Exhibit Efficiency

Exhibit Attraction is the percentage of a company's Potential Audience who remembered visiting their exhibit. The function of the physical exhibit is to attract Potential Audience. Factors which most often determine success in this regard include: awareness for a company and products among this audience, pre- and at-show promotion, exhibit design and graphics, demos and attention-getting techniques, interest in the products or services exhibited, and exhibit size.

Exhibit Efficiency is the percentage of a company's Potential Audience, with whom staff made face-to-face contact. Factors which impact Exhibit Efficiency are the number of personnel on duty, quality and performance of staff, and staff training.

Exhibit Efficiency is calculated by taking the total population who indicated having an interest in a specific company's types of products, cross-tabulated with those who visited the company's exhibit (Company X) and/or Company X's competitors' exhibits, and had a face-to-face interaction within the exhibit, Company X in this case. Table 6 presents these two measures.

Table 6. Exhibit Attraction and Exhibit Efficiency for Five Company's Exhibits

Company	% of Potential Audience	
	Exhibit Attraction	Exhibit Efficiency
Company X	95	49
Company A	92	48
Company C	92	63
Company B	65	31
Company D	41	24
Show Average	79	43

Cost per Visitor Reached (CVR)

Cost per Visitor Reached (CVR) measures the cost effectiveness of participating in the show. Exhibit Attraction CVR is the cost to attract an exhibitor's Potential Audience. Company X's CVR for each of its Potential Audience attracted to its exhibit was $124. The CVR for each of its Potential Audience who had face-to-face contact in its exhibit was $184. For comparison, our high-tech show averages are $90 and $171, respectively.

Table 7. Cost Per Visitor Reached (CVR)

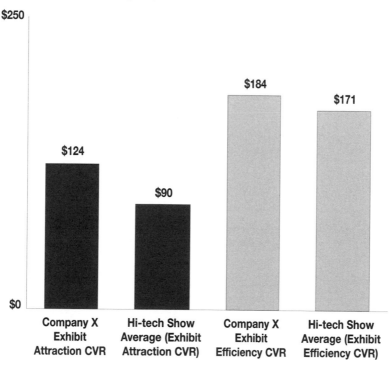

CVR is calculated by using total direct cost of exhibiting, which includes exhibit space rental, amortized construction and/or refurbishing, transportation, set-up and dismantling, promotion, demos and/or attention-getting techniques, etc. It does not include booth personnel's travel, living, and salary expenses. To determine the Exhibit Attraction CVR, divide direct costs by Exhibit Attraction. To calculate the Exhibit Efficiency CVR, divide direct costs by Exhibit Efficiency.

Other Measures

Additional measures were collected and compared to five competitors:

1. Staff performance – the helpfulness of staff
2. Overcrowded exhibit – whether an exhibit was too crowded
3. Most remembered exhibits – the companies with the most remembered exhibits in the show
4. More/less favorably inclined to purchase
5. Current use of products
6. Audience interest factor
7. Demographics – job function, industry representation, and size of company
8. Total Buying Plans (TBP) – the percentage of attendees planning to buy one or more of the products or services
9. Geographical distribution
10. Other shows attended
12. Previous attendance
12. Hours and days spent at the exhibits
13. Traffic density – measures the activity and synergism on the exhibit floor. The formula used to calculate traffic density is as follows:

$$\text{Traffic Density (TD)} = \frac{N \times tv \times 100}{A \times ts}$$

Where: N = Net Attendance = 16,322 (excludes exhibitors, press, and staff)
A = Total exhibit space = 195,000 sq. ft.
tv = Average time attendees spent at the exhibits = 9.5 hours
ts = Total hours the exhibits were open = 22 hours

Communication Strategy

This study was conducted on a proprietary basis for Key3Media and communicated in two main fashions:

1. Key3Media shared portions of the research results with exhibitors. As previously noted, this survey was conducted after the tech bubble had burst. The

industry was facing many challenges, and the show was in jeopardy. The research was used to provide exhibitors with empowering information communicating the buying power of the audience.

2. Key3Media used this information in marketing efforts not only to maintain existing exhibitors, but also to grow existing exhibitors' presence and gain new exhibitors. Independent, third-party data from a reputable source was extremely important in doing just that.

Lessons Learned

The overall takeaway from the research was that despite the health of the high-tech industry, and the significant decrease in N+I attendance compared with previous years, the overall audience quality and profile of N+I remained strong. It was more of a quantity versus quality issue. While some view a show's health based on attendance figures, the research supports that the *quality* of the audience is an important predictor of the health of a show. Furthermore, from the exhibiting perspective, about six out of every ten exhibitors at NetWorld+Interop Las Vegas performed at or above the show average in attracting their Potential Audience.

Recommendations and Use of Results

Since the research was a value-add customer service provided by Key3Media to select exhibitors, it allowed Key3Media the opportunity to meet with their customers face-to-face and talk about the show. Rather than just providing sales and marketing data that, generally, exhibitors are accustomed to, this information was different. It provided information pertaining to the voice of the attendees, not of show management. It empowered the exhibitors to make better decisions based on statistically reliable data as opposed to gut feelings or sales hype. It was a unique spin on other types of research that Key3Media had conducted as this measurement was truly for the exhibitors.

Questions for Discussion

1. How credible are these evaluation results?
2. What other ways could data be collected for this study?
3. Some of the data collected would be considered Level 0: Statistics and Indicators of the exhibit. Is it worth the time, effort, and expense to collect this level of data?
4. What are the benefits to the trade show organizer of collecting the data presented in this case study? What are the benefits of this data to the exhibitors?
5. If you were the trade show organizer of this exhibition, what could you do differently to better attract exhibitors for the next show?

About the Author

Joel Federbush is the Director of Business Development and Marketing for Exhibit Surveys. He focuses strategically on client development and serves as a highly visible face of Exhibit Surveys in the marketplace. Prior to his current position, Mr. Federbush conducted project management research for Exhibit Surveys, initiating some of the company's earliest Internet-based research and working on studies in South America and Europe. He received a Bachelor of Science degree in Business Administration from Monmouth University, Long Branch, New Jersey. Mr. Federbush can be reached by email at joel@exhibitsurveys.com or by telephone at 732.741.3170.

Editor's Notes

As shown in this case study, there are numerous factors that go into the evaluation of a trade show exhibit—both before and after an exhibit. As more trade show organizers commission studies such as this, exhibitors will grow to expect this level of data to make a decision on whether to exhibit at one show verses another. After the meeting, this level of data is valuable in determining how well the Sales and Marketing departments performed in attracting and engaging potential buyers and whether the booth should be updated, redesigned, or expanded.

Information on the number of qualified leads obtained by each exhibitor would be a useful addition to this data. Hopefully, each exhibitor is collecting this information internally and using it alongside these results to further determine the success of their trade show exhibits.

Chapter 5
Measuring Learning and Confidence

Learning is an important measure when evaluating meetings and events. Understanding how much learning has occurred is critical, particularly for meetings in which significant amounts of information, knowledge, and skills must be processed and put into action. In this case, measuring learning may be one of the greatest determinants of meeting success. This chapter focuses on simple, inexpensive techniques for learning measurement, often included with the reaction feedback.

The Importance of Measuring Learning

Several issues illustrate why learning is an important measure for the success of meetings and events. Individually, each can justify the need to measure learning. Collectively, they provide motivation for taking a more rigorous approach for measuring the amount of information, knowledge, change, or skills learned during a meeting.

Learning Versus Entertaining

The first reason for measuring learning focuses on the purpose of meetings and events. When meeting planners and event organizers are asked about the nature of their business or field, some interesting responses are provided. When pressed for the distinction of whether meetings and events represent entertainment or learning, planners will quickly indicate that the business has to be learning. If there is no learning, then the event was nothing but entertainment. This is an important issue because the measurement processes in place for the vast majority of meetings and events have focused on the entertainment perspective, creating an enjoyable atmosphere and experience. While these issues are important, they do not connect to the more vital issue of learning. The learning measure should be at the forefront of the meeting agenda. In reality, however, the learning measure tends to be overlooked in the majority of meeting evaluations.

The Learning Organization

In the last two decades, organizations have experienced rapid transformations in competitive global markets and economic changes. Organizations must learn new ways to serve customers and use innovations and technology as they attempt to be efficient, restructure, reorganize, and execute globally. To meet this change in strategy, the concept of a learning organization has evolved. This requires organizations to use learning proactively in an integrated way and to support and enhance growth for individuals, teams, and entire organizations. Learning must take place in teams and larger groups where individuals can work together to create new knowledge (Senge, 1990). With the focus on creating learning organizations— where countless activities and processes are in place to promote, encourage, and support continuous learning—meetings and events become an important learning tool.

The Compliance Issue

Organizations face an increasing number of regulations with which they must routinely comply. These regulations involve all aspects of business and government and are considered necessary to protect customers, citizens, investors, and the environment. Meetings are sometimes implemented to ensure that the organization is in compliance. When compliance is based on knowledge of regulations, measuring learning becomes the most critical measure to ensure compliance.

The Challenges of Measuring Learning

Measuring learning is not without its major challenges, which may inhibit a comprehensive approach to this issue. Measuring learning is sometimes equated with testing, which some participants fear. For example, a quiz may be administered at a product launch event to measure how well participants processed information at the event. Few people enjoy taking tests. The challenge is to make testing (or learning measurement) less threatening.

Another challenge is that learning measurement questions the professional autonomy of many individuals. Occasionally, meetings will involve engineers, scientists, accountants, physicians, lawyers, or other professional groups. These individuals often feel that, because they have satisfied professional credential requirements, they have the knowledge and expertise required for whatever issues arise in their professional roles. A learning measure may make them feel that their professional competence is in question and, therefore, may be resisted.

When tests are used, another challenge is the ethical and legal considerations. When test scores affect participants' job status, a test must be formally checked for validity and reliability. This issue is not common for the vast majority of meetings.

The challenge is to take a reasonable approach, allocating resources to check for validity or reliability when necessary. This rare issue is beyond the scope of this book. Other books cover it in more detail. (Phillips and Phillips, 2003)

A final challenge for measuring learning is the resources required. Budgets are often tight and spending excessive amounts of resources on learning measurement may not be desired or necessary. There is always a trade-off of additional resources versus the accuracy desired. Keeping the resource allocation reasonable is important. This often leads to some informal measures, combined with reaction questionnaires.

Typical Measures

Measuring learning focuses on information, knowledge, skills, and perceptions. Sometimes, these are expanded to different categories. Table 5-1 shows some typical measures collected at this level.

Table 5-1. Typical Learning Measurement Categories

Skills	Attitudes
Knowledge	Capability
Awareness	Capacity
Understanding	Readiness
Information	Confidence
Perceptions	Contacts

Knowledge is general and includes the assimilation of facts, figures, and concepts. Instead of knowledge, the terms awareness, understanding, or information may be specific categories. Sometimes, perceptions or attitudes may change based on what a participant has learned. For example, in a diversity meeting, the participants' attitudes toward having a diverse work group are altered. In other situations, the issue is developing a reservoir of knowledge and skills and referring to it when developing capability, capacity, or readiness. When individuals are capable, they are often described as being ready for the job. When participants use skills, an appropriate measure might be the confidence the participant has to use those skills in a job setting. This becomes critical in job situations where skills must be performed accurately and within a certain standard, as in customer service skills. Networking is often part of a meeting. Developing contacts is important in this case. This may be within, or external to, an organization.

Data Collection Methods

Questionnaires and Surveys

Different questionnaires and surveys were described in Chapter 4, with the focus on measuring reaction. The types of questionnaires and surveys include the two-way or true-false tests, where the participants are provided with statements and must either agree or disagree. These are easy to write and score. Rating scales are common in surveys and were described previously. The typical scale is a five-point scale, although three-, four-, seven-, and ten-point scales are used. Multiple-choice is the most common objective test and has the advantage of easy scoring. Matching exercises are also useful. They are easy to write and can be scored quickly. Fill-in-the-blank items are open-ended and easy to write, but more difficult to score, and short-answer questions can be easy to develop, but also difficult to score. Essay questions are less likely to be used because they are difficult to score and less reliable due to the subjective opinion of the scorer. The good news about using questionnaires is that the questions can be included on the reaction feedback questionnaire.

Role Playing and Skill Practices

Role plays, sometimes referred to as skill practices, require participants to practice a newly learned skill as they are observed. Participants are provided with assigned roles and specific instructions, which sometimes include an ultimate course of action. The participant then practices the skill with other individuals to accomplish the desired objectives. This exercise is intended to simulate the real-world setting to the greatest extent possible.

The success of this role-play technique also lies in the judgment of those observing. The skill of effective observation is as critical as the skill of the person playing the role. Also, the success of this method depends on the participants' willingness to participate in and adjust to the planned role. If participant resistance is extremely high, the performance in the skill practice may not reflect the actual performance on the job. Nevertheless, these skill practices can be useful, particularly in meetings where skill building is essential, in helping participants practice discussion skills.

Exercises/Activities

Some meetings involve activities or exercises that must be explored, developed, or solved during the meeting. Some of these are constructed in terms of involvement exercises, while others require individual problem-solving skills. When these tools are integrated into the meeting, several specific ways to measure learning are available:

- The results of the exercise can be submitted for review and for possible scoring by a member of the meeting team. This score becomes part of the overall measure of learning.
- The results can be discussed in a group, with a comparison of the various approaches and solutions. The group can give an assessment of how much each individual has learned. This may not be practical in many meeting settings but can work in a few narrowly focused applications.
- The solutions to the problem or exercises can be shared with the group, and the participant can provide a self-assessment indicating the degree to which the skills and/or knowledge have been obtained. This also serves as reinforcement since participants quickly see the correct solution.

Administrative Issues

A few simple administrative issues must be addressed when measuring learning, especially when the process is more structured and formal. Each of these should be part of the overall plan for administering learning measurement:

1. Exercises, assessments, or tests for measuring learning should be administered consistently from one group to another.
2. When formal testing is used (which will be extremely rare), participants should be monitored as they complete the test or other measurement processes.
3. As with reaction questionnaires, the reading level must be matched with the target audience.
4. The instrument should be pilot tested with a small group to ensure that it is understandable and focuses on the appropriate issues.
5. Scoring instructions need to be developed for the measurement process.
6. Ideally, the participants are provided with the results immediately, particularly with self-scoring tests or with group-based scoring mechanisms.

Using Learning Data

Data must be used to add value and improve processes. Although several uses of learning data are appropriate, these are most common:

1. Verify that learning has been acquired.
2. Provide feedback to build confidence.
3. Improve the meeting design.
4. Evaluate speakers.
5. Build a database for comparisons.

Final Thoughts

This chapter briefly discusses some of the key issues involved in measuring learning—an important component for the success of meetings. More than any other level, this measurement moves the meetings and events industry from entertainment to learning. Even if it is accomplished informally, learning must be assessed to determine the extent to which meeting participants learn new skills, techniques, processes, tools, and procedures. Should application problems arise later, knowing what went wrong would be difficult without this measure. Also, measuring learning provides an opportunity to make adjustments so that changes can be made to enhance learning and ensure that application can occur. A formal, objective process is usually not needed, except for major meetings where the principal focus is on learning. A less-formal, less-structured approach, perhaps a self-assessment activity, is usually appropriate for most meetings and events—often included in the reaction questionnaire.

Next are case studies in which organizations measure learning in a variety of sales meetings.

Notes

Phillips, P. J., and P. P. Phillips. *Measuring Return on Investment in Training and Performance Improvement Programs*, 2nd Edition (Burlington, MA: Butterworth-Heinemann, 2003).

Senge, P. *The Fifth Discipline: The Art and Practice of the Learning Organization* (New York: Random House, 1990).

Case Study
Evaluating a National Sales Meeting
American Transport Company

By Karen Jagatic, Ph.D., Senior Consultant with GuideStar Research

This case was prepared to serve as a basis for discussion rather than an illustration of either effective or ineffective administrative and management practices. All names, dates, places, and organizations have been disguised at the request of the author or organization.

Abstract

A national meeting of sales representatives from a large transport company was held to determine perceptions and understanding of a new corporate strategy and to conduct educational workshops. A pre-meeting survey was executed to obtain benchmark ratings about the company, and to determine what attendees hoped to learn and experience. Post-meeting survey results showed that attendees were extremely satisfied with all meeting aspects, and that perceptions about the company and new strategy were rated more favorably post-meeting. This study demonstrates how pre-meeting surveys can help planners create a meeting that satisfies the needs and desires of attendees.

Background

American Transport Company (ATC) is a large transport company comprised of six operating companies, or "brands." The company was formed through the gradual purchase of each of the brands, then independent companies. While the operating companies were generally located in different geographic areas, there was some overlap among "sister" companies.

Because ATC had been formed through the streamlining of the smaller companies, corporate executives decided to conduct a meeting with sales representatives that would allow leadership to share its new corporate strategy of "One Company." Leadership was also interested in employee feelings about various aspects of working at ATC, as well as clarifying conference expectations. The meeting was planned and executed by ATC's marketing group, in close collaboration with senior leadership.

A pre-meeting survey was planned with the following objectives:

- To measure employee perceptions about working at ATC
- To solicit input about how ATC was transitioning with respect to "One Company"
- To determine satisfaction levels regarding "One Company" communications
- To determine whether there had been obstacles to ATC's achievement of the "One Company" strategy, and the extent of those possible problems
- To measure collaboration among companies
- To solicit information regarding the upcoming national conference
- A post-meeting survey was also conducted, with the following objectives:
  - To measure employee perceptions about working at ATC, especially as compared with benchmark results obtained in the pre-meeting survey
  - To solicit input about how ATC was transitioning with respect to "One Company," also compared with findings in the pre-meeting survey
  - To learn how employees viewed their conference experience
  - To determine which conference objectives were achieved
  - To measure the impact of the conference on participants

Evaluation Methodology

The first part of the project involved completion of telephone interviews with a sample of potential conference attendees (ATC sales people). The purpose was to qualitatively determine relevant issues and topics for the pre-meeting survey, and to refine new questions.

The pre-meeting survey was then developed using these interview findings, as well as Meeting Productivity Process (MPP) methodology, which helps organizations improve the value and strategic business results of large group meetings, and the Core 7 Dimensions, a framework of measurement based on the measurable and quantifiable personal dimensions of meeting participants. The Core 7 Dimensions are:

- Knowledge/Understanding/Perceptions
- Opinions/Attitudes/Beliefs
- Issues/Concerns/Feelings
- Needs/Preferences
- Abilities
- Intentions
- Behaviors/Business Results

The pre-meeting survey contained approximately fifty multiple-choice questions, as well as eleven open-ended questions, grouped into the following sections:

- Working at ATC
- "One Company"—How Are We Doing?

- "One Company" Communications
- Transitioning to One Company
- Collaboration Among Companies
- The Upcoming National Conference

The post-meeting survey questions were also built around the Core 7 Dimensions. It included questions about company strategy and working at ATC, which appeared on the pre-survey. There were approximately sixty multiple-choice questions and six open-ended questions, grouped into the following sections:
- Working at ATC (also on pre-meeting survey)
- "One Company"—How Are We Doing? (also on pre-meeting survey)
- Your Conference Experience Overall
- Objectives Achieved
- General Sessions and Activities Ratings
- Conference Impacts

Data Collection and Data Analysis

Pre-meeting survey participants were ATC sales representatives scheduled to attend the ATC national conference. These sales people were emailed a survey invitation, which included a hyperlink to the Web-based, pre-meeting survey. Reminders, also containing hyperlinks to the survey, were mailed periodically to boost the response rate. Survey results were gathered electronically and automatically entered into a database used by survey consultants to analyze results. The same approach was used to gather data for the post-meeting survey. The pre-meeting survey had a response rate of 87% (546 respondents), while the post-meeting survey had a response rate of 79% (503 respondents). Margins of error for the surveys were good (+/- 1.5 and +/-2.0, respectively), indicating reliability of survey results.

Data was generally analyzed by reporting in table form the percentage of survey participants answering a particular question in a particular way. As many of the questions in the survey used a response scale ranging from "Strongly Disagree" to "Strongly Agree," a "% Favorable" rating was calculated by combining the number of people who answered "Agree" or "Strongly Agree" to a question. A "% Favorable" rating could also be calculated by combining responses for "Satisfied" and "Very Satisfied," where appropriate.

For questions appearing in both the pre- and post-meeting surveys, Return on Event (ROE) could be determined. ROE is calculated by taking the difference in ratings between the pre- and post-meeting surveys. A positive number means that the conference had a positive impact on the item; the larger this number, the greater the impact of the meeting on the particular item. A negative number means that the conference had a negative impact on the item.

In addition to analysis of quantitative data, qualitative data, gathered in the form of open-ended question responses, was analyzed. Participants' comments were "coded" into categories. As a result, the most frequently mentioned responses could be tallied and patterns noted.

Evaluation Results

Pre-Meeting Survey

Sales representatives scheduled to participate in ATC's national meeting were invited to complete a pre-meeting survey. They were asked about working at ATC and about how ATC was progressing with regard to its "One Company" strategy. These findings are presented with post-meeting survey results later in this case.

Sales representatives were asked with which company they identified themselves most. Responses showed 17% identified most with ATC as a whole, while 83% identified most with their particular operating company. As shown in Table 1, survey participants were also asked which of the following items would be positively impacted as a result of achieving the "One Company" strategy:

Table 1. Pre-Meeting Survey Results on Impacts of One Company Strategy

Do you agree or disagree that the following items will be positively impacted as a result of achieving the "One Company" strategy? (Opinions/Attitudes/Beliefs Core 7 Dimension)	% Agree/ Strongly Agree
Competitiveness in marketplaces	92%
ATC's financial health	87%
Customer perceptions	86%
Standardizing of job descriptions	74%
Job training programs	73%
My career development	72%
Employee motivation	64%
Employee morale	63%
My promotional opportunities	62%

Sales representatives were also asked several questions about communications at ATC. Slightly more than half (52%) said they were satisfied or very satisfied with internal communications about the "One Company" strategy, while 74% felt adequately, fairly well, or fully informed about what is going on at ATC.

The pre-meeting survey also asked sales representatives which of a number of conditions would be obstacles to achievement of the "One Company" strategy. "Customer confusion caused by company overlap" was found to be the biggest obstacle, followed by "Customer frustration with inconsistent delivery schedules among companies" and "A lack of customer service representative training." Survey participants were also asked how they rated the collaboration among operating companies: 41% rated it as average, and 23% rated it as good or excellent.

One of the most important questions asked survey participants to select which objectives they felt were important for the conference to accomplish. These findings, shown in Table 2, along with responses to an open-ended question asking participants what they wanted to learn about, were instrumental in the meeting planners' success in planning and executing the meeting.

Table 2. Pre-Meeting Survey Results on Objectives Important for Conference

Which of the following objectives do you think are important for the conference to accomplish? (Check all that apply.)	% Checked
Communicate ATC business plans and goals.	81%
Communicate a roadmap and timeline to achieve the "One Company" strategy.	69%
Emphasize common standards, processes, and procedures.	56%
Motivate people to behave as though they are a part of one company, breakdown provincial attitudes.	54%
Provide an update on company's competitive landscape and position in the market place.	51%
Communicate the company's vision, mission, and values.	48%
Provide idea sharing and best practices sessions with people in my job from other companies.	47%
Motivate people to identify with and view themselves more as part of one company.	44%
Provide social networking opportunities with people from other companies.	39%
Showcase of marketing materials and programs.	35%
Provide some training or development opportunities for people doing my job.	27%

Post-Meeting Survey

Almost all meeting participants (98%) were satisfied or very satisfied with the overall quality and professionalism of the conference. While many meetings are rated favorably overall, to obtain a rating this high with more than 500 survey participants was an achievement. Participants were also asked to rate various dimensions of the meeting. Results were generally good and are presented in Table 3.

Table 3. Post-Meeting Survey Results on Conference Dimensions

Please rate the following dimensions of the conference. (Opinions/Attitudes/Beliefs Core 7 Dimension)	% Good/ Excellent
Effectiveness of the communications in the general session presentations	97%
Overall quality of the general session presentation elements (audiovisuals, staging, etc.)	97%
Relevance of the general session presentations in addressing your issues, needs, and concerns	95%
Overall value of the conference experience for the time, money, and effort involved	92%
Company managers genuinely listened to what you had to say during your interactions with them	86%
The curriculum of the breakout sessions in meeting some of your training needs	82%
Sufficient opportunities for personal interaction and dialogue with company leadership	77%
Adequate time scheduled for the various breakouts to adequately cover the topics	63%

Participants were asked how satisfied they were with the effectiveness of the conference in achieving a number of objectives, as shown in Table 4.

Table 4. Post-Meeting Survey Results on Achievement of Objectives

How satisfied are you with the effectiveness of the conference in accomplishing the following objectives? (Opinions/Attitudes/Beliefs Core 7 Dimensions)	% Satisfied/ Very Satisfied
Providing an update on the company's competitive landscape and position in the marketplace.	92%
Providing social networking opportunities with people from other companies.	92%
Motivating people to identify with and view themselves as part of one company.	91%
Showcasing of sales/marketing materials and programs.	88%
Emphasis on common standards, processes, and procedures.	79%
Providing idea sharing and best practices sessions with people in my job from other companies.	75%
Providing training and development opportunities for people doing my job.	75%

Employees were also asked to rate whether they agreed with the following conference-related questions, as shown in Table 5. These questions covered reactions to the conference and the skills/knowledge acquired.

Table 5. Post-Meeting Results on Knowledge, Understanding, and Perceptions

As a result of your overall conference experience, please rate your level of agreement with the following: (Knowledge/Understanding/Perceptions Core 7 Dimension)	% Agree/ Strongly Agree
I understand and embrace the company's core values.	99%
I understand the key competitive challenges facing the company.	98%
I fully understand ATC's strategy of "one team" serving the customer.	95%
I can clearly communicate the company's mission, vision, and strategy to customers and coworkers.	95%
The conference was very valuable in helping me improve my professional effectiveness.	87%
The conference was very valuable in helping me improve the company's performance.	86%
Both my peers and I received appropriate recognition and appreciation at the conference for our contributions to ATC.	81%

Numerous logistics-type questions were also asked of attendees, including those related to satisfaction with accommodations, food, and entertainment. Specific break-out session questions also appeared on the post-meeting survey. Ratings were high for most questions. Survey participants were also asked a number of open-ended questions, which were grouped based on type of response.

Results shown in Table 6 illustrate that the conference was successful in many areas, including motivating employees to help ATC achieve its strategy.

Table 6. Post-Meeting Results on Opinions, Attitudes, and Beliefs

Please tell us how you feel about the following statements: (Opinions/Attitudes/Beliefs Core 7 Dimension)	% Agree/ Strongly Agree
I am personally committed to the changes that will be required to achieve our strategy.	99%
I am confident that I can make whatever changes are necessary in my attitudes and behavior to be a productive team member in achieving the "One Company" strategy.	98%
I believe I am responsible for creating and increasing shareholder value.	98%
The conference instilled a greater sense of unity among the people I was with at the conference.	90%
The company is poised to significantly improve its financial and operational performance over the next twelve to eighteen months.	91%
I am optimistic about the company's ability to become a leading national company in the industry.	89%
I am confident in the ability of the leadership team at ATC to accomplish the "One Company" strategy.	87%
I believe I have the resources I need to accomplish my objectives.	78%

Table 7 shows the comparison of the pre- and post-meeting results and the relative Return on Event (ROE). These results are outstanding for almost all survey questions, especially post-meeting. Some questions were so highly rated in the pre-meeting survey that no further significant improvement was possible. The lowest-scoring items showed the greatest change post-conference. The Return on Event (ROE) column shows the impact of the meeting on survey items. The conference had the strongest impact on satisfaction with job at ATC (ROE +7), feeling valued as an employee (ROE +8), and happiness with changes seen at ATC (ROE +11).

Table 7. Comparison of Pre- and Post-Meeting Results in Key Core 7 Dimensions

Do you agree or disagree with the following statement? (Opinions/Attitudes/Beliefs and Issues/Concerns/Feelings Core 7 Dimensions	% Agree/ Strongly Agree PRE-Meeting	% Agree/ Strongly Agree POST-Meeting	Retun on Event (REO)
I am committed to ATC's success.	100%	100%	0
My manager/supervisor holds me accountable to certain performance standards.	98%	97%	-1
I am proud to be at ATC.	97%	99%	+2
I am personally challenged and motivated by my work.	96%	97%	+1
I am committed to a long-term career at ATC.	95%	97%	+2
ATC is a good place to work.	95%	98%	+3
My manager/supervisor is a positive role model.	89%	91%	+4
I am satisfied with my job at ATC.	86%	93%	+7
I feel valued as an employee of ATC.	77%	85%	+8
I'm happy with the changes I've seen at ATC.	76%	87%	+11

ATC was also interested in results for questions related to the new "One Company" corporate strategy. As the results in Table 8 show, the conference was extremely successful in improving attendees' understanding of various aspects of the "One Company" strategy. Improvements were tremendous, including a thirty-seven-point increase in understanding how ATC will operate under the "One Company" strategy. All questions in this section improved at least fourteen points, indicating that the conference was successful in conveying key messages to attendees.

Table 8. Comparison of Pre- and Post-Meeting Results in Knowledge, Understanding, and Perceptions

Do you agree or disagree with the following statement? (Knowledge/Understanding/Perceptions Core 7 Dimension)	% Agree/ Strongly Agree PRE-	% Agree/ Strongly Agree POST-	Return on Event (ROE)
I have a clear understanding of how ATC will operate when we achieve a "One Company" strategy.	45%	82%	+37
I have a clear understanding of ATC leadership's plans for achieving a "One Company" strategy.	56%	86%	+30
How would you rate ATC leadership so far in managing the transition to being "One Company?"	59%	85%	+26
I have a clear understanding of the "One Company" strategy.	73%	95%	+22
I have a clear understanding of the business reasons for embarking on the "One Company" strategy.	83%	97%	+14

Communication Strategy

Because this was the ATC's first meeting of this nature, much of the project communication was informal. After the pre-meeting survey was conducted, results were shared with company leaders and findings were used to make changes to the meeting.

Post-meeting results were communicated in a variety of ways, including:
- e-Blasts to the sales representatives who attended the meeting
- Phone calls with sales managers
- Newsletters to all employees, including those who did not attend the conference
- Informal but lengthy discussions with company executives, both before and after the meeting

Lessons Learned, Recommendations, and Use of Results

The main lesson learned by ATC's leadership and marketing group in planning the meeting was that perceptions of the desires of sales representatives were "way off base." The pre-meeting survey results allowed meeting planners to abandon original ideas for the conference and tailor the meeting to the needs and desires expressed by participants in the survey. As a result, the meeting contained more networking opportunities, more educational sessions, and less "podium" time.

The excellent outcome of the meeting and the post-meeting survey show that when meeting planners and corporate executives understand employee expectations, a successful meeting is more likely. Post-meeting survey results were used in a different manner, turning attention away from the meeting itself and toward the company as a whole. Unfortunately, there was a major organizational change at ATC. This included the loss of the leadership and marketing team involved in organizing the meeting, making the full potential of post-meeting survey results unrealized.

The results found in this study provide a benchmark for future meetings at ATC. Learning that leadership and employees were out-of-touch was an important discovery. Other recommendations, based on survey results, as well as sentiments expressed in open-ended question responses, included:

- Leadership should continue to communicate with employees about daily activities, which will impact how well the "One Company" strategy is achieved.
- There is overlap between sister companies, which is negatively impacting customer relationships.
- As redundancies are eliminated and processes become standardized in the organization, it is important to effectively communicate changes to employees.
- Sales, customer service, and computer training is lacking and needed.
- Lack of standardized billing is an issue.
- Participants appreciated the opportunity to network with peers from other units. Leadership should continue to reinforce the relationships formed and improved at the conference by encouraging employees to work together as much as possible and rewarding them for their efforts
- Future awards ceremonies should include operations personnel, in addition to sales people and drivers.
- After the departure of the company's CEO, some employees were confused about ATC's direction. These employees were nervous, and desired more leadership communication.
- People left the meeting excited about the future. Notes should be taken on what worked well at this conference and findings should be documented so similar action can be taken when planning future conferences.

Questions for Discussion

1. Since a pre- and post-meeting survey design was used for this study, the improvements found in post-survey results can be attributed to the meeting. Do you agree with this approach? Why or why not?
2. Qualitative research in the form of interviews was conducted prior to construction of the pre-meeting survey. What are some advantages and disadvantages associated with qualitative versus quantitative research methods?
3. ROI was not calculated for this meeting. Explain how the study could have been expanded to allow for this calculation.

4. The term Return on Event (ROE) is used in this case. Does this term help or inhibit the credibility of the study?
5. Shortly after this meeting, there was a major shakeup in the company where several executives left the organization. What impact do you think this may have had on how survey results were used?
6. Several non-meeting related questions were asked of meeting participants. What was the advantage of this? Do you believe there were any disadvantages to asking non-meeting related questions, and if so, what were they?

About the Author

Karen Jagatic, Ph.D., is a Senior Consultant with GuideStar Research, a professional research and consulting service firm based in New York, New York. As an Industrial/Organizational Psychologist, she has more than a decade of experience in the design and implementation of surveys, and is skilled in data analysis and interpretation of survey results. Ms. Jagatic has worked with many Fortune 500 organizations in the technology, telecommunications, consulting, medical, and financial services sectors. She can be reached at karen@guidestarco.com.

Editor's Notes

This study emphasizes the importance of conducting a needs assessment and content planning session with meeting executives and attendees prior to the development of the meeting. The pre-meeting survey data provided meeting planners with specific information to create targeted meeting objectives, allowing for a benchmark to be established. This important benchmark was later compared with post-meeting results to isolate the impact of the meeting.

Case Study
Measuring the Success of a Sales Kickoff Meeting
Sun Microsystems

By Nancy Powell, Marketing Consultant and Project Manager

This case was prepared to serve as a basis for discussion rather than an illustration of either effective or ineffective administrative and management practices. Names, dates, places, and data may have been disguised at the request of the author or organization.

Abstract

This case study demonstrates how pre-event surveys can gauge the attitudes and perceptions of attendees to set a benchmark for post-event survey results and to influence the development of the meeting content, structure, and theme. In this case, the meeting's successful impact was greatly enhanced by leadership's embrace of the necessity, process, and results of measurement. The sales meeting, occurring in the wake of a major merger between StorageTek and Sun Microsystems, served to unite the sales force with an emphasis on education of key products and marketing strategies.

Background

For decades, Storage Technology (StorageTek) and Sun Microsystems have competed in the storage industry. On June 1, 2005, the two companies' roads intersected when Sun announced the acquisition of StorageTek. The combination of StorageTek's years of leadership in the storage and data management market and Sun's leadership in network computing solutions created an instant heavyweight in the global storage market. The value proposition of this acquisition was clear. The merged sales and service personnel now became the focus of the acquisition team. It was vital to inform, empower, motivate, and train them to move forward.

A face-to-face meeting, the "U.S. and Canada 2006 Sales Kickoff" in Denver, Colorado, offered the perfect, targeted opportunity to address the critical needs of this audience. Held at the Hyatt Regency Denver and the Colorado Convention Center on January 9–12, 2006, the meeting was mission-critical to the success of this acquisition.

Approximately 1,200 North America sales team members attended. The preliminary meeting purpose was for Sun Microsystems's Data Management Group

(DMG) to present key information on products and marketing to the StorageTek and Sun sales teams. While on-target, the preliminary goals, outlined below, did not contain specific measurable objectives.

- To bring the StorageTek and Sun's North America storage sales representatives together as "one team"
- To communicate to attendees the state of the company and a long-term strategy for success
- To update and train attendees on combined product and service offerings
- To deliver a compelling message regarding Sun's go-to market strategy and motivate the entire sales and service team to embrace that strategy
- To convey how the StorageTek sales force will be integrated in the Sun culture and reinforce the value of the partnership

Creating collaboration and unity among the StorageTek and Sun sales teams was vital and the buy-in was crucial to success. The event team called on long-time partner ProActive Inc. to deliver a targeted and creative meeting that would meet key objectives during this exciting, yet uncertain, time. ProActive, an award-winning strategic communication and events agency delivering creative, service-oriented, experiential marketing solutions has worked with StorageTek since 2001.

The Sun/ProActive team understood that after spending a significant amount of time, energy, and money on a strategic communication event, it should be clear whether messages had effectively reached the target. Analysis should not only inform its organizers how to build a better meeting. It should also strengthen the audience relationship in the future. The Sun/ProActive team was determined to do just that.

Valuable to the event team was ProActive's strategic, creative process of understanding the needs of the organization, the industry, and the audience to build content and measure success—especially when a company is undergoing this kind of significant change.

Evaluation Methodology

Full-scale qualitative and quantitative measurement tools were deployed immediately. Audience feedback became the foundation to drive the meeting's direction, content, look, and feel. Data was collected in conjunction with the sales meeting in three ways:

- A pre-event, Web-based survey in late September 2005
- A telephone pulse check in December 2005
- A post-event Web-based survey fourteen days after the conclusion of the meeting in late January 2006

The evaluation methodology used was a version of the Meeting Productivity

Process (MPP) methodology. MPP is a proven, research-driven process for designing meetings that deliver powerful, measurable results, and for accurately and scientifically measuring post-event results. It was developed by GuideStar Research, a strategic partner of ProActive, to meet the special needs of both meeting attendees and meeting managers. The process has been used in a variety of businesses to dramatically change people's understandings, perceptions, attitudes, abilities, intentions, and behaviors through the meeting medium.

For this meeting, Sun chose to use portions of the MPP process to help build specific content that would drive business objectives. The survey design was based on input from Sun, as well as standard and customized questions used by ProActive to evaluate events of this nature. A battery of questions from the pre-event survey was included in the post-event survey so attitudes and perceptions could be compared.

Pre-Event Survey

A pre-event survey solicited opinions from the employees in the Data Management Group (DMG), the newly-merged storage business unit of Sun, about the acquisition and the company's current status. Audience preferences for various strategic and operational issues to be addressed at the U.S. and Canada 2006 sales kickoff were also captured. This pre-event survey specifically measured and collected:

- Employees' views about the acquisition
- Employees' level of satisfaction with the communication around the acquisition
- Employees' level of confidence in the newly merged company and its ability to thrive in the market
- Employees' opinions about what goals and agenda items should characterize the kickoff, as well as what objectives and overarching message should define it

Eight separate sections in the survey set benchmarks for measuring success:

- Audience views about the DMG
- Confidence
- Views about the 2006 sales kickoff
- Sales meeting dimensions
- Training and breakout sessions
- Comments and suggestions
- Demographics

Pulse Check

In early December 2005, a "pulse check," which consisted of twenty phone calls to random attendees, was taken to confirm the focus and direction of the meeting and to identify any new issues or questions.

Post-Event Survey

A post-event survey was emailed to attendees fourteen days after the meeting. The objectives of this were to:

- Measure employees' views of DMG, their confidence in the company, and their perceptions of the DMG leadership
- Measure attendees' overall perceptions of the meeting and its key messages
- Gather employees' suggestions for training at future meetings
- Measure employees' understanding of and confidence in the sales strategies and tactics presented, as well as to measure their satisfaction with the organizational and product-related issues addressed

Compare pre- and post-event perceptions around several key dimensions (i.e., DMG products, the new organizational structure, DMG leadership, the company's vision and strategy)

Data Collection and Data Analysis

DMG employees who would be attending the meeting received an e-mail invitation to participate in the pre-event survey and a hyperlink to the Web-based survey. Reminders also containing hyperlinks to the survey were sent periodically to increase the response rate. Survey results were gathered electronically and entered into a database analyzed by consultants.

Pre- and post-event data was collected through anonymous Web surveys. The pre-event survey was sent to 838 employees in North America, and 534 responses were received, resulting in a 62% response rate. The post-event survey was sent to 1,280 employees, and 715 of them completed the survey—a 56% response rate.

Data was analyzed by reviewing the percentage of survey participants answering a particular question in a particular way. Many of the survey questions used a response scale ranging from "Strongly Disagree" to "Strongly Agree." A "% Favorable" rating was calculated by combining the number of people who answered "Agree" or "Strongly Agree" to a question. Favorable ratings were also calculated by combining responses for "Satisfied" and "Very Satisfied," where appropriate.

Full numerical survey results, along with the complete surveys and all open-ended comments solicited from participants, were part of the post-event survey executive summary. Both quantitative and qualitative data was analyzed, and comments were grouped by content type, strength, and number of the types of comments.

The Return on Event (ROE) was calculated by comparing ratings on pre- and post-event benchmark questions. Comparisons were made between individual questions to determine impact in singular areas, as well as between the complete ranges of questions, to determine overall ROE. A positive number indicates the meeting had a positive impact in that area, and a negative number indicates the converse.

Evaluation Results

It was vital that the initial goals set for this meeting would hit the mark and meet the needs of the audience, so tapping into those needs was imperative. Feedback from the pre-event survey quickly revealed that the sales force was hungry for information about the acquisitions' affect on their jobs, their customers, their future, and the future of the company. It became clear that this meeting required more than just product information, training, and a state-of-the-company speech. The complex emotions involved—including fear, anger, and confusion—required direct attention.

Based on this data, the meeting goals were refined to:
- Communicate to attendees the state of the company, providing a clear, accurate, and factual roadmap
- Ease negative perceptions and feelings of uncertainty about the merger and build excitement around the company's 2006 sales year
- Provide employees with critical information about the company's new organizational structure, its vision and strategies, as well as its product and services roadmap
- Offer attendees a wide range of product and sales tools training

The survey information played a key role in content and creative development, unequivocally guiding all aspects of presentations, pre- and post-communication, speaker selection, and set design. The overwhelming needs of the audience—to be given information *now* and to understand what was going to happen *next*—generated the theme of "Now and Next," brought to life in every element of the event.

Pre-Event Survey

Although the executive team had clear preliminary goals, the audience refined and adjusted those goals through its survey responses. Three main issues quickly emerged:
- Lack of clarity
  - About the acquisition, Sun's DMG vision, and strategy moving forward

- About the type of collaboration between the Sun and StorageTek teams
- About the shape and nature of the new organization
- About which products would be continued and which would be discontinued
  - Need for success
    - The sales teams had strong aspirations for success and determination to win, but did not have enough information to know how that could happen
  - Job security
    - With any merger or acquisition, there is uncertainty about job security and culture change

After becoming aware of these concerns, Sun retained the initial meeting objectives but committed to making necessary shifts in content and delivery.

The pre-event survey results were used in several key ways. Data collected through the pre-event survey and a series of creative sessions allowed ProActive to develop a theme that would speak directly to the concerns of the attendees. A targeted set design visually brought the theme to life. A bold and clear stage design and complete environment made it clear that this new entity had a roadmap, was providing direction, and had a clear vision. For example, attendees entering the ballroom experienced a sense of being on a drive, in open country, with clearly-marked road signs. The perspective of the road signs changed as they met in the center—an effect intended to make the audience feel they were moving fast-forward toward a horizon of blue sky. It clearly conveyed they were all on a road together, knowing where they were going, how to get there, and what would lie ahead.

ProActive, in collaboration with Sun's event team, designed certain aspects of the general session content to address concerns uncovered by the pre-event survey. It became clear that this kickoff needed to be more interactive and conversational, focusing on the sales force and aimed at addressing its needs, rather than just an information dump from management. Consultants coached presenters on using a more casual, relaxed, open, and engaging presentation style, and minimizing PowerPoint presentations. An effort was made to keep messaging clear, consistent, and relevant, as well as on point with Sun's vision, strategy, climate, culture, and tactics. Being made aware of the survey results, audience needs, and meeting objectives, presenters were able to accomplish this.

Pre-event survey results also guided recommendations on training and networking activities. With Sun and StorageTek sales and service team members, all from different cultures, getting acquainted, it was important to provide dedicated opportunities for attendees to interact and develop a climate of unity and collaboration, as well as a chance to individually and informally approach leadership. Such networking sessions were woven throughout the event. Focused training on products, suggested by the pre-event survey results, was offered.

Pulse Check

The responses to the December pulse check confirmed the theme "Now and Next" to be on target and identified no new issues.

Post-Event Survey

When the post-event survey was tabulated, it became clear that great strides were made in pursuit of Sun's fulfillment of its objectives for this event.

Survey results revealed the following successes at the 2006 sales kickoff:

- 80% satisfaction with the relevance of the communication in the general session presentations
- 73% liked the quality of the executive presentations
- 77% were satisfied with the meeting's effectiveness in providing an update about the company's competitive landscape and positioning in the marketplace
- 78% were satisfied with the presentation on the DMG mission and strategy

In the environment of a newly merged organization, these scores were exceptionally strong.

Overall Successes

When the pre- and post-event results were compared, the following successes—tied to the meeting objectives—emerged:

- To communicate to attendees the state of the company
    — Understanding of the DMG's strategic goals went from 36% to 76%
- To ease negative perceptions and feelings of uncertainty about the merger
    — Understanding of a viable, competitive strategy for the DMG that will result in its being a market leader went from 52% to 75%
- To provide employees with critical information about the company's new organizational structure, vision, and strategies
    — Understanding of the DMG's product roadmap, moving forward, went from 8% to 68%
- To offer attendees a wide range of product and sales tools training
    — Belief that the DMG will continue to provide its sales force with the high level of sales support StorageTek has provided in the past went from 61% to 79%

Sun accomplished its strategic goals by producing a seamless event that addressed audience needs during a critical time. Pre-event research made it painstakingly clear that if attendees were not persuaded to take a more confident view of the acquisition and its implications for their future, they would lose motivation and commitment. In other words—jump ship.

The kickoff was the ultimate deal-breaker for the coveted sales team members in their decision to stay with Sun DMG. Losing talented sales personnel, who were needed to deliver on the promise of this exciting new company, was not an option. By employing objective measurement tools and thoughtful creative response to this strategic need, the leadership created a positive atmosphere that retained employees, drove business results, and moved Sun Microsystems into its future with confidence.

Communication Strategy

Pre-event survey results were shared with the management and event teams so they could make appropriate adjustments to the meeting content and delivery strategies. The results also led to an event theme that responded to employee concerns and was used in all communication.

Post-event survey results were presented to key Sun executives in a summary that outlined results, successes, opportunities, challenges, and recommendations for continuing communication intended to further improve results around these key issues. Leadership quickly began discussing ways to leverage the meeting's gains with consistent actions and ongoing communication with its sales force.

A top-level summary on the successes of the meeting, based on the surveys, was available to attendees through the company Web site, where they could also download presentations from the kickoff.

Lessons Learned, Recommendations, and Use of Results

The positive changes in perceptions and attitudes showcased in the post-event survey results indicate that asking for—and listening to—audience input is more likely to lead to a successful meeting. This approach gives the audience a sense of being "heard" and creates an atmosphere more conducive to listening. Therefore, the likelihood is greater that the message will be absorbed and will resonate long after the closing session.

Despite the initial positive impact gained by addressing employee feedback at a meeting, the lessons learned can be lost if not carried into the future. In this case, the assessment process included providing recommendations to Sun leadership for ongoing communication, turning attention away from the meeting itself and toward the company's future. The survey results will provide a benchmark for future Sun meetings. Discovering that leadership is not always in touch with employees' needs or attitudes was important for Sun and will offer opportunities for future applications and ongoing communication with employees.

The kickoff made great strides in shifting attitudes and perceptions of a critical audience by first assessing audience concerns. Post-event feedback clearly showed an improvement in key areas, but it was important for the management team to realize there was still much work to be done to achieve 2006 goals and beyond. Sun's leadership was eager to learn more about future opportunities and challenges, and the survey results provided the perfect platform.

A summary report identified several opportunities for further communication:
- A need for additional clarity about sales procedures and processes
  - Recommendation: Provide more information and training regarding sales procedures, rules of engagement, working with ISOs, the structure of win teams, and the day-to-day operations required to pursue and close sales.
- A call for continued communication and facts to alleviate ongoing perceptions of the acquisition
  - Recommendation: While perceptions of the acquisition greatly improved as a result of the meeting, more facts and more consistent communication surrounding the unified organization need to be deployed.
- A confirmation of job security
  - Recommendation: Although the meeting delivered much improvement in this area, continued hearsay, layoffs, and leadership resignations indicate remaining uncertainty. Communication that builds confidence in the sales force, related to their place within the organization, needs to continue.
- Product and service improvement and updates
  - Recommendation: Although great opportunities exist for additional sales and customer service, widely-spread skepticism exists about the company's ability to deliver new products on time. This area should remain the target of ad hoc communication aimed at providing prompt and accurate information about progress.

Questions for Discussion

1. Sun chose to use online surveys instead of in-depth phone interviews or focus groups as a pre-event data collection method. How do you think using either of these alternate methods might have affected initial results?
2. Based on the post-event survey results, what do you think are the top three objectives on which the management team should focus to fully benefit from the success of the meeting?
3. How might an event manager best leverage the success of this meeting to

show the value of the event department?

4. The post-event survey results show significant changes in attitudes and perceptions. What would be the best way to build upon those changes to impact business imperatives?

5. Could this meeting be evaluated at Level 5, ROI? If so, how?

About the Author

Nancy Powell is a marketing consultant and project manager with more than twenty years' experience in the events and communication industry. She was a senior account manager at ProActive (www.proactiveinc.com) until December 2005 when she left to start her own consulting business. While at ProActive, Ms. Powell worked with many Fortune 500 clients, including StorageTek. She may be reached at npowell468@aol.com or 708.955.5774. To reach ProActive, please contact Sarah Polster at spolster@proactiveinc.com or 312.654.8844.

Editor's Notes

It is important to note that this meeting won Meeting Professionals International's prestigious 2006 Global Paragon Award of Excellence for Theme. It appears clear in this case study that the award was only possible due to the needs assessment data collected through the pre-event survey and telephone pulse check.

Meetings such as this, where attendee emotions and perceptions must be managed and positively influenced, are critical to an organization's strategic performance. Without these meetings and a carefully structured design and messaging, a company could fail.

This meeting could have been taken to the Level 5, ROI, measurement if the meeting attendees had been briefed on the impact study during the meeting, recognized the importance of the study, and understood what would be asked of them. However, collecting business impact data during this period of transition between the companies could have proven difficult without the right executive-level support.

Case Study
Evaluating an Internal Sales Meeting
National Telecom

By George Eberstadt, nTAG Executive Vice President
of Business Development and Operations

This case was prepared to serve as a basis for discussion rather than an illustration of either effective or ineffective administrative and management practices. All names, dates, places, and data have been disguised at the request of the author or organization.

Abstract

This case study illustrates how events can be quantifiably evaluated against learning and motivation goals (Level 2 ROI). For this internal sales meeting, attendees wore interactive name badges to make it easier to meet sales professionals outside their groups and to provide survey responses. Results were collected and tabulated in real time with an on-site, wireless event data management system.

Background

In 2006, a leading telecom company had recently experienced a merger and was in the process of combining sales organizations. This three-day sales event with 500 attendees was designed to motivate and educate sales professionals. The group needed to gel quickly to achieve new, shared goals. First, they needed to meet and make positive connections so collaboration on company objectives would be effective.

The event had many motivational elements, including inspirational speakers and contests, designed to excite the audience's competitive nature. Throughout the event, attendees had opportunities to earn points for completing activities and for attending sessions. The attendees with the most points were entered into drawings for big-ticket prizes.

To train sales professionals with different levels of knowledge and perceptions, the company organized forty-four separate breakout sessions. Each of these sessions needed to be evaluated and measured to determine if they contributed to achievement of event goals. Attendance was automatically tracked and reported to the event owner by the interactive name badge system.

Some products and product categories were new to the sales professionals. To introduce them to these products, the event included exhibit booths focused on each product category and respective sales tools. Attendees were awarded points for each booth visited. Each day, alerts on the interactive name badges reminded attendees to visit the exhibit booths.

Evaluation Methodology

The company used a five step methodology developed by nTAG Interactive to determine Level 2 ROI.

Step 1 defined the business objectives for the event and weighted their relative importance. The event owner defined four primary business goals, and then defined the weight of each goal as outlined in Table 1.

Table 1. Event Business Goals with Weights

Goal	Weight
Motivate the sales team	20%
Show appreciation, build affinity	20%
Build understanding of goals/targets	30%
Educate on product info, sales tools	30%

The event owner's goals were slightly more weighted toward the shared understanding and education goals (60% of total) than the "change in perception" goals, such as building motivation and affinity (40%).

Step 2 defined quantifiable metrics by which to measure how well the event achieved these objectives. The event organizer established the following metrics for each of the goals, shown in Table 2.

Table 2. Business Goals and Metric Used

Goal	Metric
Motivate the sales team	% of 5s (highest score) in response to survey question – "How much did attending this meeting increase your motivation to tackle the challenges of the year ahead?"
Show appreciation, build affinity	% of 5s (highest score) in response to survey question – "How well did this meeting make you feel that the company appreciates the work you do?"
Build understanding of goals/targets	% of 5s (highest score) in response to survey question – "How well did this meeting help you understand your sales goals for the coming year?"
Educate on product info, sales tools	% of 5s (highest score) in response to survey question – "How effectively did the overall meeting provide you with product information and useful sales tools?"

For this event, the organizer selected similar metric types for each goal. While this strategy simplifies calculations and data gathering, and meets the needs for this event, alternatives can be used. For example, instead of measuring performance with survey responses, the event organizer can choose to use quiz scores to determine learning levels or attendance measurements to establish the audience's excitement and motivation levels.

Step 3 determined the relationship between each goal's performance and degree of achievement. In this step, the event owner established a set point, or level, where the event results would provide no additional value to the company and a set point, or level, where the event performance would provide enough additional value to only cover the cost of the event, called the "breakeven value." Establishing a $0 value (or no additional value) and a breakeven value for each of the goals requires judgment calls rather than exact measurements. However, it does provide a starting point for discussion among event stakeholders, helps to set expectations, and provides a basis for evaluating the event. For this event, the team estimated the following $0 and breakeven values illustrated in Table 3.

Table 3. Value Scores Established to Measure Success of Goals

Goal	$0 Value Score	Breakeven Value Score
Motivate the sales team	10% of respondents give highest score	30% of respondents give highest score
Show appreciation, build affinity	0% of respondents give highest score	30% of respondents give highest score
Build understanding of goals/targets	0% of respondents give highest score	30% of respondents give highest score
Educate on product info, sales tools	0% of respondents give highest score	30% of respondents give highest score

In this case, the event stakeholders established that the $0 value scores for all the goals would be that 10% of attendees would rate each goal the highest score of five. Because the metrics and types of survey questions selected were similar, it made sense to have the same value for all the goals. But this was not a requirement. In other cases, the $0 value and breakeven scores would likely differ for each goal. The event stakeholders decided that for the meeting to break even, 30% of the meeting attendees would have to rate each goal the highest score of five.

Data Collection

In Step 4 of the methodology, actual performance data was collected for each metric. The data was collected using the nTAG Event Data Management System, which includes interactive name badges. In essence, these are lightweight, wearable computers worn by all event attendees. Attendees used these nTAGs to respond to survey questions about the sessions, in particular, and about the meeting, as a whole. The nTAG system collected and tabulated the data immediately for review by the event owner and her team.

Survey questions were used to evaluate the sessions and speakers. This data was then used to make decisions about content, speakers, and agenda for future meetings. The measurement goals, as covered in this case study, were defined by answers to the questions about the meeting as a whole.

Other data collected included attendance at sessions and visits to exhibitor booths. Each session room was equipped with a reader that received signals from the interactive name badges, automatically tracking session attendance. When an attendee visited an exhibit booth, the name badge would communicate with the name badge of the booth staffer, verifying his booth presence. The nTAG System automatically compiled attendance reports during the event, so the event organizer could determine if attendance goals were being met.

Evaluation Results

More than 90% of attendees responded to the surveys. This high response rate was due mainly to two factors—attendees were awarded points for completing each survey, and the nTAGs made completing the surveys fast and easy for them.

The results of the overall meeting survey are summarized in Table 4. Note that performance exceeded breakeven levels (established at 30%) on the first three goals, but fell short on the last goal by 6%.

Table 4. Overall Meeting Survey Results

Goal	Actual Score Achieved
Motivate the sales team	49% of respondents gave highest score
Show appreciation, build affinity	43% of respondents gave highest score
Build understanding of goals/targets	44% of respondents gave highest score
Educate on product info, sales tools	24% of respondents gave highest score

In the final step of the methodology, Level 2 ROI was calculated by comparing event performance against the $0 value and breakeven estimates, determining the added value of the event.

Given that the total cost of the event was $1,200,000 (including an estimate of the cost of attendees' time), the methodology calculated the value of each goal at the breakeven set point, or level, and the value of each set point above the $0 value. As shown in Table 5, the value per point was calculated by dividing the breakeven value for each goal by the difference between the breakeven value and $0 value scores.

Table 5. Value of Each Goal

Goal	Weight	$0 Value Score	Breakeven Value Score	Difference Between the Breakeven Value and $0 Value Scores (column C - B)	Value at Breakeven = Event cost of $1.2 Million X Weight ($1.2 Million x Column A)	Value per point above $0 Value Score (Column E /Column D)
Column	A	B	C	D	E	F
Motivate the sales team	20%	10%	30%	20	$240,000	$12,000
Show appreciation, build affinity	20%	10%	30%	20	$240,000	$12,000
Build understanding of goals/targets	30%	10%	30%	20	$360,000	$18,000
Educate on product info, sales tools	30%	10%	30%	20	$360,000	$18,000
TOTALS	100%	N/A	N/A	N/A	$1,200,000	N/A

Once the value per incremental point was calculated, the actual value for each goal was compared against the breakeven score to compute the incremental value to the company for each goal, and for the event as a whole, as shown in Table 6. The company's value of this meeting was $528,000.

Table 6. Total Value from Event

Goal	Actual Score	Breakeven Value Score	Difference Between Actual Score and Breakeven Value Score	Value per point above $0 Value Score	Net Value
Motivate the sales team	49%	30%	19	$12,000	$228,000
Show appreciation, build affinity	43%	30%	13	$12,000	$156,000
Build understanding of goals/targets	44%	30%	14	$18,000	$252,000
Educate on product info, sales tools	24%	30%	-6	$18,000	($108,000)
TOTAL VALUE FROM EVENT					$528,000

The results show that the event created value among three of the primary goals, but did not achieve desired performance levels for educating the sales team on product information and tools.

Since Table 6 shows the additional value from the event over the breakeven amount of $1.2 million, meeting benefits are derived by adding the value of

$528,000 to the breakeven amount of $1.2 million for a total of $1,728,000 as the total meeting benefits. When the total meeting benefits are compared with the total costs of the meeting, the Level 2 ROI is 44% (as shown below)

$$ROI = \frac{\text{Meeting Benefit} - \text{Meeting Costs}}{\text{Meeting Costs}} = \frac{\$1,728,000 - \$1,200,000}{\$1,200,00} \times 100 = 44\%$$

Other results from the meeting included almost perfect attendance at sessions and more than 90% survey response rates. Since the audience members, composed mainly of sales professionals, were competitive in nature, they strived to gain points by completing the defined attendance and survey tasks, which resulted in these positive results.

Communication Strategy

The nTAG System produced reports that tracked session attendance, survey responses, and visits to exhibit booths, as well as the Level 2 ROI analysis. Because automated tools were used to collect and tabulate the data, the event organizer could review results both during and immediately after the event, monitoring actual results versus objectives. She could also share results with the audience members throughout the event, motivating them to earn more points and, therefore, encouraging activity that would lead to a higher ROI.

Lessons Learned

The metrics, as well as anecdotal feedback, prove that this event was a great success in terms of motivating the sales force. The event team understood its audience and knew exactly how to inspire and encourage them.

Although an important goal of the event was learning, efforts were more focused around motivation. This caused a slight misalignment between goal definition, event implementation, and the results of the goal to "Educate on product info, sales tools."

Recommendations and Use of Results

Looking forward, event resources and programs should shift a bit from motivation to learning. For the next event, the organizer may consider providing electronic quizzes, via the nTAG, to measure the level of knowledge gained from presentations and exhibit booths. Attendees with the highest number of correct responses can then be eligible for prizes or raffles. Alternatively, the learning goal could take up a smaller proportion of the overall goals.

Although this event helped bring together separate sales teams, event stakeholders did not set goals for encouraging and measuring interactions between these groups. The interactive name badges could have been used to show areas of common interest or conversation topics when attendees meet each other (e.g., "Hi, Dan. I work in the Eastern region. I'm an expert in unified messaging.") to break the ice and make it easier to meet new colleagues.

If at the next event, company objectives include building cooperation between diverse departments or teams, the event organizer should establish a goal, metric, and measurement to track performance of this objective. With current event technology, meeting planners have provided incentives for interactions and connections among different groups to enliven the events, increase satisfaction of attendees, and increase event ROI.

Questions for Discussion
1. What additional detail is needed to improve the credibility of the study?
2. How else could attendee feedback data have been collected?
3. Is the methodology used to calculate a Level 2 ROI credible? Why or why not?
4. How could a Level 5 ROI be determined for this meeting?

About the Author
Throughout his career, George Eberstadt has found unique ways to improve business processes and uncover hidden corporate value. In 2002, Mr. Eberstadt cofounded nTAG Interactive, an event technology company focused on the $120 billion meetings and events industry. As nTAG's Executive Vice President of Business Development and Operations, he has gained and shared insight into how meetings can be designed and deployed to meet corporate objectives and contribute to the bottom line. Mr. Eberstadt received his MBA with highest honors from the University of Chicago and an AB, magna cum laude, from Harvard.

Editor's Notes
The interactive nametags used in this study showcased cutting-edge technology that can do much more than collect attendee feedback. This system can also track attendance and traffic flows, facilitate networking, and measure networking between individuals and groups.

This case study calculated the meeting's ROI by setting measurable goals, weighting each goal's importance, and assigning subjective monetary values, provided by meeting executives, to each goal. The perceived credibility of this approach could vary between organizations. Additional research would be needed to determine the actual ROI derived from the business impacts of the meeting.

Case Study
Measuring the Success of an All-Employee Sales and Information Meeting
Gaylord Palms Resort and Convention Center

By Joe Cestare, Director of Convention Services,
Gaylord Palms Resort and Convention Center;
Suzanne Stephan, Director of Marketing,
Gaylord Palms Resort and Convention Center;
and Keith Salwoski, Public Relations Manager,
Gaylord Palms Resort and Convention Center

This case was prepared to serve as a basis for discussion rather than an illustration of either effective or ineffective administrative and management practices. Names, dates, places, and data may have been disguised at the request of the authors or organization.

Abstract

This study measures the success of a sales rally for all employees at this resort hotel. The primary goal was to boost sales for the Christmas season, which is usually a slow period for the hotel and convention center. The meeting generated statistically significant improvements in knowledge, excitement, and financial understanding about the Annual Christmas Show.

Background

Gaylord Entertainment is one of America's fastest-growing specialty lodging and entertainment organizations. Gaylord owns and operates a collection of purpose-built convention resorts, deriving nearly 90% of its revenue from hotel operations. Gaylord properties include Gaylord Opryland Resort & Convention Center in Nashville, Tennessee; Gaylord Palms Resort & Convention Center, near Orlando, Florida; and Gaylord Texan Resort & Convention Center, located on Lake Grapevine, near Dallas, Texas. Currently under construction, Gaylord National Resort & Convention Center, located on the Potomac near Washington D.C., is scheduled to open in March 2008. In addition, Gaylord Entertainment owns a number of specialty entertainment and media companies, including the famed Grand Ole Opry.

Gaylord's "all-in-one-place" designs feature everything a convention could require for days of uninterrupted business and fun. Gaylord Hotels include outstanding meeting spaces, guest rooms, business services, dining, boutiques, entertainment, special events, recreational activities, childcare, spa facilities, and more.

Gaylord Palms Resort & Convention Center is a 1,406-room convention resort, located in Kissimmee, Florida—five minutes from Walt Disney World. It opened in 2002 with much fanfare, breaking industry records with room pre-sales. With 80% to 90% of its business related to meetings and conventions, the resort enjoys a healthy occupancy rate year-round. However, the Orlando convention calendar experiences occasional periods of low occupancy that the resort must overcome. In particular, the month of December is light on convention activity.

It is Gaylord Hotels' goal to be the "gold standard" in the meetings and conventions market. Although the physical product is remarkable, the company believes its most important competitive advantage lies with its people. In fact, Gaylord Hotels' management spends more time and resources than industry average to ensure an enriching and rewarding work environment for employees. Gaylord calls its employees "STARS," which stands for: Smiles, Teamwork, Attitude, Reliability, and Service with a passion. Together, Gaylord's STARS have one shared vision: flawless service. Gaylord's vision statement is "STAR employees delivering flawless service to customers seeking meeting, convention, and leisure experiences."

The service-profit chain is Gaylord's roadmap to success. Although simple in concept, the service-profit chain is a powerful phenomenon. In short, Gaylord Hotels never forgets the value of its people, both the STARS and the guests. Gaylord believes if its STARS are satisfied, happy, and productive, they are naturally poised to add value to their customers. The STARS are in position to create loyal customers, which leads to business profitability. The service-profit chain is ingrained in the company's culture. Gaylord's STARS are ultimately responsible for the success of Gaylord Hotels.

Prior to 1983, Opryland Hotel (now Gaylord Opryland Resort) was essentially empty during the month of December. Groups traditionally avoided this busy month, not wanting to conflict with holiday celebrations and other end-of-year activities. Needing to create an activity to spur December business, "Country Christmas at Opryland Hotel" was born. Over a twenty-year period, the festival grew to its current form, one of the largest Christmas celebrations in the nation. It currently includes a collection of marquee events, dinner shows, and attractions, including the "Radio City Holiday Spectacular" starring the famed Radio City Music Hall Rockettes.

Based on the success of Gaylord's Nashville resort, it was quickly established that Gaylord Palms would also "own" the Christmas holiday season within the Orlando destination. Complementing the many activities of Central Florida theme parks and attractions, Gaylord added to its resort an impressive display of holiday lights, Christmas shows, seasonal meals, and "ICE!" attraction. In 2005, the Christmas season took on a new name, celebrating the atrium's "Best of Florida" experience. The new program, called "Best of Florida Christmas," put a greater emphasis on the holiday celebrations of the Sunshine State.

Entering the 2005 holiday season, it was important that Gaylord's STARS understand the many changes introduced, including the new name. To ensure that all STARS would understand their role in the "Best of Florida Christmas" and "ICE!" events, a special ALL-STAR Rally was held.

Gaylord Palms STAR Rallies

Once a quarter, all STARS are invited to a special rally meeting. This meeting is not only required, but also desired by the resort's 1,800 STARS, who appreciate the meeting's lively production value. In addition, it is an opportunity for all STARS to hear information from the resort's General Manager and other leadership committee members about issues and topics of importance. The meetings are packed with information, including details that are not shared with employees at other hotels in the market. In the end, it is Gaylord's opportunity to get its staff synchronized, solicit support for new programs, recap successes, applaud legendary guest service, and energize the important STARS community.

Best of Florida Christmas STAR Rally

The Best of Florida Christmas STAR Rally was imaginative. Called the "ICE! All-STAR Parade," it paid tribute to the nation's Thanksgiving Day parade broadcasts. The meeting room was lined with bleachers on both sides of a carpet, painted to look like a road. At one end of the "grandstands" was the announcer's booth, which featured two actors providing funny "color commentary" during the parade. The actors were broadcast onto a giant screen above their booth.

Each portion of the All-STAR Rally was preceded by an actual "parade unit," which traveled down the parade route. Some of the units included a marching band, an Engineering Department vehicle parade, and Santa Claus. To introduce the "ICE!" and "Best of Florida Christmas" portions of the Rally, a group of elves pushed a giant gift box down the parade route. At the appropriate moment, the resort's Director of Marketing, emerged to share the exciting details about the year's events. After the "parade" concluded, all STARS were invited to grab an ice-blue parka and be among the first to visit the "ICE!" attraction. As a parting gift, all STARS were given an "ICE!" tote bag promoting the event.

Evaluation Planning

The goals for the event focused on three areas:

- STAR Knowledge of the "Best of Florida Christmas" and "ICE!" Events. The events team goal was to outline a clear, detailed message to the STARS about what the attraction entailed (i.e., costs, hours of operation, added value), so the STARS were comfortable discussing it with friends, family, and customers.
- STAR Excitement about the "Best of Florida Christmas" and "ICE!" Events. If the STARS were excited and ready to show the excitement to their family, friends, co-STARS, and customers, their enthusiasm would help generate interest.
- STAR Understanding of Financial Impact of the "Best of Florida Christmas" and "ICE!" Events. STARS needed to understand the financial importance and impact to Gaylord of these public events.

Data Collection and Analysis

A data collection plan, shown in Table 1, was established with the resort's Director of Training and Gaylord Entertainment's Research and Market Planning Team. A pre-meeting survey (shown in Figure 1) and a post-meeting survey (shown in Figure 2) were administered to Gaylord Palms STARS and Leaders. These surveys were exactly the same, except for one item. On the pre-survey, prior Best of Florida Christmas/ICE! experience was assessed while attendance at the All-STAR Rally was assessed on the post-event survey.

On each survey, a total of seventeen questions were included. They featured:

- Two items assessed prior employment and Best of Florida Christmas experience (or attendance at STAR Rally on the post-event survey)
- Five items assessed knowledge of the Best of Florida Christmas/ICE! event
- Five items assessed excitement for the Best of Florida Christmas/ICE! event
- Four items assessed STARS/Leader awareness of responsibility for financial performance of Best of Florida Christmas/ICE!
- One item assessed the respondents' current job/department at Gaylord Palms

On the fourteen items assessing STARS/Leader knowledge, excitement, and financial understanding, participants were asked to rate statements on a 7-point scale where 1 = Completely Disagree and 7 = Completely Agree.

Data from Gaylord Palms STARS was collected via a pencil-and-paper survey. Leaders, alternatively, were provided these same pre- and post-event surveys using an on-line survey tool (Zoomerang). Data were collected from 472 STARS (considered if responded to at least one item) and 159 Leaders for the pre-event survey and 211 STARS and 147 Leaders for the post-event survey.

Table 1. Data Collection Plan

DATA COLLECTION PLAN

Level	Objective(s)	Measures/Data	Data Collection Method	Data Sources	Timing
0	**Statistics, Scope, and Volume** • Identify who was employed at Gaylord Palms Resort & Convention Center during December 2004. • Identify who has personally experienced the ICE! attraction before, either as a STAR or as a guest.	Yes/no	Electronic email survey Paper survey with responses gathered verbally at department pre-shift meetings	Leaders (+/- 225 people) STARS (+/- 1000 people)	Pre-meeting Post-meeting
1	**Reaction/Satisfaction** • Think the events and entertainment will be great fun. • Think it is fun to race down the ICE! slides. • Be excited about holiday events. • Be eager to share information on events with others this year. • Look forward to bringing family and/or friends to the special STARS family preview of ICE!	7 point scale	Electronic survey (benchmarked against pre-meeting data) Paper survey with responses gathered verbally at department pre-shift meetings (benchmarked against pre-meeting data)	Leaders STARS	Pre-meeting Post-meeting
2	**Learning** • Know the operation dates/hours of events. • Understand why ticket prices have changed. • Know where to access info on events. • Understand most of the events and entertainment are free of charge to hotel guests and ICE! visitors. • Know about holiday room packages and the special priority entry pass overnight guests will get for ICE! • Understand the importance of the ICE! event in bringing additional business to Gaylord Palms Resort.	7 point scale	Electronic survey (benchmarked against pre-meeting data) Paper survey with responses gathered verbally at department pre-shift meetings (benchmarked against pre-meeting data)	Leaders STARS	Pre-meeting Post-meeting

Figure 1. Pre-Meeting Survey

Pre-Meeting Survey

Thank you for taking a few minutes to complete this brief survey regarding ICE! 2005. The survey results will be processed and compiled by the market research department at the corporate office, and your comments will be kept strictly confidential.

1. Were you employed at Gaylord Palms Resort & Convention Center during December 2004? [MARK ONE ONLY]

___ YES   ___ NO

2. Have you personally experienced the ICE! attraction before, either as a STARS or as a guest? [MARK ONE ONLY]

___ YES   ___ NO

On a scale from 1 to 7, where 1=Completely Disagree and 7=Completely Agree, please rate your level of agreement with the following statements: [CIRCLE ONE NUMBER ONLY FOR EACH STATEMENT]

	Completely Disagree				Completely Agree		
3. I know the dates and hours of operation of ICE!	1	2	3	4	5	6	7
4. I understand why ticket prices for ICE! have changed this year.	1	2	3	4	5	6	7
5. I know where to access information on Best of Florida Christmas, including the schedule of events.	1	2	3	4	5	6	7
6. I understand most of the Best of Florida Christmas events and entertainment is free of charge to hotel guests and ICE! visitors.	1	2	3	4	5	6	7
7. I know about our holiday room packages, and the special priority entry pass our overnight guests will get for ICE!	1	2	3	4	5	6	7
8. I am excited about ICE! and Best of Florida Christmas.	1	2	3	4	5	6	7
9. I am eager to share information on ICE! and Best of Florida Christmas events with others this year.	1	2	3	4	5	6	7
10. I look forward to bringing my family and/or friends to the special STARS family preview of ICE!	1	2	3	4	5	6	7
11. I think the Best of Florida Christmas entertainment will be great fun, and I can't wait to see it.	1	2	3	4	5	6	7
12. It is fun to race down the ICE! slides.	1	2	3	4	5	6	7
13. I understand the importance of the ICE! event in bringing additional business to Gaylord Palms Resort.	1	2	3	4	5	6	7
14. I understand how I can help promote the ICE! attraction in my community.	1	2	3	4	5	6	7
15. My company produces special events like ICE! to provide me with hours during what would otherwise be a slow period.	1	2	3	4	5	6	7
16. I play an important role in the success of ICE! and Best of Florida Christmas events.	1	2	3	4	5	6	7

Please indicate the area of the hotel in which you currently work: [MARK ONE ONLY]

___ Accounting
___ Banquet Services/Kitchen/ Stewarding
___ Bell Services
___ Canyon Ranch SpaClub
___ Catering/Convention Services/ Set-up/Exhibit Hall
___ Engineering
___ Food & Beverage /
___ Entertainment
___ Front Office/CID/Concierge/ Celebrity Services
___ Housekeeping
___ Human Resources/Training
___ IT/Telecommunications
___ Purchasing/Receiving
___ Reservations
___ Safety Services
___ Sales/Marketing
___ Other

Figure 2. Post-Meeting Survey

ICE! Post Rally Survey

Thank you for taking a few minutes to complete this brief survey regarding ICE! 2005. The survey results will be processed and compiled by the market research department at the corporate office, and your comments will be kept strictly confidential.

1. Were you employed at Gaylord Palms Resort & Convention Center during December 2004? [MARK ONE ONLY]
   ___ YES   ___ NO

2. Did you attend the All-STARS Rally on Thursday, November 17, 2005? [MARK ONE ONLY]
   ___ YES   ___ NO

On a scale from 1 to 7, where 1=Completely Disagree and 7=Completely Agree, please rate your level of agreement with the following statements: [CIRCLE ONE NUMBER ONLY FOR EACH STATEMENT]

	Completely Disagree				Completely Agree		
3. I know the dates and hours of operation of ICE!	1	2	3	4	5	6	7
4. I understand why ticket prices for ICE! have changed this year.	1	2	3	4	5	6	7
5. I know where to access information on Best of Florida Christmas, including the schedule of events.	1	2	3	4	5	6	7
6. I understand most of the Best of Florida Christmas events and entertainment is free of charge to hotel guests and ICE! visitors.	1	2	3	4	5	6	7
7. I know about our holiday room packages, and the special priority entry pass our overnight guests will get for ICE!	1	2	3	4	5	6	7
8. I am excited about ICE! and Best of Florida Christmas.	1	2	3	4	5	6	7
9. I am eager to share information on ICE! and Best of Florida Christmas events with others this year.	1	2	3	4	5	6	7
10. I look forward to bringing my family and/or friends to the special STARS family preview of ICE!	1	2	3	4	5	6	7
11. I think the Best of Florida Christmas entertainment will be great fun, and I can't wait to see it.	1	2	3	4	5	6	7
12. It is fun to race down the ICE! slides.	1	2	3	4	5	6	7
13. I understand the importance of the ICE! event in bringing additional business to Gaylord Palms Resort.	1	2	3	4	5	6	7
14. I understand how I can help promote the ICE! attraction in my community.	1	2	3	4	5	6	7
15. My company produces special events like ICE! to provide me with hours during what would otherwise be a slow period.	1	2	3	4	5	6	7
16. I play an important role in the success of ICE! and Best of Florida Christmas events.	1	2	3	4	5	6	7

Please indicate the area of the hotel in which you currently work: [MARK ONE ONLY]

___ Accounting
___ Banquet Services/Kitchen/Stewarding
___ Bell Services
___ Canyon Ranch SpaClub
___ Catering/Convention Services/Set-up/Exhibit Hall
___ Engineering
___ Food & Beverage /Entertainment
___ Front Office/CID/Concierge/Celebrity Services
___ Housekeeping
___ Human Resources/Training
___ IT/Telecommunications
___ Purchasing/Receiving
___ Reservations
___ Safety Services
___ Sales/Marketing
___ Other

To be conservative, only surveys that were complete (with the exception of item 17) were included in the analysis (405 and 181 for the pre-event and post-event survey, respectively). Additionally, post-event surveys from respondents who did not attend the All-STAR Rally were not included in the analysis.

As there were no identifying information collected on the pre- and post-survey, surveys could not be matched on the individual level. As such, the analysis here reflects group, rather than individual, differences. Similarly, there is no way to ensure that there were the same people in the pre- and post-event surveys.

Data from an e-mail survey were collected from Gaylord Palms Leaders. Since e-mail addresses were collected for each respondent, only those participants who responded to both the pre- and post-event surveys were used in the analysis. A total of 108 participants completed both surveys. As this survey was forced-choice and collected on-line, each one was complete (no missing responses). As such, none of these surveys were removed from the analysis. Similar to the STAR surveys, only those respondents who stated that they had attended the All-STAR Rally were included in the analysis.

Scores for the knowledge, excitement, and financial categories were created by totaling the scores from each question within the category and then dividing by the number of items within the scale. This produced a single score for each of the three categories, ranging from 1 to 7.

Results

A comparison of pre- and post-event knowledge category scores between STARS (employees) and leaders are shown in Table 2. Table 3 shows the differences in the excitement category, comparing the pre- and post-event responses. Table 4 shows the differences in the financial understanding category, also comparing the pre- and post-event responses. Most of the improvements were statistically significant.

Table 2. Comparison of Pre- and Post-Event Survey Responses for Knowledge Category Questions

Item	Leaders — All Participants		STAR (Employees) — All Participants		Leaders — Employed at Palms in Dec. 2004		STAR (Employees) — Employed at Palms in Dec. 2004		STAR (Employees) — Not Employed at Palms in Dec. 2004		Leaders — Attended ICE! Previously		STAR (Employees) — Attended ICE! Previously		Leaders — Not Attended ICE! Previously		STAR (Employees) — Not Attended ICE! Previously	
	Pre	Post	Pre	Post	Pre	Post	Pre	Post	Pre	Post	Pre	Post	Pre	Post	Pre	Post	Pre	Post
Knowledge Category	**5.94**	**6.70***	**5.77**	**6.50***	**5.97**	**6.75***	**5.8**	**6.50***	**5.66**	**6.47***	**5.95**	**6.72***	**5.84**	-	-	-	**5.55**	-
I know the dates and hours of operation of ICE!	5.86	6.65*	5.95	6.50*	5.91	6.70*	5.94	6.50*	6.01	6.5	5.88	6.66"	5.99	-	-	-	5.83	-
I understand why ticket prices for ICE! have changed this year.	5.77	6.70*	5.27	6.41*	5.81	6.80*	5.33	6.45*	5.04	6.28*	5.81	6.74*	5.37	-	-	-	4.95	-
I know where to access information on Best of Florida Christmas, including the schedule of events.	5.94	6.64*	5.91	6.50*	5.94	6.69*	5.95	6.50*	5.77	6.50*	5.91	6.66*	5.97	-	-	-	5.71	-
I understand most of the Best of Florida Christmas events and entertainment is free of charge to hotel guests and ICE! visitors.	6.45	6.86*	6.04	6.64*	6.51	6.89*	6.12	6.62*	5.76	6.68*	6.49	6.87*	6.14	-	-	-	5.73*	-
I know about our holiday room packages, and the special priority entry pass our overnight guests will get for ICE!	5.68	6.66*	5.69	6.43*	5.7	6.69*	5.69	6.43*	5.7	6.40*	5.67	6.66*	5.74	-	-	-	5.53	-
n =	108	108	405	181	99	99	313	141	92	40	101	101	305	0	7	7	100	0

*Denotes statistically significant difference.

Table 3. Comparison of Pre- and Post-Event Survey Responses to Knowledge Excitement Questions

Item	Leaders All Participants		STAR (Employees) All Participants		Leaders Employed at Palms in Dec. 2004		STAR (Employees) Employed at Palms in Dec. 2004		STAR (Employees) Not Employed at at Palms in Dec. 2004		Leaders Attended ICE! Previously		STAR (Employees) Attended ICE! Previously		Leaders Not Attended ICE! Previously		STAR (Employees) Not Attended ICE! Previously	
	Pre	Post	Pre	Post	Pre	Post	Pre	Post	Pre	Post	Pre	Post	Pre	Post	Pre	Post	Pre	Post
Excitement Category	6.31	6.54*	6.31	6.54*	6.34	6.57*	6.31	6.53*	6.31	6.59*	6.34	6.56*	6.35	-	-	-	6.2	-
I am excited about ICE! and Best of Florida Christmas.	6.36	6.58*	6.28	6.55*	6.35	6.63*	6.22	6.52*	6.47	6.68	6.37	6.60*	6.29	-	-	-	6.26	-
I am eager to share information on ICE! and Best of Florida Christmas events with others this year.	6.5	6.75*	6.37	6.61*	6.53	6.78*	6.35	6.58*	6.41	6.7	6.51	6.78*	6.39	-	-	-	6.29	-
I look forward to bringing my family and/or friends to the special STARS family preview of ICE!	6.52	6.62	6.54	6.69*	6.54	6.64	6.51	6.67	6.63	6.75	6.54	6.63	6.52	-	-	-	6.6	-
I think the Best of Florida Christmas entertainment will be great fun, and I can't wait to see it.	6.2	6.52*	6.26	6.46*	6.22	6.58*	6.26	6.46	6.26	6.48	6.22	6.55*	6.28	-	-	-	6.22	-
It is fun to race down the ICE! slides.	5.97	6.21*	6.11	6.40*	6.05	6.25	6.21	6.42	5.78	6.35	6.06	6.25	6.27	-	-	-	5.64*	-
n =	108	108	405	181	99	99	313	141	92	40	101	101	305	0	7	7	100	0

*Denotes statistically significant difference.

Table 4. Comparison of Pre- and Post-Event Survey Responses to Financial Category Questions

Item	Leaders All Participants		STAR (Employees) All Participants		Leaders Employed at Palms in Dec. 2004		STAR (Employees) Employed at Palms in Dec. 2004		STAR (Employees) Not Employed at at Palms in Dec. 2004		Leaders Attended ICE! Previously		STAR (Employees) Attended ICE! Previously		Leaders Not Attended ICE! Previously		STAR (Employees) Not Attended ICE! Previously	
	Pre	Post	Pre	Post	Pre	Post	Pre	Post	Pre	Post	Pre	Post	Pre	Post	Pre	Post	Pre	Post
Financial Category	6.48	6.70*	6.42	6.63*	6.52	6.74	6.42	6.63*	6.43	6.69*	6.5	6.71	6.45	-	-	-	6.34	-
I understand the importance of the ICE! event in bringing additional business to Gaylord Palms Resort.	6.85	6.87	6.69	6.79	6.89	6.94*	6.7	6.77	6.64	6.85	6.85	6.89*	6.72	-	-	-	6.58	-
I understand how I can help promote the ICE! attraction in my community.	6.6	6.79*	6.38	6.70*	6.64	6.82*	6.39	6.70*	6.35	6.73*	6.63	6.78*	6.41	-	-	-	6.3	-
My company produces special events like ICE! to provide me with hours during what would otherwise be a slow period.	6.02	6.42*	6.3	6.46	6.06	6.45*	6.31	6.44	6.24	6.55	6.07	6.43*	6.33	-	-	-	6.19	-
I play an important role in the success of ICE! and Best of Florida Christmas events.	6.43	6.71*	6.31	6.53*	6.48	6.77*	6.26	6.57*	6.49	6.63	6.46	6.72*	6.32	-	-	-	6.28	-
n =	108	108	405	181	99	99	313	141	92	40	101	101	305	0	7	7	100	0

*Denotes statistically significant difference.

Meeting Benefits and Conclusion

While data was collected on event attendance figures, attendee demographics, and customer satisfaction levels, the results cannot be directly tied to the employee rally. However, one could assume that if the leaders and STAR employees were knowledgeable and excited about the Best of Florida Christmas/ICE! events, customer satisfaction levels should be high during this period. In fact, guest satisfaction surveys showed an improved rating on the statement, "The staff was very helpful." While this customer satisfaction level was not isolated to the staff rally itself, it can be assumed that a portion of this score was a result of the rally.

When visitors were asked "How did you hear about ICE! at Gaylord Palms?" staff at Gaylord Palms were credited as information sources on these holiday events (as shown in Table 5). Assumptions could be made that the employee meeting caused staff to be more knowledgeable about the event and spread their excitement about it to others.

Table 5. Information Sources

Information Sources	Dec 26 - Jan 2	Cumulative
	%	%
Friends/Family	70	65
Internet/Website	22	20
Newspaper Ad	19	19
Newspaper Article	15	16
Television News Segment	13	14
Radio Ad	11	13
Email Ad/Promotion	7	7
Staff at Gaylord Palms	4	6
From Staying here for Business or Convention	3	4
Other	10	12
	n=4395	N=20729

Q: How did you hear about ICE! at Gaylord Palms?

All Gaylord STARS had access to a coupon worth $3 off the admission for Best of Florida Christmas/ICE! to share with friends, family, and customers. This was highlighted at the meeting rally. Although visitation to the attraction increased 11% from 2004, unfortunately redemption of the $3 discount coupons was down almost 13%, compared to 2004.

Compared to the previous year, total revenue for the holiday events increased 11%. Revenue was captured in three separate entries for the ICE! attraction (this does not include incremental outlet/restaurant revenue): attraction admissions,

ICE! retail sales, and commemorative photograph sales (managed by a Gaylord Palms vendor). This increase in total revenue was reflected by an 83% increase in ticket sales, a 15% increase in retail sales, and a 2% increase in photo sales. Again, this increase cannot be directly linked or isolated to the employee meeting, but it can be assumed that the employee meeting had some impact.

Questions for Discussion

1. What other objectives, if any, could have been created for a meeting such as this?
2. What could have been done to collect Level 3, Application, and/or Level 4, Business Impact, results?
3. Should a meeting like this be taken to an ROI calculation?
4. Why would it be important for Gaylord Palms to use the ROI Methodology for this meeting?

About the Authors

Joe Cestare is the Director of Convention Services at Gaylord Palms Resort and Convention Center, which hosts more than 600 meetings and conventions annually. Mr. Cestare has been with Gaylord since 2001 and has hospitality management experience with ITT Sheraton and Starwood Hotels. In July 2005, he was the first hotelier to complete the ROI Certification for Meetings and Events.

Suzanne Stephan holds a degree in psychology from Brandeis University. Though she began her career as a meeting planner for a large travel industry trade show organization, she found her true passion in marketing. Ms. Stephan has been an account manager for several advertising agencies in both New York and Orlando, including Yesawich, Pepperdine, Brown & Russell where she developed marketing programs for numerous high-profile hotel and travel accounts. She has been the Director of Marketing at Gaylord Palms Resort since 2003.

Keith Salwoski is the Public Relations Manager at Gaylord Palms Resort and Convention Center. Mr. Salwoski has a journalism degree from Michigan State University. He began his career at News-Herald Newspapers in Southgate, Michigan, before moving into public relations, where he has worked his magic for Walt Disney World, SeaWorld, and Six Flags Theme Parks.

Editor's Notes

This is an excellent study to illustrate collecting data for Inputs and Indicators (Level 0), Reaction and Perceived Value (Level 1), and Learning (Level 2). Using the service profit chain concept, the linkage between attitudes and customer service and revenue was suggested, heightening the perceived value of the meeting.

Chapter 6
Measuring Application and Implementation

Some meetings and events are designed to drive action, and they often fail because of breakdowns in application. Participants just do not use what they learned in the meeting when they should, or at the expected level of performance. Measuring application and implementation is important to understand the success or lack of success. Without successful implementation, changes in business impact will not occur. A variety of methods—such as questionnaires and action planning—are available to measure the application and implementation of meetings and events. Along with describing evaluation techniques, this chapter addresses the challenges and benefits faced with collecting data at this level.

The Importance of Measuring Application

Measuring application and implementation is necessary if the participants are expected to do something after the meeting. For some meetings, it is the most critical data set because it provides an understanding of the success of implementation, along with the barriers and enablers that influence success.

The Value of Information

The value of information increases as progress is made through the chain of impact—from reaction (Level 1) to ROI (Level 5). Therefore, information concerning application and implementation (Level 3) is more valuable to key clients than reaction and learning data. This does not discount the importance of these first two levels, but emphasizes the importance of moving up the chain of impact. Measuring the meeting's application often provides critical data about not only the success of the meetings, but the factors that can contribute to greater success in future meetings.

A Key Transition Time

The two previous measures, reaction and learning, occur during or at the end of the meeting, where attention and focus are placed on the participants' direct involvement in the meeting. Measuring application and implementation occurs later and captures the participants' use of information, knowledge, and skills in the work or life context. Essentially, measures at this level reflect the degree of post-meeting success. This key transition period makes measuring application and implementation a critical part of success.

A Key Focus of Many Meetings

Because many meetings focus directly on the need to use what is learned in meetings and events, the client often has concerns about these measures of success. Frequently, executives will request that participants take renewed action, change their approach, shift their tactics, or otherwise implement changes. Major events designed to empower employees, create teamwork, or build a loyal customer base will concentrate on the application of meeting content.

Barriers and Enablers

Often, when a meeting doesn't deliver the follow-up results, the first question asked is, "What happened?" Ideally, the first question should be, "What can we do to improve the meeting?" In either scenario, identifying barriers to success is needed. These are the problems encountered during implementation and obstacles to the actual application of the content. At this level of evaluation, these problems should always be addressed and analyzed. In many cases, the participants provide important recommendations for making improvements.

When a meeting is successful, the obvious question is, "How can we repeat this, or even improve it in the future?" The answer to this question is also found at this level of evaluation as enablers are identified. Identifying the factors that directly contribute to meeting success is always necessary. Those same items can be used to replicate the process to produce new or improved results in the future. When participants identify those issues, they provide an important prescription for success.

Challenges of Measuring Application and Implementation

Collecting application and implementation data brings into focus some key challenges for meeting planners. These challenges may inhibit an otherwise successful evaluation.

Linking with Learning

Application data should be linked closely with the learning data discussed in Chapter 5. Essentially, planners must know what participants need to accomplish.

This information is based on what the participants learned in the meeting. Application data measure the extent to which participants applied what they learned.

Applying Serious Effort to Level 3 Evaluation

Because some meetings are planned to drive impact data (e.g., sales) and actual ROI, less emphasis may be placed on measuring application and implementation. In some cases, it may be omitted or slighted in the analysis. For example, sales executives expect sales increases after a sales conference is conducted, sometimes ignoring how the sales representatives performed after the meeting. When impact is desired, Level 3 evaluation is critical. Obtaining credible, usable data will require a serious effort, beyond the usual meeting application.

Fundamental Issues

When measuring application and implementation of meetings, several important issues must be addressed. Largely, these are similar to the issues encountered when measuring reaction and learning. A few may differ slightly because of the later collection timeframe.

Methods

When collecting application data, several methods are available. These involve traditional methods of surveys and questionnaires but also include classic methods for qualitative data collection such as observation, interviews, and focus groups. Action planning, where individuals plan their parts of the implementation in the meeting, is also useful. Sometimes, performance records are monitored to capture movements in key measures. These methods are described in more detail later and are the principal focus of this chapter.

Objectives

As with the other levels, data collection begins with objectives that are set for the meeting's application and implementation. Objectives define expected actions. Without objectives at this level, collecting data is difficult. Chapter 2 described the basic principles for developing these objectives.

Topics to Explore

The topics addressed at this level parallel many of those identified in Chapters 4 and 5. Therefore, many of the areas can be mapped into this level. However, because of the timeframe, additional opportunities to measure success are available. For example, questions about the intent to apply what is learned in the meeting are logical issues to measure at this time—when the application and implementation occurs. Application focuses on activity or action, not the consequences (which is impact), and the number of activities to measure can be mind boggling. Table 6-1 shows some coverage areas for application. These examples can vary.

Table 6-2. Examples of Coverage Areas for Application

Action	Explanation	Example of Objective
Increase	Increasing a particular activity or action.	Increase the use of a probing skill.
Decrease	Decreasing a particular activity or action.	Decrease the number of times the inspection reports are checked.
Eliminate	Stop or remove a particular task or activity.	Eliminate a face-to-face meeting, and replace it with a virtual meeting.
Maintain	Keep the same level of activity for a particular process.	Continue to monitor each complaint.
Create	Design, build, or implement a new procedure, process, or activity.	Create a process for resolving the differences among team members.
Use	Use a particular process, procedure, or activity.	Use the salesforce.com software to track prospects.
Perform	Conduct or do a particular task, process, or procedure.	Perform a post-audit review at the end of each new contract.
Participate	Become involved in various activities, projects, or meetings.	Submit a suggestion for reducing costs.
Enroll	Sign up for a particular program.	Enroll in the career advancement program.
Respond	React to groups, individuals, or systems.	Respond to customer inquiries within 15 minutes.
Network	Facilitate productive relationships with contacts.	Follow-up with contacts on, at least, a quarterly basis.

Sources and Timing

The sources of data are straightforward. The meeting participants are the most likely source. In some situations, the managers of participants may be a source. In other cases, organizational records or systems are the source. In exhibitor studies, the exhibitor would be a source.

The timing of data collection can vary. Since this is a follow up after the meeting, the issue is to determine the best time for a post-meeting evaluation. The challenge is to analyze the nature and scope of the application and determine the earliest time that an action will be taken or completed. This occurs when the application becomes routine, the task is complete, and the implementation is progressing significantly. When to collect data is a judgment call. Collecting as early as possible is important so that potential adjustments can still be made. At the same time, evaluations must allow for desired changes so that the implementation can be measured. In most meetings, this time will be in the three-week to three-month range.

Convenience and constraints also influence the timing of data collection. Perhaps the participants are conveniently involved with another meeting or special event. This would be an excellent opportunity to collect data. Sometimes, constraints are placed on data collection. Clients or other executives are anxious to have the data and to make decisions about the success of the meeting, which moves data collection earlier than the ideal time.

Responsibilities

Measuring application and implementation involves the responsibility and work of others. Because these measures occur after the meeting, an important question may surface in terms of who is responsible for this follow up. Many possibilities exist, from the planner to the client staff, as well as the possibility of external, independent contractors. This matter should be addressed in the planning stage so that no misunderstandings about the distribution of responsibilities occur. More importantly, those who are responsible must understand the nature and scope of their roles and what is needed to collect the data.

Questionnaires and Surveys

Questionnaires have become a mainstream data collection tool for application and implementation measures because of their flexibility, low cost, and convenience. The factors involved in questionnaire design discussed in Chapter 5 apply equally to questionnaire development for measuring application and implementation.

Content

One of the most difficult tasks is to determine specific factors that need to be addressed on a follow-up questionnaire. Although the content items can be the same as those used in reaction and learning questionnaires, additional items are necessary for capturing application and implementation. Figure 6-1 presents a questionnaire used in a follow-up evaluation of a meeting to create a sales culture.

Figure 6-1. Sample Questionnaire for Measuring Application and Implementation

---

Sales Culture at Progress Bank
Follow-up Questionnaire

Are you currently in a sales capacity at a branch?　　　Yes　☐　　　No　☐

Listed below are the objectives of the sales culture meeting. After reflecting on these, please indicate the degree of success in meeting the objectives. Use the following scale:

1. No success at all
2. Limited success
3. Moderate success
4. Generally successful
5. Very successful

As a result of this meeting, participants will:	1	2	3	4	5
a. Convince customers to buy/use Progress Bank products and services.	☐	☐	☐	☐	☐
b. Build a productive, long-term relationship with customers.	☐	☐	☐	☐	☐
c. Increase sales of each product line offered in the branch.	☐	☐	☐	☐	☐

2. Have you used the job aids provided during the meeting?

Yes　☐　　　No　☐

Please explain. _____

_____

_____

_____

3. Please indicate the change in the application of knowledge and skills as a result of your participation in the sales culture meeting. Use the following scale:

1. No change
2. Limited change
3. Moderate change
4. Much change
5. Very much change

	1	2	3	4	5	No Opportunity To Use Skill
a. Probing for customer needs.	☐	☐	☐	☐	☐	☐
b. Helping the customer solve problems.	☐	☐	☐	☐	☐	☐
c. Understanding the features and benefits of all products and services.	☐	☐	☐	☐	☐	☐
d. Comparing products and services to those of competitors.	☐	☐	☐	☐	☐	☐
e. Selecting appropriate products and services.	☐	☐	☐	☐	☐	☐
f. Using persuasive selling techniques.	☐	☐	☐	☐	☐	☐
g. Using follow-up techniques to stay In touch with the customer.	☐	☐	☐	☐	☐	☐
h. Using new software routines for data access and transactions.	☐	☐	☐	☐	☐	☐

4. What has changed about your work (actions, tasks, activities) as a result of this meeting?

_____

_____

_____

_____

5. Please identify any specific accomplishments/improvements that can be linked to this meeting.

_____

_____

_____

_____

6. Indicate the extent to which you think this meeting has influenced each of these measures in your branch. Use the following scale:

    1. No influence
    2. Limited influence
    3. Moderate influence
    4. Much influence
    5. Very much influence

	1	2	3	4	5
a. Sales	☐	☐	☐	☐	☐
b. Productivity	☐	☐	☐	☐	☐
c. Customer Response Time	☐	☐	☐	☐	☐
c. Cross-Sales Ratio	☐	☐	☐	☐	☐
d. Cost Control	☐	☐	☐	☐	☐
e. Employee Satisfaction	☐	☐	☐	☐	☐
f. Customer Satisfaction	☐	☐	☐	☐	☐
g. Quality	☐	☐	☐	☐	☐
Other _____	☐	☐	☐	☐	☐

7. What barriers, if any, have you encountered that prevented this meeting from being successful. Please explain, if possible.

_____

_____

_____

_____

8. What has helped this meeting be successful? Please explain.

_____

_____

_____

_____

9. Which of the following statements best describes the level of management support?

    ☐ There was no management support.
    ☐ There was limited management support.
    ☐ There was a moderate amount management support.
    ☐ There was much management support.
    ☐ There was very much management support.

10. What specific suggestions do you have for improving this meeting?

_____

_____

_____

_____

11. Other comments about this meeting:

_____

_____

_____

_____

Developing a checklist of the content issues to include on a follow-up questionnaire may be useful. Figure 6-2 shows a checklist of the key issues presented in the example discussed here and reflects much of the follow-up data that is often needed to measure application and implementation, and in this case, actual business impact. (Note that the "Linkage with Measures" question is an impact (Level 4) question.)

Figure 6-2. Questionnaire Content Checklist

☐ Progress with objectives	☐ Other benefits
☐ Use of materials	☐ Barriers
☐ Knowledge/skill enhancement	☐ Enablers
☐ Skills used	☐ Management support
☐ Changes with work/actions	☐ Suggestions for improvement
☐ Linkage with measures	☐ Other comments

Improving Response Rates

For most evaluations at this level, questionnaires and surveys will be used to collect a wide range of information. However, asking for too much detail in the follow-up questionnaire can negatively impact the response rate. The challenge, therefore, is to approach questionnaire and survey design and administration for maximum response rate. Table 6-3 shows the actions that can be taken to ensure a successful response rate. Although the term questionnaire is used, the list also applies to surveys.

Table 6-3. Techniques for Increasing Response Rates

- Provide advance communication about the questionnaire.
- Clearly communicate the reason for the questionnaire.
- Indicate who will see the results of the questionnaire.
- Show how the data will be integrated with other data.
- Keep the questionnaire simple and as brief as possible.
- Keep questionnaire responses anonymous—or at least confidential.
- Make it easy to respond; include a self-addressed, stamped envelope/e-mail.
- Use a local coordinator to help distribute and collect questionnaires.
- If appropriate, let the target audience know that they are part of a carefully selected sample.
- Use one or two follow-up reminders.
- Have the introduction letter signed by a top executive.
- Enclose a giveaway item with the questionnaire (pen, money, etc.).
- Provide an incentive (or chance of incentive) for quick response.
- Send a summary of results to target audience.
- Distribute questionnaire to a captive audience.
- Consider an alternative distribution channel, such as e-mail.

- Have a third party gather and analyze data.
- Communicate the time limit for submitting responses.
- Consider paying for the time it takes to complete the questionnaire.
- Review the questionnaire at the end of the formal session.
- Carefully select the survey sample.
- Allow completion of the survey during work hours.
- Design questionnaire to attract attention, with a professional format.
- Let participants know what actions will be taken with the data.
- Provide options to respond (paper, email, Web-site).
- Frame questions so participants can respond appropriately and make the questions relevant.
- Add emotional appeal.

Collectively, these items help boost response rates of follow-up questionnaires. Using all these strategies can result in a sixty to eighty percent response rate—even for lengthy questionnaires that might take thirty minutes to complete.

For a specific technique, some individuals will respond to it (while others will not), bringing in a few more percentage points of return rate, perhaps three to eight percent. Some techniques are more powerful. For example, reviewing a questionnaire at the end of the meeting will often secure about fifteen to twenty percent when the participants have a chance to understand the reason for the questionnaire, the questions, the data needed, and how the data will be used. As each technique is used, the desired response rate can be achieved, often in the range of sixty to ninety percent. This requires determination, focus, and discipline. Too often, meeting planners do not put the effort into collecting data and have a miserable response rate. In reality, this is about changing culture, since the planner essentially has a dialogue with the participants. When this dialogue is perceived as productive, trusting, and helpful, a tremendous amount of data can be collected.

Interviews, Focus Groups, and Observation

In addition to questionnaires and surveys, interviews, focus groups, and observations may be used. As this brief section shows, they have important identities, but all have the disadvantage of increased cost. Because they will rarely be used in evaluations, detailed information is not presented here. It is included in other references, such as *The Handbook of Training Evaluation and Measurement Methods*, 4th Edition, by Jack J. Phillips and Patricia Pulliam Phillips, published by Butterworth-Heinemann, 2007.

Data Collection with Interviews

Interviews may be conducted by the planner or a third party. Interviews can secure data that is difficult to obtain. Also, interviews can uncover success stories that can be useful in communicating the success of the meeting. Respondents may be reluctant to describe their results in a questionnaire but will volunteer the information to a skillful interviewer who uses probing techniques. The interview is versatile and appropriate for application and implementation data. A major disadvantage of the interview is that it consumes time, which increases the cost of data collection. It also requires preparation by the interviewers to ensure consistency.

There are two basic types of interviews: structured and unstructured. A structured interview is similar to a questionnaire. Specific questions are asked with little room to deviate from desired responses. The advantages of the structured interviews over questionnaires are that the interview process can ensure that the questionnaire is completed and that the interviewer understands the responses supplied by the person interviewed. The unstructured interview permits probing for additional information. This type of interview uses a few general questions that may lead to more detailed information as data are uncovered.

Data Collection with Focus Groups

Focus groups are helpful when in-depth feedback is needed. The focus group, designed to solicit qualitative judgments on a topic or issue, involves a small group discussion conducted by an experienced facilitator. Group members are all required to provide input, as individual input builds on group input.

When compared to questionnaires, surveys, or interviews, the focus group approach has several advantages. The basic premise of using focus groups is that when quality judgments are subjective, several individual judgments are better than one. The group process, where participants often motivate one another, is an effective method for generating and clarifying ideas and hypotheses. On the downside, it is much more expensive than questionnaires, but less expensive than the one-on-one interview.

On-the-Job Observation

A rare data collection method is observing participants on the job and recording any changes in behavior and specific actions taken. This technique is particularly useful when knowing how participants use new skills, knowledge, tasks, procedures, or systems is important. The observer may be the planner, the participant's manager, a member of a peer group, or an external resource, such as a mystery shopper. The most common observer, and probably the most practical, is an external resource. Observation is expensive and is used only in special situations.

Action Plans

The action plan is a common data collection tool. With this approach, participants are required to develop action plans as part of the meeting. Action plans contain the detailed steps necessary to accomplish specific objectives related to the meeting. The process is one of the most effective ways to enhance support of a meeting and build the ownership needed for successful application and implementation.

The plan is typically prepared on a printed form, such as the one shown in Figure 6-3. The action plan shows what is to be done, by whom, and the date the objectives should be accomplished. The action-plan approach is a straightforward, easy-to-use method for determining how participants will change their behavior on the job and achieve success with the meeting implementation.

Developing the Action Plan

The development of the action plan requires two major tasks: determining the areas for action and writing the action items. Both tasks should be completed during the meeting and, at the same time, be related to on-the-job, meeting-related activities. A list of areas for action can be developed with the help of a speaker or facilitator. The list may include an area needing improvement or an opportunity for increased performance. Examples of typical questions that should be answered before determining the areas for action are:

- Is it related to the meeting?
- How much time will this action take?
- Is this expected?
- Are the skills for accomplishing this action item available?
- Who has the authority to implement the actions?
- Will this action have an effect on other individuals?
- Are there any organizational constraints for accomplishing this action item?

Usually, writing specific action items is more difficult than identifying the action areas. The most important characteristic of an action item is that it is written so that everyone involved will know when it is accomplished. One way to help achieve this goal is to use specific action verbs and set deadlines for the completion of each action item.

Figure 6-3. Action Plan

| Name _____ | Speaker/Facilitator Signature _____ | Follow-Up Date _____ |

Objective _____

SPECIFIC STEPS: *I will do this*	Date	Evaluation Period ___ to ___	END RESULT: *So that*
1. _____			
2. _____			
3. _____			
4. _____			
5. _____			
6. _____			
7. _____			

Expected Intangible Benefits

Barriers: What Got in the Way?	Enablers: What Helped the Process?

Some examples of action items are:
- Identify and secure a new customer account by (date).
- Handle every piece of paper only once to improve my personal time management by (date).
- Analyze the causes of absenteeism by (date).
- Probe my employees directly about a particular problem by (date).

If appropriate, each action item should indicate other individuals or resources needed for its completion. Planned behavior changes should be observable. It should be obvious to the participant and to others when the change takes place. Action plans, as used in this context, do not require the prior approval or input from the participant's manager, although, as in any case, manager support may be helpful.

Successful Use of Action Plans

The action-plan process can be an integral part of implementation and is not necessarily considered an add-on or optional activity. To gain maximum effectiveness from action plans for data collection, the following steps should be implemented:
- Communicate the action plan requirement early.
- Announce the action planning process at the beginning of the meeting.
- Describe the action planning process.
- Allow time to develop the plan.
- Have someone review the action plans for relevance and completeness.
- Explain the follow-up mechanism.
- Collect action plans at predetermined follow-up times.
- Summarize and report the data.

Action Plan Advantages and Disadvantages

Although there are many advantages to using action plans, at least two concerns exist:
- The process relies on direct input from the participant, usually with no assurance of anonymity. As such, the information can sometimes be biased and unreliable.
- Action plans can be time consuming for the participant, and if the participant's manager is not involved in the process, the participant may not complete the assignment.

As this section has illustrated, the action plan approach has many inherent advantages. Action plans are:

- Simple and relatively easy to administer
- Easily understood by participants
- Suitable to a wide variety of meetings
- Appropriate for all types of data
- Able to measure reaction, learning, behavior changes, and impact
- Usable with or without other evaluation methods

Because of the flexibility and versatility of the process, action plans have become important data collection tools for meeting evaluation.

Data Use

Data becomes meaningless if it is not used properly. As we move up the chain, the data becomes more valuable in the minds of clients, key executives, and other stakeholders with a strong interest in the meeting. While data can be used in dozens of ways, the following are the principal uses for data after it is collected:

1. Review and report results
2. Adjust meeting design and implementation strategy
3. Reinforce desired actions—let them know what is expected
4. Improve management support for meetings and events
5. Market future meetings

Final Thoughts

This chapter outlined techniques for measuring application and implementation—a critical issue in determining the success of a meeting. This essential measure determines not only the success achieved, but areas where improvement is needed and areas where the success can be replicated in the future. A variety of techniques are available, ranging from questionnaires to action plans. The method chosen must match the scope of the meeting and resources available to collect data. Complicated meetings require a comprehensive approach that measures all the issues involved in application and implementation. Simple meetings can have a less formal approach and collect data only from a questionnaire.

Two case studies follow that demonstrate how to evaluate a communication meeting and a leadership conference at Level 3.

Case Study
Measuring the Success of a
Strategic Communication Meeting
Great Property Real Estate Company

By Sue Tinnish, Principal, S.E.A.L. Inc.

This case was prepared to serve as a basis for discussion rather than an illustration of either effective or ineffective administrative and management practices. All names, dates, places, and organizations have been disguised at the request of the author or organization.

Abstract

Many companies hold internal meetings in which senior management sets forth the strategic direction of the organization to align disparate business units and employee behavior. These meetings are critical for a firm's future success. It is important to determine how effectively meeting participants transfer the information received at a meeting to others within the organization. This case study explores the effectiveness of a strategic communication meeting and the subsequent sharing of information. It also examines the extent to which new behaviors supporting the firm's strategic direction were modeled in the workplace.

Background

The Great Property Real Estate Company (hereafter referred to as Great Property) provides real estate and investment management expertise. It operates locally and globally to supply real estate related services to owner, occupier, and investor clients. Services provided include:

- Facility management
- Investment advice and execution
- Corporate finance (access to global debt and equity capital markets for acquisition and dispositions)
- Workouts/turnaround and advisory services
- Tenant representation
- Leasing
- Strategic consulting
- Construction management

At the outset of each year, Great Property conducts a strategic communication meeting with senior-level management throughout the United States. In 2006, this one-day meeting featured an awards ceremony held the night before and updates from executive management and various business units. The purpose of the meeting was for participants to obtain updates on the company, network with peers, and learn about the company's strategy. Great Property's 2006 strategy required that all employees break out of their "silo" mentality and convey to clients information about the firm's entire resources and services (not simply their areas of expertise).

Rationale for Study

The Strategic Communication Meeting is executive management's vehicle for communicating key information to a large audience with emotional appeal. It is their one opportunity to get everyone on the same page. However, the Chief Operating Officer questioned whether inviting senior vice presidents (SVPs) and vice presidents was necessary. For the 2006 meeting, the firm scaled down the participant list to include only SVP-level employees. Accordingly, the Chief Operating Officer wanted to use the results from the impact study to make a decision about future meetings and the appropriate audience for them. The Chief Operating Officer planned to use the results to decide whether restricting the size of the meeting audience reduced the impact and communication of the message about the firm's strategy and direction across the employee base.

In addition to assessing the ability of participants to cascade the meeting's key messages throughout the organization, Great Property was also interested in:
- Capturing reaction to changes in the meeting
- Quantifying the amount of networking occurring during the meeting
- Assessing behavioral change in keeping with the firm's new strategy

Evaluation Methodology

The Phillips ROI Methodology was adopted as the evaluation methodology. (Phillips, 2003) This approach was expected to produce three types of data:
- Reaction and planned action
- Learning and confidence
- Application and implementation

Reaction and learning data would be collected post-meeting, while application and implementation data would be collected three months after the meeting. Executive management believed this level of analysis would yield the information they sought.

Evaluation Planning

Specific and measurable objectives at each level of measurement were created and agreed upon by all key stakeholders.

Level 1: Reaction Objectives

Reaction objectives were established to assist in improving the meeting process and to provide indicators that new behaviors supporting the organization's strategic direction would be modeled. Specific objectives focused on participants' perception of the meeting would be:

- A valuable use of time
- Full of new and valuable information important to the job
- Well-executed
- Conducted by effective speakers presenting relevant information
- Action-oriented—they can carry forward the message from the meeting to their teams and departments
- Valuable for developing new contacts
- Motivating

There was also an expectation that attendees would plan to execute new behaviors that support Great Property's strategic direction.

Level 2: Learning Objectives

To ensure that participants would understand the strategic direction and could successfully communicate and execute this strategy, learning objectives were established. These objectives focused on participants' ability to:

- Articulate the company's strategies and activities
- Cross-pollinate the firm's services through new relationships established
- Identify firm services outside their business units

Level 3: Application and Implementation Objectives

While the intent of the strategic communication meeting was to set the direction of the organization, the ultimate objective was to prepare participants to effectively communicate the strategy, not only through words, but also through behaviors. These behaviors should then influence the perception of others toward the strategic direction and prepare them to carry out the corporate strategy. Specific application and implementation objectives focused on participants:

- Conveying the firm's strategy to colleagues
- Modeling behavior that supports the firm's strategic direction

If each participant executes the call to action from the meeting (shares information with their team), then accordingly other colleagues within the firm will:

- Be knowledgeable about Great Property's strategies and direction
- Acknowledge the importance of the company's strategies and direction on the job
- Observe changes in management to support strategies and direction
- Change their behavior to support strategies and direction

Data Collection and Analysis

Table 1 shows the Data Collection Plan that identifies objectives at each level of measurement, the data collection method used, the data sources, the timing of data collection, and who is responsible for that data collection.

Questionnaires were used to collect feedback from the meeting attendees. Great Property emailed an electronic post-meeting questionnaire (available for download at www.roiinstitute.net) to participants. This questionnaire focused on Level 1 and 2 measures, with an open-ended question for improvement recommendations. The questionnaire was divided into four sections:

1. Overall Impressions
2. Meeting Content
3. Value of the Meeting
4. Executing the Messages of the Meeting

There was a 39% participant response rate to the post-meeting questionnaire.

A follow-up electronic questionnaire (available for download at www.roiinstitute.net) was emailed to all employees three months after the meeting. This timeframe was selected because of the importance in disseminating information to all employees.

This questionnaire, akin to an evaluation used in $360°$ human resources reporting, covered:

- Key messages and strategies from the meeting cascaded through the organization
- Observable changes were evident in the attitudes and behavior of SVPs (modeling the mindset and behavior required to support the firm's strategies)
- All employees planned changes related to the new behavioral and business norms

At the SVP level, that call to action from the meeting was manifested in two ways:

1. Communicate strategy to team members
2. Model behavior necessary to cross-sell firm's services

Table 1. Data Collection Plan

Level	Objective(s)	Data Collection Plan				
		Measures/Data	Data Collection	Data Sources	Timing	Responsibilities
0	**Indicators and Statistics** • Sources of previously acquired info • Preferences for receiving info	Indicate sources Rank preferences	Electronic Survey Questionnaire	Attendees	Post-meeting	Communications Department
1	**Reaction/Satisfaction** • Valuable use of time • Content important to job • Well-executed meeting • Format of dinner/awards ceremony • Accommodations/service at venue • Value of question and answer session • Value of learning about other groups in firm • Effectiveness of presenters • Relevance of presentations • Amount of new information presented • General comments/ recommendations.	4.0 out of 5 on a 5-point scale on value, content, execution, dinner/awards, etc. 50% of info is new Open-ended responses	Electronic Survey Questionnaire	Attendees	Post-meeting	Communications Department
2	**Planned Action** • Intent to use tools/processes to cascade message • Intent to apply knowledge • Intent to undertake new business activities	60+% intend to use meeting highlights video; 60+% intend to use personal communication tools; 30+% intend to use other tools 80% agree or strongly agree Each attendee intends to undertake 2 or more new business activities	Electronic Survey Questionnaire	Attendees	Post-meeting	Communications Departmen

3	Learning				
	• More informed about strategies and activities • Meeting helped motivate attendees to perform at best • Equipped to educate team about strategies/ direction • Belief that culture supports making mistakes • Meeting helped attendees connect with colleagues from other areas • Number of new relationships created at meeting	75% agree or strongly agree 80% agree or strongly agree (on equipped objective) 4.3 out of 5 on "Meeting helped me connect with colleagues from other areas of the firm" 66% to have made 4 – 10 new contacts	Electronic Survey Questionnaire	Attendees	Post-meeting	Meetings Departmen
4	Application/Implementation				
	• Perceived barriers and enablers to application	Indicate which barriers/enablers	Electronic Survey Questionnaire	Attendees	Post-meeting	Meetings Department

Application/Implementation				
• Identify vehicles in 2005 used to learn about strategic direction	Indicate which vehicles used	Electronic Survey Questionnaire	Attendees	3 months following meeting	Communications Department
• Identify vehicles in 2006 used to learn about strategic direction				
• Importance of company's strategies and direction to current job	Indicate which activities taken/planned			
• Activities undertaken to support strategic direction				
• Activities planned during next few months	80% agree or strongly agree on knowledge and understanding of company strategies, meeting theme, priorities, role			
• Knowledgeable about company's strategies and direction				
• Know about global priorities				
• Understand how global priorities relate to the US				
• Familiar with meeting theme				
• Know the 4 priorities	80% Agree or Strongly Agree on feeling equipped			
• Understand how employee's role aligns with strategies				
• Feels well equipped to help execute company strategies	50% indicate yes; average 2 observed changes			
• Observed changes in manager to support strategies and direction				
• Perceived/actual barriers and enablers to application	Indicate which barriers/enablers			

For all other employees, the effective execution would become apparent in four ways:

1. Knowledge about Great Property's strategies
2. Ability to execute the company's strategies
3. New behaviors adopted
4. Planned new behaviors

To ensure adequate response rates, several extra steps were taken. The electronic questionnaires were sent by email with a cover letter mentioning the evaluation study, signed by the Chief Operating Officer. The email with the survey link also included the reason for the questionnaires, a response deadline, and emphasized anonymous and confidential responses. During the meeting, SVPs were also told of the forthcoming questionnaires. Two follow-up reminders were sent to questionnaire non-respondents encouraging responses.

Results

Results were developed and reported at the end of the meeting and three months following the meeting.

Level 1: Reaction

Table 2 shows the attendee reaction and satisfaction from the end-of-meeting questionnaire. Most of the reaction measures exceeded the goal of 4.0. The notable exceptions are the question and answer session and the networking via table-top displays. Relevance of meeting content was slightly below the goal.

Table 2. Reaction Data from Attendees

Issue	Rating*
Meeting was a valuable use of time	4.22
Meeting content is important to my job	3.98
Meeting was well-organized	4.51
Format of dinner/awards ceremony	4.49
Accommodations/service at the venue	4.28
Value of question and answer session during the meeting	3.41
Value of learning about other groups in firm via table-top displays	3.28

*Rating scale: 1 = Strongly Disagree; 5 = Strongly Agree

Nineteen presentations comprised meeting content. Results on relevance of this content ranged from a high of 4.48 to a low of 3.4. On the effectiveness measure, the range was from 4.4 to 2.97. Using a 5-point scale, the midpoint 3 reflects neutrality. Combining the top two ratings, 4 and 5 (Agree and Strongly Agree), measures the total positive responses. Of the nineteen presentations, nine generated

75% or more responses of "Agree or Strongly Agree" in relevance and effectiveness.

Another measure taken at Level 1 was intent to apply information and knowledge acquired during the meeting, where 91% either agreed or strongly agreed that they intended to apply the knowledge learned. Only 8% provided a neutral response and only 1% indicated no intention to apply by selecting the "Strongly Disagree" option. A further intended action was actual planned changes in behavior. Survey results indicte 4.25 planned changes per respondent.

Level 2: Learning

Executive management set a goal of 75% of participants responding "Agree" or "Strongly Agree" to several areas of new knowledge. The meeting was highly successful in two areas—being more informed about strategies and activities and connecting with colleagues from other areas—99% and 94%, respectively. The meeting met the goal of being motivational, but fell short of creating a culture within Great Property that supports mistakes. These results are summarized in Table 3 below.

Table 3. Learning Data from Attendees (SVPs)

Issue	Percentage of Agree and Strongly Agree Responses
More informed about strategies and activities	99%
Meeting helped motivate attendees to perform at best	76%
Belief that culture supports making mistakes	48%
Meeting helped me connect with colleagues from other areas	94%

The most significant learning goals focused on attendees' competence to deliver the message about strategy and direction—83% of attendees agreed or strongly agreed that after the meeting they were well-equipped to educate their team on the company's strategy. Table 4 summarizes the results.

Table 4. Learning Data from Attendees (SVPs)

I feel well equipped to educate my team about the company's strategies and direction.	Percentage of Responses
Strongly Agree	23%
Agree	60%
Neutral	10%
Disagree	5%
Strongly Disagree	1%

While competence to deliver the message was important, executive management had also set an objective for participants to establish new relationships throughout the organization. Table 5 indicates that 60% of respondents reported that they created more than four new relationships during the meeting. Another 25% reported meeting eleven or more new colleagues. Overall, this surpassed the firm's goal of 66% of participants meeting four to ten new people.

Table 5. Number of New Relationships Developed

Number of New Relationships	Percentage of Responses
4 – 6	32%
7 – 10	28%
1 – 3	14%
15+	13%
11 – 15	12%

Level 3: Application and Implementation

Information was solicited on potential barriers and enablers to help executive management act to assist in implementing the strategy. SVPs reported at the end of the meeting that lack of time would potentially be the greatest barrier to successful application, with 49% selecting this item.

Meeting attendees expressed that potential enablers to implementation included existing relationships with colleagues and support from senior management.

Follow-Up Results

For the strategic communication meeting to be successful, action (execution) was required from the SVP-level employees to impact all other employees. If the SVPs communicated key meeting messages to their teams, the assumption was that then all employees would become knowledgeable about Great Property's strategies. As shown in Table 4, 83% of the meeting participants felt well-equipped to educate their teams as indicated in their "Strongly Agree" and "Agree" responses. This slightly exceeds the firms' expectation of 80%. The resulting impact of the SVPs delivering the message was that 66% of Great Property employees felt knowledgeable about the firm's strategies (combination of "Agree" and "Strongly Agree" responses, as shown in Table 8). This is below the desired rate of 80%. Forty-six percent of all employees below the SVP level felt well-equipped to execute Great Property's strategies.

Table 8. Communicating Meeting Message to All Employees

Possible Responses	End-of-Meeting Questionnaire	Follow-Up Questionnaire	
	I feel well equipped to educate my team about the company's strategies and direction.	I am knowledgeable our company's strategies.	I feel well equipped to help execute the company's strategies.
	SVP Level	Below SVP Level	Below SVP Level
Strongly agree	23%	9%	8%
Agree	60%	57%	38%
Neutral	10%	23%	32%
Disagree	5%	9%	18%
Strongly Disagree	1%	2%	4%

Further, the employees responding to the follow-up survey demonstrated their acumen about the firm's priorities, as indicated in Table 9.

Table 9. Knowledge Level of All Employees as Captured on the Follow-Up

Survey Question	Percentage of Agree and Strongly Agree Responses
I know about the global priorities.	59%
I understand how the global priorities relate to our role in North America.	46%
I am familiar with the concept of the "meeting theme."	73%
I know about the 4 priorities.	41%
The company's strategies are important to my current job.	69%
I understand how my role within the company aligns with our strategies.	56%

Through 2005 and 2006, the majority of people received their information about Great Properties' strategies and direction from a variety of sources, including:

- Executive e-mail messages
- Conference calls
- Their manager

These top three responses increased in the percentage of employees selecting that vehicle in 2006, as attending the strategic communications meeting was eliminated for all below the SVP level in 2006. The general population also relied heavily on:

- 2006 Strategic Communication Meeting DVD, increased reliance by 22%
- Company training sessions, increased reliance by 6%
- Meeting Materials on intranet, increased reliance by 5%

Table 10 summarizes results regarding the extent of reliance on the various communication vehicles.

Table 10. Vehicles for Learning about Strategies and Direction of Great Property

Vehicles	Percentages of Respondents	
	2005	2006
Executive e-mail messages	54%	72%
Conference Calls	49%	53%
My manager	35%	43%
Intranet	27%	36%
News publications	25%	34%
Informal conversations with colleagues	18%	22%
None, I did not work for Great Property in 2005	18%	–
Attending the 2005 Strategic Communication Meeting	16%	–
Company training sessions	14%	20%
Strategic Communications Meeting Materials on intranet	7%	12%
Other	6%	–
2006 Strategic Communication Meeting DVD	–	22%

If the SVPs executed on their intended activities, then employees would observe the changes in their manager's behavior. Of the top activities planned by SVPs, the teams observed these behaviors in 31% to 62% of the activities, as summarized in Table 11. Great Property had set a target of 50% observation rate for each of the activities. On a positive note, 60% of employees indicated their managers encouraged the team to collaborate with colleagues in other areas.

Table 11. Observation of Behavior Change at SVP Level

Possible Activities or Changes	End-of-Meeting Questionnaire	Follow-Up Questionnaire
	SVP Level Responses to "What activities do you plan to undertake?"	Below SVP Level Responses to "What changes have you observed in your manager's behavior?"
Reach out—my team to provide additional services	62%	62%
Reach out—their team to provide additional services	51%	45%
Introduce other business practices to staff	50%	48%
Reach out—my team support pitches	50%	30%
Connect with senior leaders in other markets	50%	31%
Proactively bring new ideas to clients	50%	40%

If employees at the SVP level educated their teams about Great Property's strategies and modeled behavior supporting these strategies, the assumption was that an effective internalization of the message would result in these same employees exhibiting the desired behavior. As shown in Table 12, between 36% and 18% of employees indicated they had undertaken seven desired behaviors. Another 25% of all employees intended to add these seven desired behaviors in the future. Only two areas of behavior fell below 25%—adoption or planned adoption.

Table 12. Intention of Employees below SVP Level to Execute Behavior

Possible Activities	Follow-Up Questionnaire	
	"What activities have you undertaken to support the strategic direction?"	"What additional activities do you plan to undertake?"
	2006	Next Months
Reach out—my team to provide additional services	36%	38%
Proactively bring ideas to clients	24%	35%
Reach out—my team to provide additional services	23%	29%
Include information in pitches	23%	23%
Reach out—my team support pitches	22%	26%
Introduce colleagues to my clients	19%	20%
Connect with colleagues while traveling	18%	25%
Nothing—already doing	3%	25%
None—I was already doing	3%	—
None—I do not see value	1%	—
None—do not apply	35%	—

Similar analysis was performed on the average number of behaviors. The total number of survey responses for each behavior were summed and divided by the number of survey respondents resulting in an average number of behavior changes per respondent. In the follow-up questionnaire, survey respondents on average cited they had made 1.75 changes in their behavior and intended to make another two changes. Total expected changes of 3.75 compares favorably with intended changes in behavior at the SVP level of 4.25.

Barriers and Enablers to Application

Perceived and actual barriers and enablers to implementation were determined to help executive management plan follow-up steps to promote cultural change. As illustrated in Table 13, lack of time was the largest barrier to implementation across the workforce. Additionally, people below the SVP level indicated the need to identify correct contacts and the need for more training/information about product. However, an insignificant number of SVPs identified these two areas as perceived barriers (8% and 9%, respectively).

This perception of barriers is not surprising. By the nature of their positions, likely tenure, and responsibilities, people at the SVP level have access to more information and more people than those below the SVP level.

The SVP results on enablers further documented this gap or difference between the two levels. In identifying perceived enablers captured in the post-meeting questionnaire, 61% at the SVP level indicated that existing relationships with colleagues would help them execute Great Property's strategy.

Table 13. Barriers to Implementation

Barriers	End-of-Meeting Questionnaire	Follow-Up Questionnaire
	SVP Level	Below SVP Level
Lack of Time	49%	55%
Uncertainty about compensation	10%	19%
Don't know who to contact	8%	32%
Don't see direct benefit to client	3%	7%
Insufficient information about other product lines	9%	41%
Nothing—already doing	42%	8%

As shown in Table 14, both groups felt that support from senior management and ongoing communication were two significant factors enabling them to implement Great Properties' strategies.

Table 14. Enablers to Implementation

Enablers	End-of-Meeting Questionnaire	Follow-Up Questionnaire
	SVP Level	Below SVP Level
Compensation	21%	30%
Existing relationships with colleagues	61%	44%
Additional forums for networking	44%	45%
Client satisfaction	37%	48%
Ongoing communication	55%	66%
Support from senior management	60%	64%

Communication Strategy

Executive Management, the Meetings Department, and Communications Department received a final report documenting the results of the survey. It was recommended that the results be shared with all employees.

SVPs would be able to use the data to better communicate and manage their teams and eliminate perceived barriers. Sharing data would help management validate future actions.

Lessons Learned and Recommendations

The process of measuring the meeting created a laser-like focus on the agenda elements. In this case, simply planning an impact study created additional clarity on the meeting's call to action.

While communicating these key messages to the team was an obvious call to action for the SVPs, the reality of business and the culture at Great Property was that this action may get pushed aside due to time constraints, pressure for revenue, client issues, and current projects. In this case, participants cited lack of time as the top barrier. However, the follow-up survey, executed in a 360° mode, created a sense of urgency and, in essence, a deadline for the SVPs.

Anecdotally, one follow-up survey respondent noted that his/her SVP delivered the message only days before the survey's release. It is important to note that a message was sent to SVPs prior to the survey reminding them to discuss the key meeting messages with their team and the tools available to help them deliver the messages. While such incidents are not desirable, the reality is "what gets measured gets managed." Without the existence of the follow-up survey, more barriers would remain in the way of executing the meeting's call to action.

While generally the vice presidents were unhappy about not being included in the 2006 Strategic Communication Meeting, the survey results do not indicate that they should have been included or needed to be included in future meetings. Interestingly, Great Property employees (of which the vice presidents were a part) indicated that in 2005 they received their information primarily from email messages (54%), followed by conference calls (49%). Attending the Strategic Communication Meeting in 2005 ranked sixth on the list of information sources.

As long as executive management can supply employees with consistent messaging through a variety of mediums (SVPs, email, conference calls, etc.), communication appears to cascade throughout the organization. Overwhelmingly, respondents indicated that email (52%) and conference calls (29%) were their preferred channel for receiving information about the company's strategies. These preferences support using alternative methods of communication rather than face-to-face meetings. Consistent messaging, combined with ongoing networking opportunities, ongoing communication, and support from senior and executive management, allows employees not in attendance to understand, integrate, and internalize the important strategic direction of Great Property.

Use of Results

The results of this impact study were used to confirm a strategy for next year's meeting. Executive management also has data on which to base additional communication to company employees and to benchmark the results of future Great Property meetings.

Resources

Heathfield, S. M., *360 Degree Feedback: The Good, the Bad, and the Ugly*, http://humanresources. about.com/od/360feedback/a/360feedback.htm

Phillips, J. J., *Return on Investment in Training and Performance Improvement Programs*, 2nd Edition (Butterworth-Heinemann, Burlington, MA, 2003).

Questions for Discussion

1. Was taking this meeting to a Level 3 evaluation the most appropriate way to measure the meeting?
2. How could the employee follow-up questionnaire results have been isolated to show the impact of the meeting?
3. What alternative approaches could have been used to derive Level 3, Application, data?
4. Could this meeting have been evaluated at a higher level? What level would have provided superior information?

About the Author

Sue Tinnish is a Principal at S.E.A.L. Inc. She provides services to bridge people and performance, including facilitation, consulting, training, teambuilding, and ROI analysis. Her focus in the meetings industry is on improving the actual content of the meeting itself. Ms. Tinnish is a well-known industry speaker and author. She can be contacted by phone at 847.394.9857 or by email at stinnish@ ameritech.net.

Editor's Notes

The strategic communication meeting, as presented in this case study, was the perfect type of meeting to take to a Level 3 evaluation. It would have been a challenge to determine the business impacts and subsequent ROI of this meeting; however, that was not needed. This case study provides a template of how meetings with similar objectives can be evaluated through the use of questionnaires.

Case Study
Measuring the Success of a Leadership Conference
Express Personnel Services

By James B. McDonough, Director,
Meetings and Training Services, Fusion Productions and
Teresa Burris, CMP, Event Marketing Manager, Express Personnel Services

This case was prepared to serve as a basis for discussion rather than an illustration of either effective or ineffective administrative and management practices. Names, dates, places, and data may have been disguised at the request of the author or organization.

Abstract

Today, an increasing number of meetings and conferences are being evaluated to make improvements, to make decisions about their future, and to determine the connection between the meeting and performance within the organization. In this case, Express Personnel conducted surveys and focus groups to capture meeting desires and needs, attendee reaction, learning acquired, and the subsequent application of the knowledge, skills, and contacts acquired at the meeting. Since Express Personnel is a franchise organization, the success of the attendees meant success for them as well.

Company Background

Express Personnel Services, founded by Robert A. Funk and William H. Stoller in 1983, is the largest privately-owned staffing firm in the world. Headquartered in Oklahoma City, Oklahoma, the franchise company has approximately 440 locations and offers a full range of staffing services, including temporary placement, evaluation hire, flexible staffing, and professional search.

The culture of the company is like a family. Franchisees are provided the expertise and support materials to be successful, and they in turn apply their hard work and knowledge toward helping the people of their communities. Often, these franchisees are owned and operated by married couples.

The company reflects the personal and business ethics of its founders. Robert Funk says, "For many people who have lost their jobs, often through no fault of their own, we provide great hope. Our mission is to help people find jobs and our client companies find good employees, and to help those clients make those jobs and those employees even better."

Meeting Background

The International Leadership Conference (ILC) is one of many conferences provided each year by Express Personnel Services for their franchisees. It is the largest and most prestigious Express conference. Attracting approximately 850 attendees, this annual, three-day conference, held in 2005, provided breakfast meetings, educational sessions, general sessions, a trade show, networking functions, and several awards presentations. The participants were 60% female, representing three countries (United States, Canada, and South Africa). The conference theme was "Focus" with an underlying theme of "It's all about *you*. It's all because of *you*. It's been designed for *you* by *you*."

No fee is charged to participants attending this conference. However, attendees must pay their own travel and hotel expenses. Therefore, the need to show value from the attendees' perspectives and the parent organizations' perspectives is critical.

The stakeholders for this conference are listed below:
- Express Personnel Founders, Bob Funk and Bill Stoller
- Express Personnel home office including:
    — HQ Corporate Management Team
    — Strategic Sales Department
    — Meetings and Conferences
    — Administration
- Franchisee owners from the United States, Canada, and South Africa
- Franchisee managers from around the world
- Vendor exhibitors

The conference objectives established for attendees were:
1) By the close of the conference, be able to state the vision Bob Funk has for improved success.
2) Be able to state the value of the components of the Express marketing strategy (i.e., neighborhood marketing, four-walls marketing, and helping people succeed).
3) Gain three new ideas from the networking functions and apply them at their offices within twelve weeks of the Leadership Conference.
4) Within twelve weeks of the Leadership Conference, be able to apply the tools Bill Stoller will present.

5) Within twelve weeks of the Leadership Conference, be able to apply the components of the Express marketing strategy at their own offices.

Evaluation Methodology

The Express Personnel Headquarters Corporate Management Team always felt they had a great program. On-site attendees were not shy and were quick to let staff know what they liked and disliked. Through the years, post-conference satisfaction evaluations had been favorable.

However, the meeting management team was always seeking ways to enhance and improve the program. An increasing number of meetings and conferences were being evaluated to provide important data to make improvements and decisions about their future. Express Personnel was interested in knowing the actual contribution of training and content delivery.

Therefore, an evaluation study was designed to measure the success of the International Leadership Conference. Its four key objectives were to improve the program using specific data to make adjustments and changes to ensure more effective learning; provide presenter feedback so that adjustments could be made to improve training delivery; determine the extent of skill and knowledge transfer to the workplace; and measure the specific contribution of the training to the franchisees' and the headquarters' business.

The team agreed to redesign their traditional evaluation plan. Rather than one conference-wide, post-conference evaluation, they decided to measure the satisfaction and learning at each general session and workshop. Specific paper evaluation forms were created for each session. They would also collect additional, intangible information through on-site focus groups and post-conference telephone conversations.

Using the Phillips ROI Methodology, their goals were to measure:
- Level 1 – Reaction and Planned Action (during the conference and post-conference)
- Level 2 – Learning and Confidence (during the conference and post-conference)
- Level 3 – Application and Implementation of the skills, knowledge, and contacts acquired at the meeting (three months follow-up).

Evaluation Planning

To evaluate the meeting with the objectives and success in mind, a comprehensive evaluation strategy was created. Beginning with a detailed analysis of the evaluations of previous programs, the evaluation strategy included:

- Stakeholder analysis to identify needs and wants
- A data collection plan (shown in Table 1) to identify what to measure and how to measure specific areas of the conference
- Interviews with all corporate stakeholders
- Theories on what to improve and enhance were developed and tested through a pre-conference survey of all attendees (available for download at www.roiinstitute.net)
- Data collection tools consisting of general session and breakout session questionnaires; a post-conference, overall evaluation; and a three-month follow-up on the application of the information via scripted conference calls (breakout and general session questions can be downloaded at www.roiinstitute.net)
- Creation and distribution of attendee action planning sheets (Figure 1) designed to facilitate application of the learning
- An on-site focus group to gain "gut-level" reaction to the conference design and measurement process
- Follow-up conference calls (conducted with a pool of people from the focus group to collect the Level 3 application data)

To support the evaluation study and meeting objectives, the following were done:

- Marketing materials included the statement: "All breakout sessions are 'Field-Driven' and based on your responses to our pre-conference survey."
- During the general sessions, attendees were consistently exposed to two messages in the general session speeches:
    — "This conference is designed to provide you everything you need to be successful. It is designed to be the best ever. It has been designed by you."
    — "We will continue to seek your input throughout the conference with detailed session evaluations and a focus group."
- EPS' vision and strategic goals were delivered by Bob Funk in a way that demonstrated culture and professionalism to franchise brokers.
- Bob Stoller presented the Seven Habits of a Successful Franchisee and reaffirmed this message throughout the meeting.
- Walk-in and walk-out slides were designed and used, which reinforced each of the major general session topics.
- A sales contest was launched during the meeting.
- Breakout workshop topics were selected based on the survey responses, listing importance of educational topics:

—The account penetration topic ranked number one; therefore, a guest presenter was brought in to address this.

—Recruiting/retention ranked number two, so a panel was organized to demonstrate best practices.

—The seven habits of successful franchisees ranked number three and was addressed in both a breakout session and in Bill Stoller's general session. Printed cards listing the seven habits of successful franchisees were inserted in every registration packet to reinforce this message.

- Presenters were asked to identify at least three learning outcomes for their sessions. Teleconferences were conducted with guest speakers to identify the goals of the meeting and for customizing their message to Express.
- The last fifteen minutes of each breakout session were dedicated to filling out the session evaluation sheet and for "formal networking," allowing attendees to discuss what they learned and how they might apply the information at their offices.
- Blank action plans were distributed in registration packets. Attendees were encouraged to write the actions they would take upon returning to their businesses.
- Since the majority of the attendees read the Daily ILC newsletter, articles which reinforced the learning objectives were included.

Data Collection

Several opportunities to collect data availed themselves including:
- Pre- and post-conference surveys
- Focus groups
- Breakout and general sessions
- Follow-up evaluation

Pre-Conference Survey and Focus Groups

A pre-conference survey was sent electronically to all attendees before the conference to identify stakeholder needs. As part of the pre-conference data collection, an on-site focus group made up of franchisees from every size market and length of operation was conducted with eighty participants. Pre-registered conference participants were invited to participate. The goals of the focus group were to enlist their buy-in to the post-conference measurement process, inform them of the evaluation process, test their knowledge of the general sessions to date, and gather their opinions on the new designs.

Breakout and General Sessions

Monitors were assigned to collect completed, breakout session evaluation forms. Attendees were asked to rate the sessions on:

- Whether course content was relevant, clear, and informative and if program objectives were met
- Quality of presentations—speakers knowledge and presentation style
- Quality of presentation materials—slide support and use of presentation materials
- Extent to which course met expectations
- If new, applicable information was provided

Attendees were also asked to name at least one learning outcome from each session. Along with data collected at the end of each breakout session, participants provided data at the end of five general sessions, via questionnaire. This form included categories similar to those on the breakout session forms.

Post-Conference Survey

A post-conference survey was administered within three weeks of the meeting's conclusion. This survey gave attendees a final opportunity to provide their perceptions of workshops, awards, and general sessions as well as indication that new knowledge was acquired.

Follow-Up Evaluation

Conference calls with select focus group participants were conducted in May 2005 to determine the implementation and application of knowledge and skills acquired at the ILC and the subsequent impact on their business. Twenty-eight members of the focus group were contacted. The intent was to collect data with regard to successful application of knowledge acquired during the leadership conference. Knowledge was defined as skills and information applicable to the job, as well as new people met during the conference that could broaden an attendee's sphere of influence.

Results

Pre-Conference Survey and Focus Group

Based on 2004 evaluations, a pre-event survey was created for the 2005 conference, and attendees were specifically asked why they were attending and what knowledge they hoped to gain. The results of the survey included networking as the primary reason for attendance, followed by education and motivation; recognition and awards were listed last. Major findings of the surveys showed that attendees most wanted time to network. When asked what motivates them at ILC, they listed guest speakers, interaction, education, hearing from the founders, awards, and the energy and enthusiasm at the meeting. Challenges to growth, ranked in order included:

    (1) Recruiting shortage

    (3) Market share

    (4) Business mix

    (5) Differentiation

The on-site focus group found that:

- All participants could articulate the 2009 goals as stated by Bob Funk.
- All participants were consistent and passionate about the EPS culture and maintaining that culture in the face of wide-spread growth over the next five years.
- Participants in the focus group recognized the new design of the awards, but felt that the awards could not be part of the social functions. They wanted either to network or give the awardees their recognition. Both couldn't be done at the same time.
- The group unanimously agreed that networking was the most beneficial form of learning.
- If a mentor program was created, they suggested pairing those with two to four years' experience with the new franchisees. Those with five to ten years' experience could be paired with those having two to four years' experience.
- The group preferred the rounds and crescent style seating in the workshops.
- The group wanted facilitated learning sessions designed to share and discuss best practices.
- Informal settings using round tables in the foyer would allow people to gather during breaks, thereby enhancing networking opportunities.
- Participants desired an opportunity for late-night discussions, possibly via an after-hours "coffee bar."

Breakout and General Sessions

Thirteen breakout sessions were evaluated on the following objectives:

- Relevance
- Clarity/informative
- Meets program objectives

The results found that:

- 82.6% to 100% good to excellent in relevance

- 76.5% to 100% good to excellent on clarity/informative
- 77.7% to 100% good to excellent on meeting program objectives

Breakout speakers' knowledge of subject and presentation style attained similar scores.

The founders' and the guest speakers' general sessions were rated along similar measures. The results showed:
- 89.9% to 98.9% good to excellent in relevance
- 89.2% to 98.3% good to excellent on clarity/informative
- 87.7% to 97.5% good to excellent on meeting the conference objectives

Post-Conference Survey

About 85% of attendees submitted responses to the online post-conference evaluation. The post-course evaluation measured reaction and knowledge gain. The findings showed:
- Respondents could list four out of five company goals.
- Approximately 90% of those responding correctly listed the seven habits of successful franchisees.
- 38% indicated that not enough to somewhat enough time was given to networking. Only 60% of respondents indicated that enough time was given. However, the quality of information gained through networking ranked 78% valuable to very valuable.
- 79% of respondents rated the knowledge and expertise needed to grow respondents' businesses effectively to be provided.
- The majority of respondents anticipated increases in sales, profitability, productivity and staff training as a consequence of applying newly acquired knowledge and skills.

Follow-Up Evaluation

The follow-up conference calls with focus group participants attempted to find the extent to which participants applied knowledge acquired and took advantage of new people through networking. Additional data on costs of the conference was also obtained.

Universally the answer was "yes" to the question "Have they applied some aspect of what they have learned from the ILC on the job?" This indicated that application had occurred. While focus group participants indicated positive consequences occurred as a result of the conference, monetary values were not offered. Respondents estimated they spent $2,000 to $7,000, including travel, lodging, and time away from work. While they could not compare these costs to monetary benefits, respondents did not seem to mind the investment. As one respondent put it, "Cost is not a factor. I will come for connection, networking, and motivation."

Communication Strategy

Results were reported to all the stakeholder groups with an analysis, supporting data, and suggested changes for continuous improvement. An overall report, created by the Meetings and Conferences team, was distributed via e-mail to the Management Team. Individual face-to-face meetings were then held with the founders and the VPs of Sales and Marketing to discuss the findings and the recommendations for improvement. Session and presenter evaluations were only sent to specific presenters. Individual team leaders, such as Sales or Marketing, received the evaluations that were specific to their responsibilities.

The Meetings and Conferences team continue to meet on the specific actions for improvement. The attendees received a brief synopsis of the report as a pre-conference marketing piece in preparation for the next conference. Each report met with an overall positive response.

The study was a validation of what they thought—the ILC meets the needs of the attendees and the franchise organization. The study also identified specific areas for improvement. Meetings and Conferences received additional recognition from senior management and focus group participants for conducting the study.

Lessons Learned

Many lessons were learned and suggestions given for continuous improvements. One suggestion was that attendees be given more clearly defined learning objectives for general sessions and breakout sessions. Also, the presentation content should be measured against the attendees' expectations to determine where the content should be placed (i.e., in breakout or general sessions).

Pre-approval of presentations, presenter training—including presentation tips, teleprompter training, and staging techniques—and inclusion of networking opportunities during presentations was recommended. Investigation into other adult learning techniques to reinforce conference content was also suggested. Finally, formal networking opportunities—investigative roundtable discussions, mentoring, foyer discussion groups, and post-conference communications of best practices—were suggested.

Questions for Discussion

1. Discuss the ways in which this conference was aligned to the specific needs of the organization.

2. Does this study provide sufficient evidence of success at Level 3? How could this evaluation study be made more credible?
3. How could Level 4 business impact data be obtained?
4. Does this study illustrate the value of the International Leadership Conference to the sponsoring organization?

About the Authors

As the Event Marketing Manager for Express Services, Inc., Franchisor for Express Personnel Services, Teresa Burris, CMP, is responsible for the strategy, planning, and implementation of meetings and special events, including coordination of all meeting management functions, logistics, measurements, and program development. She leads a team that plans and implements seventy-five events per year, ensuring that the conferences under her direction align with the goals and objectives of the leadership team and directly impact sales growth and training outcomes. These events range from large corporate conferences to appearances of the Express Personnel Clydesdales. Ms. Burris received the Certified Meeting Professional (CMP) designation in 2005 and is a member of Meeting Professionals International (MPI). She has been with Express Services for nine years.

During his twenty years with Fusion Productions, Jamie B. McDonough, Director of Meetings and Conferences, has designed and produced numerous meetings, conferences, and instructional experiences. His clients include Price WaterhouseCoopers, Bausch & Lomb, American Society for Training and Development (ASTD), Eastman Kodak, and the Project Management Institute. A member of (MPI) since 1992, he has had the honor of producing numerous MPI annual conferences, the MPI Foundation/Marriott Program "Maximizing Your ROI", the first ROI Summit at the 2004 MPI World Education Congress; and the 2005 ROI Platinum program. He received his Masters of Science degree in Instructional Design from the Rochester Institute of Technology in 1989. Jamie is currently serving as 2006-2007 chair of the MPI International Chapter Leaders Committee.

Editor's Notes

The evaluation team in this case study used questionnaires, a focus group, and interviews to collect data from conference attendees. While questionnaires are often the easiest and quickest way to collect data, other data collection methods can be used and are often necessary to obtain the type of feedback required. In this case, a focus group was needed to generate a rich and focused discussion among the attendees and for the facilitator to clarify responses.

During the conference, attendees were asked to complete an action plan to determine how the skills, knowledge, and contacts acquired at the conference could be applied in the work setting. For meetings that are taken to a Level 4, Business Impact, or Level 5, ROI, evaluation, attendee action plans can also help determine how the content and professional contacts from the meeting can be applied in the workplace to impact certain pre-defined business measures. As a follow-up to the meeting, attendees can be contacted to provide the subsequent monetary values or benefits gained from completing their action plans.

Table 1. Data Collection Plan

Data Collection Plan

Level	Objective(s)	Measures/Data	Data Collection Method	Data Sources	Timing	Responsibilities
1	**Workshop** **Reaction/Satisfaction** • Positive reaction to the program, materials, presentations • Create action plans indicating planned action	80% score in the areas of relevance, clarity/informative, meeting program objectives 100% of participants would create one or more action plans	Workshop questionnaire Attendee action plan	Participants	End of each session End of conference	Facilitator ROI team
	General Sessions **Reaction/Satisfaction** • Positive reaction to presentations • State action plans	80% score in the the areas of relevance, clarity/informative, meeting program objectives Applause When asked, state action plan	Facilitators asks random questions General session questionnaire	Participants	During each session At the end of each session	Facilitator ROI Team

2	**Workshop Learning** • Answer questions based on stated objectives of the sessions and the above objectives	State one or more learner outcomes from workshop	Breakout session questionnaire	Participants	During Session	Facilitator
3	**General Sessions Learning** • State learning	State one or more items learned	Focus group	Focus group of participants	During conference	Facilitator
	Application/ Implementation • Apply skills and knowledge at the work place	Use tools/content provided at the job site	Post-conference questionnaire Follow-up call	All participants Select members of focus group	Three months following conference	Meetings group administrator Call back center

Figure 1. Action Plan

Presenter(s): _____

Key Points:

How will I apply this information?

Timeline:

Who is responsible?

Action Plans:

Goal:

Express Personnel Services International Leadership Conference

February 23-26, 2005 ? Anaheim, California

Chapter 7
Measuring and Isolating the Impact of Meetings and Events

This chapter focuses on tracking business performance measures connected to meetings and events and is the last chapter on collecting data. Executives regard business impact data as the most important data type because of its connection to business success. In many cases, a less-than-desired performance in one or more business measures (a business need) created the need for the meeting. This chapter covers the methods needed to collect the business measures and includes monitoring the business records, collecting action plans, and using questionnaires. These three processes account for most opportunities available for collecting impact data.

When a significant increase in business performance is noted after a meeting or event has been conducted, the challenge is to link it to the meeting. Other factors may have contributed to the improvement, as well. This chapter explores useful techniques for isolating the effects of the meeting. If this issue is not addressed, the link to business impact is not credible.

The Importance of Measuring Business Impact

Although several obvious reasons exist for measuring impact, several specific issues support the rationale for collecting business impact data related to a meeting or event.

A Business Driver for Meetings

For many meetings and events, business impact data represent the initial drivers for the meeting. The problem of deteriorating (or less-than-desired) performance or the opportunity for improvement of a business measure often leads to the need for the meeting. If the business needs defined by business measures are the drivers, then the key measures for evaluating the meeting are those same business measures. These measures often represent hard, indisputable facts that reflect performance that is critical to the business and operating part of an organization. The extent to which measures have changed is the principal determinant of the success of the meeting. These are the measures often desired by the ultimate client—the individual who funds the meeting.

Monetary Data

Business impact measures offer more valuable data than measures at lower levels. Impact data are the consequence of the application and implementation of a meeting. They represent the bottom-line measures that are positively influenced when a meeting is successful. For some stakeholders, these are the most valuable data. At this level, the actual money is developed when necessary for an ROI calculation. Impact data, influenced by the meeting, can be converted to monetary value to show the monetary contribution of the meeting. Although this conversion is actually a separate step, it is derived from the business impact data collected in this step. This makes this level of data collection one of the most critical for ROI analysis.

Easy to Measure

Business impact data are often easy to measure and readily available. Hard and soft data measures at this level reflect key measures found in plentiful numbers throughout an organization. It is not unusual for an organization to have hundreds, or even thousands, of measures reflecting specific business impact items. The challenge is to connect the objectives of the meeting to the appropriate business measures. This is more easily accomplished at the beginning of the meeting due to the availability and ease with which many of the data items can be located.

The irony of this level of data collection is that these data types are the most common. When measuring reaction, learning, or application, the measures have to be created. However, at the business impact level, the data have been created, except for rare exceptions where data development is necessary. The good news is that these are common data items tracked and monitored by someone.

Types of Impact Measures

Hard Versus Soft Data

To help focus on the desired measures, a distinction is made in two general categories of data: hard data and soft data, described in Chapter 2. Hard data are the primary measurements of improvement, presented through rational, undisputed facts that are easily gathered. Much of the criteria for measuring the effectiveness of management rest on hard data items, such as productivity, profitability, cost control, and quality control. Table 2-1 in Chapter 2, provides examples of hard data grouped into categories of output, quality, costs, and time.

Soft data are more difficult to collect and analyze but are used when hard data are unavailable. Soft data are difficult to convert to monetary values. They are subjectively based, in many cases, and are less credible as a performance measurement. Table 2-2 in Chapter 2 provides a list of typical soft data items grouped into typical categories. The preference of hard data in meetings does not reduce the value of soft data. Soft data are essential for a complete evaluation of a meeting as success may rest on soft data measurements.

Tangible Versus Intangible

The confusion about the categories of soft data and the often reduced value placed on soft data were discussed in Chapter 2. This leads to a critical definition in this book. While the terms hard and soft data can be used to discuss impact data, the terms tangible and intangible can also be used. Tangible data represent a category that can or has been converted to monetary value. Intangibles are defined as data purposely not converted to monetary value (i.e., if data cannot be converted to monetary value credibly with a reasonable amount of resources, then it is left as an intangible). This is consistent with the thinking of many professionals who place tremendous value on the intangible measures.

Specific Measures Linked to Meetings

An important issue that often surfaces when considering ROI applications is to identify specific measures often driven by specific meetings. While there are no standard answers, Table 7-1 represents a summary of some typical payoff measures for specific types of meetings. The measures are broad for some meetings. For example, an association general meeting may pay off in a variety of measures, such as improved productivity, enhanced revenues, improved quality, cycle-time reduction, direct cost savings, and employee job satisfaction. In other meetings, the influenced measures are narrow. For example, a meeting on diversity typically influences turnover, complaints, absenteeism, and employee satisfaction. The measures influenced depend on the objectives and the design of the meeting. The table also illustrates the immense number of measures that can be driven or influenced. A word of caution is needed. Presenting specific measures linked to a typical meeting may give the impression that these are the only measures influenced. In practice, a particular meeting can have many outcomes.

Table 7-1. Typical Measures for Meetings and Events

Project	Key Impact Measurements
Anti-social behavior Conferences	Complaints, turnover, absenteeism, productivity, employee satisfaction
Association meetings	Productivity, sales, quality, time, costs, customer service, turnover, absenteeism, job satisfaction
Business Coaching Conferences	Productivity/output, quality, time savings, efficiency, costs, employees satisfaction, customer satisfaction
Career-Focused Meetings	Enrollments, promotions, recruiting expenses, turnover, job satisfaction.
Communications meetings	Errors, stress, conflicts, productivity, job satisfaction
Compliance meetings	Penalties/fines, charges, settlements, losses
Dealer meetings	Sales, market share, cost of sales, quality efficiency, customer loyalty
Diversity meetings	Turnover, absenteeism, complaints, charges, settlements, losses
Employee retention meetings	Turnover, engagement, job satisfaction, promotions
Engineering/technical conferences	Productivity/output, quality, waste, downtime, cycle time, process time, costs, customer satisfaction, job satisfaction
Executive conferences	Productivity, sales, quality, time, costs, customer service, market share, turnover, absenteeism, job satisfaction
Golfing events	Sales, market share, customer loyalty, new accounts, upselling
Indoctrination/orientation meetings	Early turnover, training time, productivity, performance
Labor-management conferences	Work stoppages, grievances, absenteeism, job satisfaction
Leadership retreats	Productivity/output, quality, efficiency, cost/time savings, employee satisfaction, engagement
Management conferences	Productivity, sales, quality, time, costs, customer service, turnover, absenteeism, job satisfaction
Medical meetings	Medical costs, quality, compliance, efficiency, patient satisfaction
Personal productivity meetings	Time savings, productivity, stress reduction, job satisfaction
Project management conferences	Time savings, quality improvement, budgets
Quality meetings	Defects, rework, response times, cycle times, costs
Safety meetings	Accident frequency rates, accident severity rates, first aid treatments
Sales meetings	Sales, market share, customer loyalty, new accounts, brand awareness
Supervisor/team leader meetings	Productivity, sales, quality, time, costs, customer service, turnover, absenteeism, job satisfaction
Team-building sessions	Productivity, sales, quality, time, costs, customer service, turnover, absenteeism, job satisfaction
Wellness/fitness meetings	Stress, turnover, medical costs, accidents, absenteeism

The good news is that most meetings and events are driving business measures. The measures are based on what is being changed in the various business units, divisions, regions, and individual workplaces. These are the measures that matter to senior executives. The difficulty often comes in ensuring that the connection to the meeting exists. This is accomplished through a variety of techniques which isolate the effects of the meeting on the particular business measures and will be discussed later.

Monitoring Business Performance Data

Data to measure business performance are available in every organization. Monitoring performance data enables management to measure performance in terms of output, quality, costs, time, job satisfaction, and customer satisfaction, among other measures. In determining the source of data in the evaluation, the first consideration should be existing databases, reports, and scorecards. In most organizations, performance data suitable for measuring meeting-related improvement are available. If not, additional record-keeping systems will have to be developed for measurement and analysis. At this point, the question of economics surfaces. Is it economical to develop the record-keeping systems necessary to evaluate a meeting? If the costs are greater than the expected benefits, developing those systems is pointless.

The Use of Action Plans to Develop Business Impact Data

For many meetings, business data are readily available. However, at times, data will not be easily accessible to the planner. Sometimes, data are maintained at the individual, work unit, or department level and may not be known to anyone outside that area. Tracking down those data sets may be too expensive and time consuming. When this is the case, other data collection methods such as action plans may be used to capture data sets and make them available for the planner. Action plans can capture application and implementation data, as discussed in Chapter 6. They can also be a useful tool for capturing business impact data. For business impact data, the action plan is more focused and credible than a questionnaire. The basic design principles involved in developing and administering action plans are the same for business impact data as they are for application and implementation data. However, a few elements unique to business impact are presented in this section.

Set Goals and Targets

As shown in Figure 7-1, an action plan can be developed with a direct focus on business impact data. The plan presented in this figure requires participants to develop an overall objective for the plan, which is usually the primary objective of the meeting. In some cases, a meeting may have more than one objective, which requires more action plans. In addition to the objective, the improvement measure and the current levels of performance are identified. This information requires that the participant anticipate the application of skills and set goals for specific performances that can be realized.

Complete the Action Plan

The action plan is completed during the meeting, often with input and assistance from the speaker or facilitator. The facilitator actually approves the plan, indicating that it meets the requirements of being specific, motivating, achievable, realistic, and time-based (SMART). The plan can actually be developed in less than a one-hour timeframe and often begins with action steps related to the meeting. These action steps are Level 3 activities that detail application and implementation. All these steps build support for, and are linked to, the business impact measures defined on the plan.

Advantages of Action Plans

The action-planning process has several inherent advantages as a useful way to collect business impact data. Most of the data are taken directly from participants and often have the credibility needed for the analysis. Also, much of the responsibility for the analysis and evaluation is shifted to the participants as they address three of the most critical parts of the process. In effect, they collect data to show improvements, isolate the effects of the meeting, and convert data to monetary values. This enables the evaluation to be conducted with limited resources and shifts much of the responsibility to those who apply and implement the ideas, information, and knowledge from the meeting. For more information on the action-planning process, see other references. (Phillips, 2003, *Return on Investment in Training and Performance Improvement Programs*, 2nd Edition, Woburn, MA, Butterworth-Heinemann)

The Use of Questionnaires to Collect Impact Data

As described in previous chapters, the questionnaire is one of the most versatile data collection tools and can be appropriate for Level 1, 2, 3, and 4 data. Chapter 6 presented a sample questionnaire in which application and implementation data (Level 3) are collected. Some of the questionnaire issues discussed in the previous chapter apply equally in collecting business impact data. Essentially, the design principles and the content issues are the same. However, questionnaires developed for a business impact evaluation will contain additional questions to capture impact data items.

Figure 7-1. Using the action plan process

ACTION PLAN

Name: _____

Facilitator Signature _____

Follow-Up Date _____

Objective: _____

Evaluation Period _____ to _____

Improvement Measure: _____

Current Performance _____ Target Performance _____

Action Steps	Analysis
1. _____	A. What is the unit of measure? _____
2. _____	B. What is the value (cost) of one unit? $ _____
3. _____	C. How did you arrive at this value? _____
4. _____	
5. _____	D. How much did the measure change during the evaluation period? (monthly value) _____
6. _____	E. List the other factors that have influenced this change. _____
7. _____	F. What percent of this change was actually caused by this meeting? _____ %
Intangible Benefits: _____	G. What level of confidence do you place on the above information? (100%=Certainty and 0%=No Confidence) _____ %

Comments: _____

Using questionnaires for impact data collection brings both good and bad news. The good news is that questionnaires are easy to implement and the cost is minimal. Data analysis is efficient, and the time to provide the data is often short, making them among the least disruptive data collection methods. However, the bad news is that the data can be distorted, inaccurate, and sometimes missing. The challenge is to take all the steps necessary to ensure that questionnaires are complete and accurate and are returned.

Unfortunately, because of the disadvantages, questionnaires represent one of the weakest methods of data collection. Paradoxically, it is the most used method because of its advantages. Questionnaires are popular, convenient, low-cost, and a way of life. The challenge is to make them better. The philosophy in the use of the ROI Methodology is to make the weakest method as credible as possible. Therefore, the challenge is to make questionnaires credible and useful by ensuring that they capture all the necessary data, participants provide accurate and complete data, and the return rates are in the seventy- to eighty-percent range.

The reason return rates need to be so high is based on Guiding Principle 6 in the ROI Methodology—no data, no improvement. If an individual provides no improvement data, the assumption is that the person had no improvement. This is a conservative principle but necessary for the credibility of the results. Therefore, using questionnaires will require effort, discipline, and personal attention to ensure proper response rates. It is helpful to remember that this is the least preferred method and is used only when the other methods do not work (i.e., business performance data cannot be easily monitored or action plans are not feasible). Three scenarios for questionnaire use are possible.

When You Don't Have a Clue

In the worse-case situation, the meeting planner does not have a clue which measures have been driven or influenced by the meeting. For some, this situation may be inconceivable, but in practice it occurs routinely. Consider the tremendous amount of money poured into meetings and events with most of them implemented without knowing how they will add value or improve a specific measure. When this is the case, the data collection instrument would follow the series of questions shown in Figure 7-2. This is much like a fishing expedition as the meeting planner attempts to uncover a particular business measure connected to the meeting. Still, it could be a useful exercise with some surprising results.

Figure 7-2. Chain of Impact Questions When the Measure Is Unknown

Scenerio 1, When You Don't Have a Clue

1. How did you use the material from this meeting?
2. What influence did it have in your work? Team?
3. What specific measure was influenced? Define it.
4. What is the unit value of the measure? (Profit or Cost)
5. What is the basis of this value?
6. How much did the measure change since the meeting was conducted?
7. What is the frequency of the measure? (Daily, weekly, monthly, etc.)
8. What is the total annual value of the improvement?
9. List the other factors that could have caused this total improvement?
10. What percent of the total improvement can be attributed to this meeting?
11. What is your confidence estimate, expressed as a percent, for the above data?
    0% = no confidence; 100% = certainty

Question 1 is an attempt to connect the meeting to the work environment—it is the transition. It is essentially a Level 3 question about application. The goal is to get the participant to reflect on actions taken because of the meeting. Question 2 examines consequences, defining or explaining more specifically the outcomes of their actions, implementation, and behaviors. The influence could be with individual work, the team, or even the organization. Question 3 asks for the specifics, defining the measure. In many cases, more than one measure may be involved, and these questions can have multiple responses. Question 4 is the actual unit value, which is profit if it is a sales-related output measure or costs if it is a quality, productivity, or time measure. This is a difficult challenge, but it is achievable in most organizations because the unit values are already developed. Question 5 gauges the credibility of the data provided in Question 4. The participant explains how he or she arrived at the unit value. If Question 5 is left blank, the data item is thrown out (but the participants know this from the instructions given). In essence, this would be an unsupported claim that is omitted from the analysis (Guiding Principle 8).

Question 6 documents the change, the difference in the pre-meeting measure and the post-meeting measure. Question 7 details the specific frequency. The frequency is necessary to calculate the total annual improvement asked for in Question 8. This is the first-year value of improvement. Most meetings will only pay off on the first year of value, although long-term meetings will have a longer period. Question 9 requires participants to think through other factors that might have influenced the specific measure they reported. This is a way of validating the reported change. Initially, the participant may think that the improvement is all directly connected to this meeting. In reality, other factors are there. This question provides an opportunity for participants to reflect on the links to other factors.

Question 10 then asks the participants to decide, after thinking about other possible factors, what percentage of the improvement came directly from the meeting, isolating the effects of the meeting from other influences. Because this is an estimate, it is adjusted for error, asked for in Question 11. Participant estimate as an isolation technique is described later in the chapter.

Participants must not be surprised with these questions. They must know that they are coming, and every effort must be made to solicit a response. Still, many professionals may consider this series of questions a futile exercise—that participants cannot provide responses. Fortunately, the research does not support this position. In hundreds of studies in which this kind of approach is taken, participants can and will provide data connected to the meeting, assuming that a connection to a business measure exists.

The skeptics often consider participants to be unknowing, uncooperative, and irresponsible, validating their point that the data would not be forthcoming. However, participants will provide data for four basic reasons:

1. They are the most credible source, since they are directly involved and understand the full scope of the meeting and its consequences.
2. It is their work, and they know more about it than anyone. Their performance is being reported and analyzed.
3 This process recognizes their roles as experts. The question suggests that they are in a position to know, and they appreciate the recognition that they have the expertise to provide the data.
4. They are responsible. For the most part, participants will provide data if they understand why the data is needed and how it will be used.

Of course, not every participant will warm up to this exercise. It works extremely well for professional, engineering, administrative, management, and technical personnel. Operators, laborers, and entry-level clerical staff may have more difficulty. But in most situations, the participants are responsible and knowledgeable and care about the process. Because of this, the quality and quantity of the data may be surprising.

When the Measure Is a Defined Set

A slightly modified approach to these questions is to assume that the meeting is influencing a set of measures in a distinct category or group. Figure 7-3 shows such an example. Question 1 lists a group of measures that logically could be directly connected to the meeting. (This is a little easier than the previous scenario where the set of measures was not known.) This series of questions requires participants to think about specific outcomes but is triggered by potential or possibility. This is even more powerful when the measures are focused on the possible or probable outcomes of the meeting. The other questions and analysis are similar to what was contained in the previous scenario. This approach has the advantage of being more credible because it connects to a given set of measures.

Figure 7-3. Chain of Impact Questions When the Measure Is in a Defined Set.

Scenario 2, When the Measure Is in a Defined Set

1. To what extent did this meeting positively influence the following measures:

	Significant Influence				No Influence	
	5	4	3	2	1	n/a
productivity	○	○	○	○	○	○
sales	○	○	○	○	○	○
quality	○	○	○	○	○	○
cost	○	○	○	○	○	○
efficiency	○	○	○	○	○	○
time savings	○	○	○	○	○	○
employee satisfaction	○	○	○	○	○	○
customer satisfaction	○	○	○	○	○	○
other	○	○	○	○	○	○

2. What other measures were positively influenced by this meeting?

3. Of the measures listed above, which *one* is most directly linked to the project? (check only one)
   - ☐ productivity   ☐ sales   ☐ quality
   - ☐ cost   ☐ efficiency   ☐ time
   - ☐ employee satisfaction   ☐ customer satisfaction   ☐ other

4. Please define the measure above.

To complete this questionnaire, questions 4 – 11 from Figure 7-2 are repeated.

When the Measure Is Known

Fortunately, with some meetings, the actual measures are known. These are the measures tied to the meeting in the beginning and are often the measures that drive the meeting. When these are known, the questionnaire can be focused, specific, and credible. Essentially, questions 3 – 11 in Figure 7-2 are asked when the measure is known. The important point here is that the participant defines the measure precisely and in some cases it is provided to them on the questionnaire. This scenario is more credible than the previous two, as it focuses on a specific measure that was defined in the beginning and is driving the meeting.

Response Rates

To ensure an appropriate response for all three scenarios, the techniques outlined in Chapter 6 apply equally to follow-up questionnaires where business impact data are collected. Questionnaires must be thoroughly explained and, if possible, reviewed during the meeting. The list of techniques presented in the previous chapter will not be repeated.

Isolating the Effects of the Meeting

In almost every situation, multiple influences drive the business measures. With multiple influences, measuring the effect of each influence is imperative, at least to the extent that it is attributed to the meeting. Without this isolation step, meeting success will be in question. The results will be overstated if it is suggested that all the change in the business impact measure is attributed to the meeting. When this issue is ignored, the impact study is considered invalid and inconclusive. This places tremendous pressure on meeting planners to show the business value of the meetings when compared to other factors.

The cause-and-effect relationship between a meeting and business impact can be confusing and difficult to prove, but can be shown with an acceptable degree of accuracy. The challenge is to develop one or more specific techniques to isolate the effects of the meeting early in the process, usually as part of an evaluation plan conducted before the meeting is planned. Up-front attention ensures that appropriate techniques will be used with minimum costs and time commitments.

Using Control Groups

The most accurate approach for isolating the impact of a meeting is the use of control groups in an experimental design process. This approach involves the comparison of one group attending the meeting (experimental group) and a control group that is not involved. The composition of both groups should be as identical as possible and, if feasible, participants for each group should be assigned randomly. When this is achieved, and both groups are subjected to the same environmental influences, the difference in the performance of the two groups can be attributed to the meeting.

One concern with the use of a control group is that it may create an image of a laboratory setting, which can make some executives and administrators uncomfortable. To avoid this stigma, some organizations conduct a pilot meeting using participants as the experimental group. A similarly matched, non-participating control group is assigned but does not attend or receive any communication about the meeting. The terms pilot and comparison group are less threatening than experimental group and control group.

The control group approach does have some inherent problems that may make it difficult to apply in practice. The first major problem is assigning the groups. Having identical control and experimental groups is impossible. Dozens of factors can affect performance, some of them individual, others contextual. To address this problem on a practical basis, it is best to select four to six variables that will have the greatest influence on performance, using the concept of Pareto principle. With the eighty/twenty rule, the factors that might account for eighty percent of the difference and the most important factors are used.

For example, in a sales meeting for Dell Computer Corporation, a control group arrangement was used. The meeting involved regional sales managers, account managers, account executives, account representatives, and sales representatives. The output measures were quota attainment, total revenue attainment, profit margin, and various sales volumes. An experimental group was involved in the meeting and was carefully matched with a control group that was not involved. The equivalent number of participants for the control group was assigned at random using the company database. To ensure that the control group and the meeting group were equivalent, assignments were made on three criteria: job positions, job levels, and experience.

Another major problem with control groups is that the process is inappropriate for many situations. Withholding the meeting from one group while it is implemented in another may not be appropriate. This is particularly important for critical solutions that are needed immediately. This barrier keeps many control groups from being implemented.

Because the use of control groups is an effective approach for isolating impact, it should be considered as a technique when a major ROI impact study is planned. In these situations, isolating the meeting's impact with a high level of accuracy is important, and the primary advantage of the control group process is accuracy. Additional information on the use of control groups is found in other references, such as *The Handbook of Training Evaluation and Measurement Methods*, 4th Edition, by Jack J. Phillips and Patricia Pulliam Phillips, published by Butterworth-Heinemann, 2007.

Trend Line Analysis

Another useful technique for approximating the impact of a meeting is trend line analysis. With this approach, a trend line is drawn to project the future, before the meeting is conducted, using previous performance as a base. After the meeting is conducted, actual performance is compared to the trend line projection. Any improvement in performance over what the trend line predicted can then be reasonably attributed to the meeting, if certain conditions are met. While this is not an exact process, it provides a reasonable estimation of the meeting's impact.

Figure 7-4 shows an example of a trend line analysis taken from sales data from a division of a consumer producer's company. Data are presented before and after a sales meeting in July. As shown in the figure, an upward trend on the data began prior to the sales meeting. Although the meeting apparently had an effect on shipment productivity, the trend line shows that some improvement would have occurred anyway, based on the trend that had previously been established. The meeting planner may have been tempted to measure the improvement by comparing the average six months' sales prior to the meeting (87.3 million) to the average six months after the meeting (92.3 million), yielding a 7.1 million difference. However, a more accurate comparison is the six-month average after the meeting compared to the trend line (92.3 million). In this analysis, the difference is 2.1 million. Using this more conservative measure increases the accuracy and credibility of the process to isolate the impact of the meeting.

To use this technique, two conditions must be met:

- The trend that has developed prior to the meeting is expected to continue if the meeting had not been conducted (i.e., would this trend continue on the same path established before the participants attended the meeting?). The process owner(s) should be able to provide input to reach this conclusion. If the answer is "no," the trend-line analysis will not be used. If the answer is "yes," the second condition is considered.

- No new variables or influences entered the process during the evaluation period. The key word is "new," realizing that the trend has been established because of the influences already in place, and no additional influences enter the process beyond conducting the meeting. If the answer is "yes," another method would have to be used. If the answer is "no," the trend line analysis develops a reasonable estimate of the impact of this meeting.

Pre-meeting data must be available before this technique can be used, and the data should have some reasonable degree of stability. If the variance of the data is high, the stability of the trend line becomes an issue. The trend line can be projected directly from historical data using a simple routine that is available with many calculators and software packages, such as Microsoft Excel™.

Figure 7-4. Trend Line Analysis

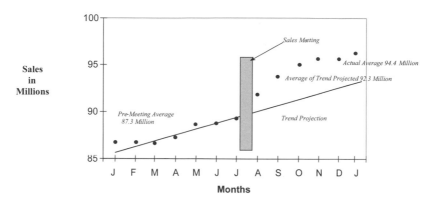

Estimates

Unfortunately, the most common method of isolating the effects of a meeting is the use of estimates. Estimating the amount of improvement connected to a particular meeting is the least effective method from an analytical viewpoint. Because it is the weakest method, every step should be taken to make it as credible as possible. The good news is that this can be a very credible process if some precautions are taken, as described in this section.

The beginning point in using this method is ensuring that the isolation is performed by the most credible source, and that is often the participant. The individual who provides this information must be able to understand how the meeting affects the impact measures. Essentially, there are four categories of input. Often, the most credible are the participants directly involved in the meeting. The managers of the participants may be credible if they are close to the situation. Customers give credible estimates in unique situations where they are involved. External experts may also be helpful. These are all described in this section.

An easily implemented method for isolating the impact of a meeting is to obtain information directly from participants. The effectiveness of this approach rests on the assumption that participants are capable of determining or estimating how much of a performance improvement is related to the meeting. Because their actions have produced the improvement, participants may have accurate input on the issue. They should know how much of the business impact change was caused by implementing the meeting content. Although an estimate, this value will usually have considerable credibility with management because they know participants are at the center of the change or improvement. Participant estimation is obtained by asking participants this series of questions:

- What other factors have contributed to this improvement in performance?
- What is the link between these factors and the improvement?
- What percentage of this improvement can be attributed to the meeting?
- What confidence do you have in this estimate, expressed as a percentage? (0% = No confidence; 100% = Complete confidence)
- What other individuals or groups could estimate this percentage to determine the amount attributed to this meeting?

Table 7-2 illustrates this approach with an example of one participant's estimations. Participants who do not provide information on the questions are excluded from the analysis. Also, erroneous, incomplete, and extreme information should be discarded before analysis. To be conservative, the confidence percentage is factored into the values. The confidence percentage is a reflection of the error in the estimate. Therefore, an eighty percent confidence level equates to a potential error range of plus or minus twenty percent. With this approach, the level of confidence is multiplied by the estimate. In the example, the participant allocates sixty percent of the improvement to the meeting and is eighty percent confident in the estimate. The confidence percentage is multiplied by the estimate to develop a usable value of forty-eight percent. This adjusted percentage is then multiplied by the actual amount of the improvement (post-meeting minus pre-meeting value) to isolate the portion attributed to the meeting. The adjusted improvement is now ready for conversion to monetary values and, ultimately, use in the return on investment calculation.

Table 7-2. Example of a Participant's Estimation

Factor That Influenced Improvement	% of Improvement Caused by	Confidence Expressed as a %	Adjusted % of Improvement Caused by
Meeting	60%	80%	48%
Process changes	15%	70%	10.5%
Environmental changes	5%	60%	3%
Compensation changes	20%	80%	16%
Other	__%	__%	__%
Total	100%		

In lieu of, or in addition to, participant estimates, the participants' managers may be asked to provide input as to the meeting's influence on improved performance. In some settings, the participants' managers may be more familiar with the other influencing factors. Therefore, they may be better equipped to provide impact estimates. The recommended questions to ask managers, after describing the improvement, are similar to those asked of the participants.

Another helpful approach in some narrowly focused meetings is to solicit input on the impact of meetings directly from customers. In these situations, customers are asked why they chose a particular product or service or to explain how their reaction to the product or service has been influenced by individuals involved in the meeting. This technique often focuses directly on what the meeting is designed to improve. Routine customer surveys provide an excellent opportunity to collect input directly from customers concerning their reactions to an assessment of new or improved products, services, processes, or procedures. Pre- and post-data can pinpoint the changes related to an improvement driven by a customer-focused meeting.

External or internal experts can sometimes estimate the portion of results that can be attributed to a meeting. When using this technique, experts must be carefully selected based on their knowledge of the process, meeting, and situation. For example, an expert in quality might be able to provide estimates of how much change in a quality measure can be attributed to a meeting regarding quality improvements and how much can be attributed to other factors.

Final Thoughts

The good news is that business impact data are readily available and credible. After describing the types of data that reflect business impact, this chapter provides an overview of several data collection approaches that can be used to capture business data. Several options are available. Some methods are gaining more acceptance for use in impact and ROI analysis. Performance monitoring, follow-up questionnaires, and action plans are used regularly to collect data for impact analysis. Because credibility of data will always be an issue when this level of data is collected and analyzed, this chapter also presents a variety of techniques for isolating the effects of a meeting or event. The techniques represent the most effective approaches available to address this issue and are used by some of the most progressive organizations. Too often, results are reported and linked with the meeting without any attempt to isolate the exact portion that can be attributed to it. If meeting and event professionals are committed to improving the images of their functions, as well as meeting their responsibilities for obtaining results, this issue must be addressed early in the process for all major meetings and events.

Chapter 8
Monetary Benefits, Costs, and ROI

To calculate the ROI, two additional steps are necessary: calculating monetary benefits by converting data to monetary values and tabulating the fully-loaded costs for meetings. While results at lower evaluation levels are important, converting the positive outcomes into monetary amounts and weighing them against the cost of the meeting is more valuable from an executive viewpoint. This is the ultimate level in the six-level evaluation framework presented in Chapter 1.

This chapter also explores the costs of meetings and events, identifying the specific costs that should be captured and some economical ways in which they can be developed. Some costs are hidden and not usually counted. The conservative philosophy presented here is to account for all costs, direct and indirect. The monetary values for the benefits are combined with meeting cost data to calculate the return on investment. This chapter also explores the techniques, processes, and issues involved in calculating the ROI. It explains how meetings and events planners pushing the evaluation envelope to the development of monetary values and calculating ROI.

The Importance of Monetary Benefits and ROI

A meeting could be labeled a success without converting to monetary values, just by using business impact data showing the amount of improvement directly attributed to the meeting. For example, a change in sales, quality, cycle time, market share, or customer satisfaction could represent significant improvements linked directly to a meeting. For most meetings, this evaluation would be sufficient. However, a few executives and key clients need the actual monetary value and ROI calculation.

Value Equals Money

For some executives, the most important value is money. There are many different types of value. However, money is becoming one of the most important values as the economic benefits of meetings are desired. This is particularly true for executives, sponsors, clients, administrators, and top leaders. They are concerned about the allocation of funds and want to see the contribution of a meeting in monetary values. Anything short of this value for these key stakeholders would be unsatisfactory.

For some meetings, the impact is more understandable when the monetary value is developed. For example, consider the impact of a leadership retreat aimed at middle managers. As part of the retreat, the managers were asked to address at least two measures that matter to them and need to improve for those managers to meet specific goals. These could represent dozens, if not hundreds, of different measures. When the meeting impact was captured, all these measures had changed, leaving a myriad of improvements, difficult to appreciate without a conversion to monetary value. When the first-year monetary value was developed for each of the measures, the results provided the planner and client with a sense of the impact of the meeting. Without converting to monetary values, understanding the contribution was difficult.

Money Is Necessary for ROI

Monetary value is required to develop ROI. As described in earlier chapters, a monetary value is needed to compare to costs to develop the benefits/costs ratio, the ROI (as a percent), or the payback period. In fact, the monetary benefits become the other half of the equation and are absolutely essential.

Key Steps to Convert Data to Money

Before describing specific techniques to convert both hard and soft data to monetary values, five general steps should be completed for each data item.

1. **Focus on a unit of measure.** First, define a unit of measure. For output data, the unit of measure is the item produced (one item assembled), service provided (one package shipped), or sale completed. Time measures might include the time to complete a meeting, cycle time, or customer-response time, and the unit is usually expressed in minutes, hours, or days. Quality is a common measure, with a unit being defined as one error, reject, defect, or reworked item. Soft data measures vary, with a unit of improvement representing such things as a complaint or a one-point change in the customer satisfaction index. Table 8-1 provides examples of these units.

Table 8-1. Breaking Down the Units of Measure

One sale made	One lost time accident
One package delivered	One grievance
One patient served	One unplanned absence
One student enrolled	One voluntary turnover
One loan approved	One hour of downtime
One unit produced	One minute of wait time
One project completed	One day of delay
One call escalation	One hour of cycle time
One FTE employee	One hour of employee time
One reject	One hour of overtime
One rework	One customer complaint
One error	

2. **Determine the value of each unit.** Now, the challenge. Place a value (V) on the unit identified in the first step. The techniques described in this chapter provide an array of approaches for making this determination or conversion. When more than one value is available, usually the most credible or the lowest value is used in the calculation.

3. **Calculate the change in performance data.** Calculate the change in output data after the effects of the meeting have been isolated from other influences. The change (Δ) is the performance improvement, measured as hard or soft data, that is directly attributed to the meeting. The value may represent the performance improvement for an individual, a team, a group of participants, or several groups of participants.

4. **Determine an annual amount for the change.** Annualize the D value to develop a total change in the performance data for at least one year (ΔP). Using annual values has become a standard approach for planners seeking to capture the benefits of a particular meeting, although the benefits may not remain constant throughout the entire year. First year benefits are used even when the meeting produces benefits beyond one year. This approach is considered conservative. More will be discussed about this later.

5. **Calculate the annual value of the improvement.** Arrive at the total value of improvement by multiplying the annual performance change (ΔP) by the unit value (V) for the group in question. For example, if one group of participants is involved in the meeting being evaluated, the total value will include total improvement for all participants in the group. This value for annual meeting benefits is then compared to the costs of the meeting, usually with the ROI formula presented in this chapter.

Table 8-2 shows how the steps are applied to a meeting of franchise owners for a flooring company. The calculations are based on one of the measures influenced by the meeting.

Table 8-2. Converting Sales Data to Monetary Values

Setting: Annual Franchise Meeting for Flooring Company

Step 1   **Define the Unit of Measure.**
Weekly sales per office location.

Step 2   **Determine the Value of Each Unit.**
The profit margin is needed. This value is a standard value already developed by the accounting staff. (V = 30% of sales)

Step 3   **Calculate the Change in Performance Data.**
Six months after the meeting, total sales per week increased by $2,100 per office. With 155 office locations, this represents a total value of $325,500. An estimated 32% of this value is related to the meeting as determined by franchise owners. (Isolating the effects of the meeting) The adjusted amount (Δ) is $325, 500 x 0.32 = $104,160.

Step 4   **Determine an Annual Amount for the Change.**
The weekly value yields an annual improvement of $5,416,320. ($\Delta P$ = 104,160 x 52)

Step 5   **Calculate the Annual Value of the Improvement.**
Annual Value = ΔP times V
                = $5,416,320 x 30%
                = $1,624,896

Standard Monetary Values

Most hard data items have been converted to monetary values and have standard values. By definition, a standard value is a monetary value placed on a unit of measurement that is accepted by key stakeholders. These standards have been developed because they are often the measures that matter in the organization. They are important. They reflect problems, and because of that, efforts have been made to convert them to monetary values to show their impact on the operational and financial well-being of the organization. The best way to understand the magnitude of any problem is to place a monetary value on it.

Converting Output Data to Money

When a meeting produces a change in output, the value of the increased output can usually be determined from the organization's accounting or operating records. For organizations operating on a profit basis, this value is typically the marginal profit contribution of an additional unit of production or service provided. For example, a team within a major appliance manufacturer was able to boost the sales of small refrigerators after a business development conference. The unit of improvement was the profit margin of one refrigerator. For organizations that are performance-driven rather than profit-driven, this value is usually reflected in the savings accumulated when an additional unit of output is realized for the same input. For example, in the visa section of a government office, an additional visa application was processed at no additional cost. Therefore, an increase in output translated into a cost savings equal to the unit cost of processing a visa application.

Perhaps no area is more dramatic with the standard values than those in the sales and marketing area. Table 8-3 shows a sampling of measures in the sales and marketing area that are routinely calculated and are considered to be standard values. (Farris, et al, 2006) For example, the first two entries go together. The sales cannot be used in an ROI value until they have been converted to profit. Sales are usually affected by the profit percentage to generate the actual value of the improvement. Other profit margins can be developed for a particular unit, a product line, or even a customer. Retention rates and return rates are routinely developed as are the lifetime value of a customer. Even these days, the market share and loyalty are developed because they all translate directly into additional sales. For the most part—with the exception of workload and inventories—the value is developed through profits. Even market share and customer loyalty are valued based on sales or additional sales obtained from the customer.

Table 8-3. Examples of Standard Values from Sales and Marketing

Standard Values in Sales and Marketing

Metric	Definition	Converting Issues
Sales	The sale of the product or service recorded in a variety of different ways: by product, by time period, by customer.	This data must be converted to monetary value by applying the profit margin for a particular sales category.
Profit Margin (%)	$\dfrac{Price-Cost}{Cost}$ for the product, customer, time period.	The most common way factored to convert sales to data.
Unit Margin	Unit Price less the Unit Cost	This shows the value of incremental sales.
Channel Margin	Channel profits as a percent of channel selling price.	This would be used to show the value of sales through a particular marketing channel.
Retention Rate	The ratio of customers retained to the number of customers at risk of leaving.	The value is the money saved to retain a new replacement customer.

Churn Rate	Churn rate is the complement of the retention rate. It is the percent of customers leaving compared to the number who are at risk of leaving.	The value is the money saved for acquiring a new customer.
Customer Profit	The difference between the revenues earned from and the cost associated with the customer relationship during the specified period.	The monetary value add is the additional profit obtained from customers. It all goes to the bottom line.
Customer Value Lifetime	The present value of the future cash flows attributed to the customer relationship.	This is bottom line as customer value increases, it adds directly to the profits. Also, as a new customer is added, the incremental value is the customer lifetime average.
Cannibalization Rate	The percent of the new product sales taken from existing product lines.	This needs to be minimized because it is an adverse effect on existing product with the value add being the loss of profits from the sales loss.
Workload	Hours required to service clients and prospects.	The salaries and commissions and benefits from the time the sales staff spends on the workloads.
Inventories	The total amount of product or brand available for sale in a particular channel	Since the inventories are valued at the cost of carrying the inventory, space, handling, and the time value of money. Insufficient inventories is the cost of expediting the new inventory or loss sales because of the inventory outage.
Market Share	The sales revenue as a percent of total market sales.	The actual sales are converted to money through the profit margins. This is a measure of competitiveness.
Loyalty	This includes the length of time the customer stays with the organization, the willingness to pay a premium, and the willingness to search.	The additional profit from the sale or the profit on the premium

Adapted from *Marketing Metrics: 50+ Metrics Every Executive Should Master* by Paul W. Farris, Neil T. Bendle, Phillip E. Pfeifer, and David J. Ribstein. (Upper Saddle River, NJ: Wharton School Publishing, 2006), p.46 – 47.

Converting Quality to Money

Quality and the cost of quality are important issues in most manufacturing and service firms. Because many meetings are designed to increase quality, the meeting planner may have to place a value on the improvement of certain quality measures. With some quality measures, the task is easy. For example, if quality is measured with the defect rate, the value of the improvement is the cost to repair or replace the product. The most obvious cost of poor quality is the scrap or waste generated by mistakes. Defective products, spoiled raw materials, and discarded paperwork are all the result of poor quality. Scrap and waste translate directly into a monetary value. In a production environment, for example, the cost of a defective product is the total cost incurred up to the point that the mistake is identified, minus the salvage value. In the service environment, a defective service is the cost incurred up to the point that the deficiency is identified, plus the cost to correct the problem, plus the cost to make the customer happy, plus the loss of customer loyalty.

Employee mistakes and errors can be expensive. The most costly rework occurs when a product or service is delivered to a customer and must be returned for correction. The cost of rework includes both labor and direct costs. In some organizations, rework costs can be as much as thirty-five percent of operating expenses.

As with output data, the good news is that a tremendous number of quality measures have been converted to standard values.

Converting Employee Time to Money

Saving employee time is an objective for some meetings and events. In a team environment, a meeting may enable the team to complete tasks in less time or with fewer people. On an individual basis, a new technology tool introduced in a meeting may be designed to help professional, sales, and managerial employees save time in performing daily tasks. The value of the time saved is an important measure, and determining the monetary value for it is relatively easy. The monetary savings are found by multiplying the hours saved by the labor cost per hour. For example, after attending a time management meeting, participants estimated they saved an average of 74 minutes per day, worth $31.25 per day, or $7,500 per year. The time savings were based on the average salary plus benefits for the typical participant.

When developing time savings, caution is needed. Savings are only realized when the amount of time saved translates into other productive work. Having participants estimate the percentage of time saved that is used on productive work may be helpful, followed by a request for examples of how the time was used. If a team-based meeting sparks a new process that eliminates several hours of work each day, the actual savings will be based on a reduction in staff or overtime pay. Therefore, an important preliminary step in developing time savings is determining whether the expected savings will be genuine. This will only happen if the time saved is put to productive use.

Finding Standard Values

As this section has illustrated, standard values are available for all types of hard data and are available in all types of functions and departments. Essentially, every major department will develop standard values that are tracked and monitored in that area. Sometimes, it is a matter of understanding the data set that they monitor, collect, and publish. Thanks to enterprise-wide systems software, these functions, including the standard values in some cases, are integrated and available for access to a variety of people. Access may be an issue, and access may need to be addressed or changed to ensure that the data can be obtained.

Data Conversion when Standard Values Are not Available

When standard values are not available, several strategies for converting data to monetary values are accessible. Some are appropriate for a specific type of data or data category, while others may be used with virtually any type of data. The challenge is to select the strategy that best fits the situation. These strategies are presented next, beginning with the most credible approach.

Using Historical Costs from Records

Sometimes, historical records contain the value of a measure and reflect the cost (or value) of a unit of improvement. This strategy relies on identifying the appropriate records, files, and statements and tabulating the actual cost components for the item in question. For example, a large construction firm organized a meeting to improve safety. The meeting was designed to improve several safety-related performance measures, ranging from safety fines to total workers' compensation costs. By examining the company's records using one year of data, the average cost for each safety measure was developed. This involved the direct costs of medical payments, insurance payments, insurance premiums, investigation services, and lost-time payments to employees as well as payments for legal expenses, fines, and other direct services. Also, the amount of time used to investigate, resolve, and correct any of the issues had to be included. This time involved not only the health and safety staff, but other staff members, as well. In addition, the cost of lost productivity, the disruption of services, morale, and dissatisfaction is also estimated to obtain a fully-loaded cost. Corresponding costs for each item are then developed.

This quick example shows the difficulty in working to use records and databases to find a value for a particular data item. This raises several concerns about this method. Sorting through databases, cost statements, financial records, and a variety of activity reports takes a tremendous amount of time, time that may not be available. Keeping this part of the process in perspective is helpful. This is only one step in the ROI Methodology (converting data to monetary value) and only one of the measures that may need to be converted to monetary value. Resources need to be conserved. Fortunately, other methods are available.

Using Input from Experts to Convert Soft Data

Using input from experts might be a viable option to convert data to money. Internal experts provide the cost (or value) of one unit of improvement. Individuals with knowledge of the situation and the respect of management must be willing to provide estimates—as well as the assumptions made in arriving at the estimates. Most experts have their own methodology for developing these values. So when requesting their input, explaining the full scope of what is needed, providing as many specifics as possible, is critical.

Internally, experts are not difficult to find. Sometimes, it is the obvious department, where the data originated or the department that was involved in collecting the data. For example, the quality department generates quality measures, the IT department generates IT data, the sales department generates sales data, and so forth. In some cases, the expert(s) is the individual or individuals who send the report. The report is sent either electronically or entered into a database and the origins are usually known. If it is sent on a routine basis, the person sending the report may be the expert or at least can lead to the expert.

Fortunately, many experts are available who work directly with important measures, such as employee attitudes, customer satisfaction, market share, turnover, absenteeism, and customer complaints.

Using Values from External Databases

For some data, using cost (or value) estimates based on the work and research of others may be appropriate. This technique taps external databases that contain studies and research programs focusing on the cost of data items. Fortunately, many databases include cost studies of data items related to meetings, and most are accessible through the Internet. Data are available on the cost of customer complaints, turnover, absenteeism, accidents, and even customer satisfaction. The difficulty is in finding a database with studies or research appropriate to the specific measure. Ideally, the data should come from a similar setting in the same industry, but that is not always possible. Sometimes, data on all industries or organizations are sufficient, perhaps with some adjustments to suit the context of the meeting. For some, the Web holds the most promise for finding monetary values for data not readily available from standard values and experts. Tremendous progress has been made—and continues to be made—in Web searches to develop monetary values.

Linking with Other Measures

When standard values, records, experts, and external studies are not available, a feasible approach might be to find a relationship between the measure in question and some other measure that may be easily converted to a monetary value. This involves identifying existing relationships, if possible, that show a strong correlation between one measure and another with a standard value.

For example, a classical relationship, depicted in Figure 8-1, shows a correlation between increasing customer satisfaction and revenue. In a meeting designed to improve customer satisfaction, a value is needed for changes in the customer satisfaction index. A predetermined relationship showing the correlation between improvements in customer satisfaction and increases in revenue can link the changes directly to turnover. Using the profit margin (a standard value), the revenue can easily be developed as described earlier. Therefore, a change in customer satisfaction is converted to a monetary value or, at least, an approximate value using this relationship.

Figure 8-1. Relationship Between Customer Satisfaction and Revenue

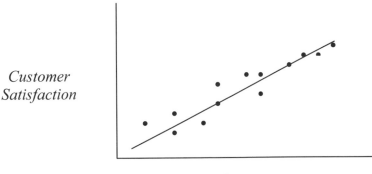

Using Estimates from Participants

In some cases, participants in the meeting should estimate the value of improvement. This technique is appropriate when participants are capable of providing estimates of the cost (or value) of the unit of measure improved with the meeting. When using this approach, participants should be provided with clear instructions, along with examples of the type of information needed.

Using Estimates from the Management Team

Sometimes, participants may be incapable of placing a value on the improvement. Their work may be so far removed from the value of the process that they cannot reliably provide estimates. In these cases, the team leaders, supervisors, or managers of participants may be capable of providing estimates. In some cases, senior management provides estimates of the value of data. With this approach, senior managers interested in the meeting are asked to place a value on the improvement based on their perception of its worth. This approach is used when it is difficult to calculate the value or when other sources of estimation are unavailable or unreliable.

All the formulas presented in this chapter use annualized values so that the first-year impact of the meeting is calculated. Using annualized values is an accepted practice for developing the ROI. This approach is a conservative way to develop the ROI, since some meetings have added value in the second or third year.

Selecting the Method

With so many techniques available, the challenge is selecting one or more strategies appropriate for the situation and available resources. Developing a table or list of values or techniques appropriate for the situation may be helpful. Credibility is the key issue. Table 8-4 provides help to determine the proper selection and finalize the values.

Table 8-4 The Accuracy of the Techniques to Convert to Money

Accuracy	Technique Using:	Comment
Most Accurate	Standard Values	80% of measures that matter have standard values, monetary values that are accepted by stakeholders
	Company Records and Cost Statements	Use only if complete and fully loaded. Unfortunately it takes much time to complete.
	Experts	Most have a comprehensive knowledge of the issue and can be unbiased and neutral.
	External Databases of Other Studies	The Internet has opened many opportunities. The studies must have similar settings.
	Linking with Other Measures	More relationships are being developed.
Least Accurate	Estimates	Use most credible source.

Monitoring Meeting Costs

Monitoring the cost of the meeting or event is an essential step in developing the ROI calculation because it represents the denominator in the ROI formula. It is just as important to capture costs as it is to capture benefits. In practice, however, costs are often more easily captured than benefits, and meeting planners have an excellent track record for capturing costs. The direct cost of the meeting is usually calculated in the proposal for the meeting.

Fundamental Cost Issues

The first step in monitoring costs is to define several issues relating to a cost-control system:

1. Costs do not have to be precise.
2. Disclose all costs.
3. Use fully-loaded costs in ROI calculations.
4. Use caution when reporting costs without benefits.

The most important task is to define which costs should be included in meeting costs. This task involves decisions that will be made by the meeting planner and are usually approved by the client. If appropriate, the client's finance and accounting staff may need to approve the list. Table 8-5 shows the recommended cost categories for a fully-loaded, conservative approach to estimating costs.

Table 8-5. Cost Categories

Cost Item	Prorated*	Expensed
Needs Assessment	✔	
Design, Development and Production	✔	
Acquisition of specific training workshops to be held during the meeting, meetings/registration software, etc.	✔	
Administration Expenses, Salaries/Benefits, and/or Fees – Before Meeting		✔
Marketing/Promotion		✔
Legal Fees		✔
Insurance (general liability, cancellation, etc.)		✔
Registration Expenses		✔
Meeting Delivery:		
• Salaries/Benefits and/or Honoraria/Fees – Facilitators, Presenters, Entertainers, Meetings Staff, Production Staff, etc.		✔
• Meeting Materials (handouts, signage, decoration, etc.)		✔
• Travel (staff, meeting participants, facilitators, presenters, etc.)		✔
• Housing/Sleeping Rooms		✔
• Food & Beverage		✔
• Facility Rental(s)		✔
• Audio Visual Rental and Services		✔
• Transportation		✔
• Translation and Interpretation		✔
• Exhibitions		✔
• Tips and Gratuities		✔
• Participant and Staff Salaries/Benefits – Contact Time		✔
• Participant and Staff Travel Time		✔
• Participant Preparation Time		✔
Evaluation		✔
Overhead	✔	

*In some situations, major expenditures may be prorated if they can be used in other meetings.

Calculating the ROI

As discussed earlier, ROI is becoming a critical measure demanded by many stakeholders, including clients and senior executives. It is the ultimate level of evaluation showing the actual payoff of the meeting, expressed as a percentage and based on the same formula used for other types of investments. Because of its perceived value and familiarity to senior management, it is now a common requirement for meeting evaluation. When ROI is required or needed, it must be calculated. Otherwise, it may be optional, unless some compelling reason exists to take the evaluation to this level.

When selecting the approach to measure ROI, communicating to the target audience the formula used and the assumptions made in arriving at the decision to use this formula are important. This helps avoid misunderstandings and confusion surrounding how the ROI value was actually developed. Although several approaches are described in this chapter, two stand out as preferred methods: the benefits/costs ratio and the basic ROI formula. These two approaches are described next.

Benefits/Costs Ratio

The benefits/costs ratio compares the monetary benefits of the meeting to the costs, using a simple ratio. In formula form, the ratio is:

$$BCR = \frac{\text{Meeting Benefits \$}}{\text{Meeting Costs \$}}$$

In simple terms, the BCR compares the annual economic benefits of the meeting to the costs of the meeting. A BCR of one means that the benefits equal the costs. A BCR of two, usually written as 2:1, indicates that for each dollar spent on the meeting, two dollars in benefits are realized. For example, an annual agents' conference for an insurance company was conducted. In a follow-up evaluation, the first-year payoff for the meeting was $2,091,880. The total, fully-loaded meeting costs were $1,369,745. Therefore, the ratio was:

$$BCR = \frac{\$2,091,880}{\$1,369,745} = 1.53$$

For every dollar invested in this meeting, 1.53 dollars in benefits were received.

ROI Formula

Perhaps the most appropriate formula is net meeting benefits divided by costs. This is the traditional financial ROI and is directly related to the BCR. The ratio is expressed as a percentage when the fractional values are multiplied by one hundred. In formula form, the ROI becomes:

$$\text{ROI (\%)} \quad = \quad \frac{\text{Net Meeting Benefits \$}}{\text{Meeting Costs \$}} \quad \text{x } 100$$

Net benefits are meeting benefits minus costs. The ROI value is related to the BCR by a factor of one. Another way to calculate the ROI is to subtract one from the BCR and multiply by one hundred to get the ROI percentage. For example, a BCR of 2.45 is the same as an ROI value of 145 percent (1.45 x 100%). This formula is essentially the same as the ROI for capital investments. For example, when a firm builds a new plant, the ROI is developed by dividing annual earnings by the investment. The annual earnings are comparable to net meeting benefits (annual benefits minus the costs). The investment is comparable to fully-loaded meeting costs, which represent the investment in the meeting.

An ROI on a meeting of 50 percent means that the costs are recovered and an additional 50 percent of the costs are reported as "earnings." In the agents' conference described earlier, the benefits were \$2,091,880. The costs were \$1,369,745. Therefore, the return on investment was:

$$\text{ROI (\%)} \quad = \quad \frac{\$2,091,880 - \$1,369,745}{\$1,369,745} \quad \text{x } 100 \quad = 53\%$$

Using the ROI formula essentially places meetings and events investments on a level playing field with other investments using the same formula and similar concepts. The ROI calculation is easily understood by key management and financial executives who regularly use ROI with other investments.

Profits can be generated through increased sales or cost savings. In practice, more opportunities for cost savings occur than for profits. Cost savings can be generated when improvement in productivity, quality, efficiency, cycle time, or actual cost reduction occurs as a result of a meeting or event.

Table 8-5 shows some misuse of financial terms in the literature. Terms such as return on intelligence (involvement or information), abbreviated as ROI, do nothing but confuse the CFO, who is thinking that ROI is the actual return on investment described above. Sometimes, return on expectations or event (ROE), return on anticipation (ROA), or return on client expectations (ROCE) are used, confusing the CFO, who is thinking return on equity, return on assets, and return on capital employed, respectively. Use of these terms will do nothing but confuse and perhaps lose the support of the finance and accounting staff.

Table 8-5. Misuse of Financial Terms

TERM	MISUSE	CFO DEFINITION
ROI	Return of Information	
	Return of Intelligence	Return on Investment
ROE	Return on Expectation	
	Return on Event	Return on Equity
ROA	Return on Anticipation	Return on Assets
ROCE	Return on Client Expectation	Return on Capital Employed
ROP	Return on People	??
ROO	Return on Objectives	??
ROM	Return on Meeting	??

ROI from Different Perspectives

Most of the analysis and comments contained in this book have perfected the use of ROI from one perspective, the organizations funding a meeting. This will be the case for many corporate meetings, as the corporation is concerned about its return on investment. However, a return on investment from the association's perspective may be needed, as well as the ROI from the attendee or participant perspective. In addition, an ROI calculation from the exhibitor or sponsor perspective may be needed. All perspectives work well with this analysis. All the costs from the perspective are captured, and all the benefits connected to that same perspective are captured. The costs versus the benefits are compared for each perspective. Even in the corporate environment, multiple perspectives may be appropriate. Franchise meetings, where the franchise owner pays some or part of the expenses to come to the meeting, may be an ideal setting for multiple perspectives. The company is interested in the ROI for organizing the conference. The franchisee is concerned about the ROI for those attending the conference. Multiple perspectives must be considered when appropriate.

ROI Objectives

Specific expectations for ROI should be developed before an evaluation study is undertaken. While no generally accepted standards exist, four strategies have been used to establish a minimum acceptable requirement, or hurdle rate, for ROI in a meeting. The first approach is to set the ROI using the same values used to invest in capital expenditures, such as equipment, facilities, and new companies. For North America, Western Europe, and most of the Asian Pacific area (including Australia and New Zealand), the cost of capital is low and this internal hurdle rate for ROI is usually in the fifteen-to-twenty percent range. Therefore, using this strategy, the planner would set the expected ROI at the same value expected from other investments.

A second strategy is to use an ROI minimum that represents a higher standard than the value required. This target value is above the percentage required for other types of investments. The rationale: the ROI process for meetings is still relatively new and often involves subjective input, including estimations.

A third strategy is to set the ROI value at a break-even point. A zero percent ROI represents break-even. The rationale for this approach is an eagerness to recapture the cost of the meeting only. This is the ROI objective for many government planners. If the funds expended for the meeting can be recovered, additional value has been realized in the intangible measures, which are not converted to monetary values.

Finally, a fourth, and sometimes recommended, strategy is to let the client set the minimum acceptable ROI value. In this scenario, the individual who initiates, approves, sponsors, or supports the meeting, establishes the acceptable ROI.

ROI is not for Every Meeting

The ROI Methodology should not be applied to every meeting. Creating a valid and credible ROI study takes time and resources. ROI is appropriate for meetings that:

- Are important to the organization in meeting its operating goals. These meetings are designed to add value. ROI may be helpful to show that value.
- Are closely linked to the strategic initiatives. Anything this important needs a high level of accountability.
- Are expensive. An expensive meeting, using large amounts of resources, should be subjected to this level of accountability.
- Are highly visible and sometimes controversial. These meetings often require this level of accountability to satisfy the critics.
- Have large audiences.
- Command the interest of top executives and administrators. If top executives are interested in knowing the impact, the ROI Methodology should be applied.

These are only guidelines and should be considered within the context of the situation and the organization. Other criteria may also be appropriate.

It is also helpful to consider the meetings where the ROI Methodology is not appropriate. ROI is seldom appropriate for meetings that:

- Are short in duration.
- Are inexpensive.
- Are legislated or required by regulation and would be difficult to change anything as a result of this evaluation.

- Are required by senior management. It may be that these meetings will continue, unchanged, regardless of the findings.
- Serve as basic or required information for specific jobs. It may be more appropriate to measure only at Levels 1, 2, and 3 to ensure that participants know how to use the information and are using it properly.

This is not meant to imply that the ROI Methodology cannot be implemented for these types of meetings. However, when considering limited resources for measurement and evaluation, careful use of these resources and time will result in evaluating more strategic meetings.

Final Thoughts

With some meetings, ROI is an important value. Meeting planners are being aggressive in defining the monetary benefits of a meeting and developing ROI. Meeting planners are no longer satisfied to simply report the meeting success with application and impact data. Instead, they take additional steps to convert impact data to monetary values and weigh them against the meeting costs. In doing so, they achieve the ultimate level of evaluation: the return on investment. This chapter presented several strategies used to convert business results to monetary values, offering an array of techniques to fit any situation or meeting.

Costs are important, and because of the scrutiny involved in ROI calculations, all costs should be included, even if this goes beyond the requirements of the policy. After the benefits are collected and converted to monetary values and the meeting costs are tabulated, the ROI calculation becomes an easy step. Plugging the values into the appropriate formula is the final step. This chapter presented the two basic approaches for calculating the return; the ROI formula and the benefits/costs ratio.

Notes
Farris, P. W., N. T. Bendle, P. E. Pfeifer, and D. J. Ribstein. *Marketing Metrics: 50+ Metrics Every Executive Should Master* (Upper Saddle River, NJ: Wharton School Publishing, 2006).

Case Study
Measuring the ROI in a National Summer Institute Comprehensive Adult Student Assessment System (CASAS)

By Amy S Anderson, CMP, CASAS Event Coordinator and Marketing Specialist and Carol Farrell, CASAS Research and Planning Specialist

This case was prepared to serve as a basis for discussion rather than an illustration of either effective or ineffective administrative and management practices. Names, dates, places, and data may have been disguised at the request of the author or organization.

Abstract

Many non-profit organizations and associations hold annual meetings for current and potential members, customers, and clients. These meetings can be evaluated from the perspectives of both the meeting organizers and the meeting attendees. This case study tackles both perspectives through the use of questionnaires, performance records, and financial documents.

Organization/Setting

The mission of Comprehensive Adult Student Assessment System (CASAS) is to assist youth (sixteen years and older) and adults functioning at or below a high school level in attaining the basic literacy skills needed to function effectively on the job, in the community, and in the family. CASAS accomplishes this by developing and implementing accountability, assessment, and evaluation systems for adult education programs. To ensure validity, CASAS links these systems to national and state program content and performance standards.

CASAS receives funding from U.S. federal and state agencies to provide adult education and employment training programs with curriculum management, assessment, and program evaluation support services and materials. Additional funding is obtained through sales of materials, training, and technical assistance. These funds are used to support some research and development of educational assessments.

Background

The CASAS National Summer Institute is a three-day educational event held annually in San Diego, California. During more than 180 sessions, the Institute provides ongoing training and technical assistance to the staff responsible for implementing CASAS systems in their agencies. It is also a primary vehicle for identifying emerging needs from the field, for initiating new development efforts, and for marketing CASAS systems and services. The Institute attracts potential new customers as well as promoting quality program implementation and use with current customers.

Hosted by CASAS, the Institute does not include exhibitors or sponsors. Fewer than fifty participants attended the first event in 1980. In 2006, nine hundred participants from across the United States and abroad attended. These attendees included program administrators and instructional staff, such as instructors, trainers, coordinators, counselors, administrators, and human resources personnel from both educational and business settings.

Summer Institute presenters are CASAS certified trainers skilled at facilitating professional development for educational agencies, community-based organizations, and business and industry. They use data collected across states to prepare seminar discussions and training workshops.

The Summer Institute must be self-supporting, while generating funds for the National Consortium and Policy Council meetings throughout the year. However, attendee registration fees are modest compared to industry norms. The financial success of the Summer Institute reflects the value customers place on CASAS products and services.

CASAS found that the Institute's primary value is the opportunity to collaborate with and gain direction from industry professionals. Such networking supports continued research and development and greatly contributes to keeping CASAS products and services current in the marketplace.

Evaluation Methodology

Through the years, CASAS has analyzed and streamlined the financial aspects of this event. The monetary ROI is well-understood. This study investigated the intangible value of the event and used three parameters to determine the value of the Summer Institute for CASAS and its customers:

1. Number of current customers receiving training certification
2. Number of new customers receiving training certification
3. Additions in pilot programs or field-testing sites

Data Collection and Analysis

On-site session evaluation forms were used to collect attendee feedback at the end of each session. Seven subjective questions with value ratings from one (strongly disagree) to six (strongly agree) measure the subjective value as consistently as possible. Although five of the seven questions evaluated the session presenter and organization, two of the questions assessed the perceived value of these sessions to the attendee. The Summer Institute planning team took these paper forms, tallied the scores, and documented subjective comments.

Within two weeks of attending the Institute, participants were e-mailed an online survey link. Since attendees entered responses into an Internet evaluation service provider's system, they were tallied automatically.

Actual conference revenue and operating expenses compiled by CASAS staff were another source of evaluation data.

Results

Level 0: Meeting Indicators and Statistics

Registration records and demographic information collected told the story of who attended the Institute program. See Table 1 for details.

Table 1. Meeting Indicators and Statistics

Total Number of Participants:	900	
Professional Representation	State Adult Education Directors	
	Program Administrators	
	Instructional Staff	
	• Trainers	
	• Coordinators	
	• Counselors	
	• Administrators	
	• Human Resources Personnel	
Industry Representation	Correctional Education	30%
	Other Federal or State-funded	69%
	Business or Private CBO	1%
Geographic Representation	California	75%
	Other U.S. States	24%
	International	1%
CASAS Representation	CASAS Staff	5%
	CASAS Certified Trainer	8%
	National Consortium Member	4%

Level 1: Reaction/Satisfaction and Planned Action

Institute attendees were asked to complete and return a session evaluation (shown in Figure 1) for each session attended. This resulted in a total of 1,585 completed session evaluation forms. The percentages of respondents indicating "strongly agree" with statements about sessions are listed in Table 2. In total, 71% of respondents understood the main concepts within the sessions and felt they would be able to apply these concepts. Sixty-eight percent of respondents, a lower-than-desired percentage, felt the sessions met their needs.

CASAS estimated the return rate compared to the number of session participants to be approximately 60%. However, the return rate can only be calculated for sessions on one of the days, due to participant required sign-in for those sessions.

Table 2. Attendee Responses to Session Evaluations

Topic	Total	Total % Satisfied
Participant Understood the Main Concepts and Feels Able to Apply Them	1122	71%
Session Met Participant Needs	1078	68%
Total Number of Session Evaluations Received	**1585**	

Within two weeks of the 2006 Summer Institute, 750 post-event e-mail surveys were sent to registered participants with valid e-mail addresses. CASAS received 138 responses for an 18% return rate. These responses are summarized in Table 3. Ninety-five percent of respondents indicated that the quality and variety of sessions were "excellent" or "good." Fifty-one percent of respondents felt there were an appropriate number of workshops offered. Twenty-six percent of respondents indicated they received a training certificate from the meeting. Approximately two-thirds of the respondents indicated an intention to attend the Summer Institute next year.

Table 3. Response to Post-Event Survey

Topic	% Responses				
Quality and Variety of Workshops	42% Excellent	53% Good	2% Fair	0% Poor	3% No response
Quantity of Workshops	35% Too Many	51% Appropriate	9% Too Few	5% No response	
Received Training Certificate	26% Yes	54% No	20% No response		
Participants Responding to Survey	76% From California		24% From Outside California		
Number of Years Attending Summer Institute	36% First Time	42% Second TO Fifth Time	15% Sixth To Ninth Time	7% Tenth or Greater Time	
Planning to Attend in 2007	61% Yes	7% No	31% Not Sure	1% No response	

Level 2: Learning

The Summer Institute provided an opportunity for educators to learn more about CASAS assessments, data analysis, reporting, and curriculum development resources. CASAS requires training prior to authorizing customers to purchase assessments. More than half the 2006 Summer Institute participants (495) had previously received CASAS training. They attended the event to network and gain further knowledge, ideas, and updates and to expand the use of the system to other programs in their agencies or states.

CASAS measured the training goal achievement through the collection of signed verification forms at the end of training sessions. Twenty-five percent of the participants (approximately 225) received certificates for training during the Summer Institute, authorizing them to purchase CASAS instruments.

Level 3: Application of Knowledge and Skills on the Job

During the meeting, participants often indicated additional needs for:
• Training for pilot programs to consider CASAS instruments
• Field-testing programs for research on new assessment systems

After learning more about CASAS programs during the meeting, a Texas state director scheduled one large agency in late November 2006 in Houston to begin a pilot program (including training). The program serves English Language Learners (ELL) using CASAS assessments. Field-testing of new listening assessments, writing assessments, and a research study on high school exit skills were also scheduled as a result of attendee planning occurring at the 2006 Summer Institute.

Level 4: Business Impact, Directly Linked the Meeting

The Summer Institute budget closed with a $70,000 surplus available to support CASAS National Consortium and Policy Council mid-year meetings and sub-committee work groups, and to fund initial planning of the 2007 Summer Institute.

Although 25% of attendees received training certificates, authorizing them to purchase CASAS instruments, no specific data was available as to whether these attendees actually purchased CASAS products and services. It was also unknown whether previously certified attendees made purchases as a result of the meeting.

Level 5: Return on Investment for CASAS

A separate Summer Institute account tracks the budget with actual revenue and expenses. The value of the time spent by planning team members is included. For those employees who prepare account-specific presentations for the program, time is charged to that account and not the Summer Institute.

To conform to nonprofit status, the budget dictates a zero balance. Ideally, CASAS realizes an approximate $45,000 surplus to cover annual costs for National Consortium and Policy Council meetings and to fund initial costs for planning the next year's Institute. This does not include the revenue for the following year's conference. Table 4 summarizes the budget and actual revenue and expenses for the 2006 fiscal year. When the number of attendees is divided by the total meeting costs, the cost per attendee was $329.88.

Table 4. Budget versus Actual Figures

Institute Budget Revenue / Operating Expenses	Actual Expenses	Actual Revenue	Actual Surplus
$357,776	$296,889	$367,097	$70,208

The benefits/costs ratio (BCR) for the 2006 Institute is calculated as follows:

$$BCR = \frac{\text{Total Benefits}}{\text{Total Costs}} = \frac{\$367,097}{\$296,889} = \$1.24$$

For every dollar spent by CASAS for this conference, $1.24 was returned.

The return on investment is calculated as follows:

$$ROI = \frac{\text{Meeting Benefits} - \text{Meeting Costs}}{\text{Meeting Costs}} = \frac{\$367,097 - \$296,889}{\$296,889} \times 100 = 23.64\%$$

The 2006 Summer Institute generated a 23.64% return on investment for CASAS.

Intangible Benefits

Since CASAS is a nonprofit organization with a small marketing budget, it relies on word-of-mouth to grow its customer base. The Summer Institute benefits from word-of-mouth marketing, but is unable to be quantified in monetary terms.

By certifying new customers and strengthening existing customer relationships, the Institute increases the potential for expanding the use of CASAS systems and services within existing states and agencies and expanding its use in new markets. Adding 221 trained participants (local facilitators) to the CASAS customer database in 2006 was significant, but further research would be necessary to demonstrate any financial benefit.

Another intangible benefit from the meeting was the opportunity for CASAS to collaborate with and gain direction from industry professionals. Such networking supports continued research and development and greatly contributes to keeping CASAS systems and services current in the marketplace.

More than half the 2006 post-event survey respondents indicated an intention to return in 2007. Twenty-two percent of these respondents indicated that they have already attended six or more years. It is assumed that these repeat participants return to the Summer Institute each year because they perceive value. A dollar amount cannot easily be attached to their perceived value or to the value CASAS believes it realizes as an organization.

A fundamental intangible for attendees was the opportunity for participants with varying degrees of CASAS product experience to network. Although the majority of attendees were from California, all participants learned from the way California and non-California programs integrate CASAS assessments with curriculum. The opportunity to compare data across states further benefited the networking dynamic.

Communication Strategy

This report and reference paperwork was posted in a physical binder within the CASAS office for all to review. Electronic copies (Microsoft Word documents) were shared with CASAS executives.

Lessons Learned

The financial value of the Summer Institute to CASAS remains steady. The full value of the Summer Institute is significant, but difficult to measure because it consists primarily of intangibles.

This study demonstrates that participants definitely perceive value in attending the Institute. By quantifying that perceived monetary value, potential participants would be better able to justify paying the registration fees.

One state has correlated increased student income with adult education program completion to demonstrate ROI. Its study justifies the cost of providing the programs by demonstrating increased earnings of the students. In the same way, the cost of attending the Summer Institute may be justifiable by demonstrating an increase in program and student success (as measured by individual programs or by CASAS, using a generic, universal parameter).

In addition, the evaluation and survey process gathered a number of valuable comments from anonymous participants. In 2007, CASAS will ask participants to volunteer contact information for follow up.

Recommendations and Use of Results

CASAS executives used these study results for strategic planning, identifying emerging needs and trends, and in establishing the goals and objectives for the next program. These goals and objectives will focus on research and development priorities, professional development, technical assistance needs, improving marketing, field communication, and evaluation of effectiveness of program implementation. The study results will directly influence:

- Sessions that CASAS will repeat at the 2007 Summer Institute
- Topics or issues that need to be addressed
- Theme or strands of sessions to be addressed
- Areas requiring development to improve participant satisfaction and increase perceived value
- Design of future sessions

Future survey questions will query participants about the value of the Summer Institute related to behavioral changes in agency policies, procedures to improve program quality, and long-term success of students due to achievement of learning outcomes. Also, post-event survey respondents will be given an opportunity to request follow-up contact from CASAS.

To determine more accurate business impacts of the meeting, CASAS will create a database to track the purchases of products and services by Institute attendees.

Resources

Phillips, J. J. and Phillips, P. P. *The ROI Quiz: The Myths and Mysteries of ROI.* From the ROI Institute Web site, 2005.

Questions for Discussion

1. If CASAS included the value of staff time planning, implementing, and attending the Institute, would the ROI continue to be positive? Should non-profit organizations include the fully-loaded costs in ROI calculations?

2. Does this study demonstrate the value of the CASAS Summer Institute to potential attendees? Explain.
3. What role should CASAS play in helping attendees determine ROI?
4. Could CASAS place a monetary value on one or more of the intangibles listed? If so how?

About the Authors

Amy S. Anderson has more than fourteen years of experience in the field of health and medicine from serving as a certified nursing assistant to a speech-language pathologist. For the past seven years, Ms. Anderson worked in the field of event planning for a conference center. She currently serves as an Event Coordinator & Marketing Specialist for CASAS. She obtained Certified Meeting Professional (CMP) status in 2003 and looks forward to obtaining Certified Meeting Management (CMM) status. Ms. Anderson's passion is data mining and using data analysis to combine event marketing with event planning for highly successful results.

Carol Farrell has worked with many organizations ranging from multinational corporations to "mom-and-pop" businesses. Her expertise lies in making that first written impression. Her current projects include proposal management, design and production of collateral materials, corporate communications, and technical writing. The case authors can be contacted at 1.800.255.1036 or casas-si@casas.org.

Editor's Notes

Calculating the financial ROI on a revenue-generating meeting can be a simple comparison of actual expenses verses actual revenues. However, capturing a more complete picture of the monetary meeting benefits, as well as the fully-loaded costs, can be challenging. This case study examines what one non-profit organization has done to take steps toward a richer and more beneficial evaluation of their annual Summer Institute.

This case also touches on the importance of determining the business impacts and ROI for the meeting attendee. ROI calculations from multiple perspectives are often needed. Results of an evaluation study from the perspective of the attendee can be used for future marketing efforts, to refine future meeting objectives to more successfully meet the needs of attendees, and ultimately to help the meeting organizer fulfill his mission.

Case Study
Measuring the ROI in a Symposium
A Human Capital ROI Approach
KnowledgeAdvisors

By Jeffrey Berk, Vice President of Products and Strategy, KnowledgeAdvisors

This case was prepared to serve as a basis for discussion rather than an illustration of either effective or ineffective administrative and management practices. Names, dates, places, and data may have been disguised at the request of the author or organization.

Abstract

This case study presents a model of how ROI can be calculated using Level 3 data. For this industry symposium, an electronic questionnaire was used to gather data at the end of the symposium and sixty days post-symposium. Monetary value was placed on improvement in job performance as a result of the symposium.

Background

KnowledgeAdvisors is a learning measurement and analytics technology company based in Chicago, Illinois. It helps organizations understand how to better train and develop employees, partners, and customers. KnowledgeAdvisors' solutions automate the data collection, storage, processing, and reporting of all components of learning analytics. Metrics that Matter®, its major technology offering, is a Web-based evaluation and analytics system that allows organizations to measure learning impact and to improve performance.

KnowledgeAdvisors has planned, organized, and implemented a three-day Learning Analytics Symposium in the United States annually since 2003. This annual training and development industry event educates attendees on the latest challenges, best practices, and tools and techniques for measuring, communicating, and improving the effectiveness of learning investments. It consists of more than fifteen sessions featuring keynotes, panel discussions, workshops, and networking events.

Before planning the first symposium, KnowledgeAdvisors interviewed clients about their desires for a symposium of this nature. Since then, an annual needs assessment has been conducted through a review of the prior year's symposium evaluation results and a scan of current industry trends.

In 2006, approximately 150 learning and development practitioners and executives attended. Some attendees were current KnowledgeAdvisor clients. All attendees paid a symposium registration fee and covered their own travel and lodging costs.

Evaluation Purpose

Because the symposium's content focused on measurement and evaluation of learning and development programs, KnowledgeAdvisors felt the symposium needed to be evaluated with the same level of intensity as they suggest their clients take—they strive to practice what they preach. Therefore, the data collection instruments, processes, and tools recommended as best practices during the symposium were also used to evaluate the symposium.

The following symposium elements were evaluated:
- Reaction and satisfaction with the sessions (content and speakers)
- Reaction and satisfaction with the facility and environment
- Effectiveness of the meeting as an engaging learning experience
- Impact that the meeting could and did have on attendees' jobs
- Macro-level business results that were improved by the meeting
- Attendee's ROI from the meeting

Evaluation Methodology

An evaluation methodology based on the Phillips ROI Methodology was used to evaluate this symposium. This methodology was selected because KnowledgeAdvisors uses it with its customers, and it is an accepted methodology among learning practitioners.

Data Collection

The data was collected via KnowledgeAdvisor's online learning analytics tool, Metrics that Matter® (MTM). MTM is a data collection, storage, processing, and reporting system that automates Levels 1 to 5 using standard data collection instruments to trend prior results, calculate current results, and compare against the MTM database of performance benchmarks. Standard MTM data collection instruments used to evaluate this symposium are the same questionnaires used by KnowledgeAdvisor clients to evaluate their training programs and meetings.

At past symposiums, the response rate of paper-based questionnaires distributed on-site was lower than desired, so only electronic, on-line questionnaires were used to collect data for this symposium. These questionnaires were used to increase response rates and save money and time since the results could be aggregated electronically through the MTM system.

In the past, attendees had been willing to complete the electronic questionnaires, thereby producing high response rates. To ensure an acceptable response rate, speakers alerted attendees at multiple points during the symposium that they would be asked to complete end-of-conference and follow-up questionnaires. Speakers also reinforced the importance of attendee feedback and indicated how this feedback would be used to evaluate the meeting and influence next year's symposium. KnowledgeAdvisors considered a giveaway for all those who responded to the questionnaires, but decided against it because it might be perceived as a gimmick.

An end-of-conference questionnaire, shown in Figure 1, was sent via email to all attendees on the final day of the symposium to measure Level 1 and Level 2 data and to show reasonable, forecasted predictions of Levels 3, 4, and 5 data. The survey categories included on the end-of-conference questionnaire were:

- Sessions
- Networking
- Conference operations
- Learning effectiveness
- Job impact
- Business results
- Return on investment
- Overall

Figure 1. Knowledge Advisors End-of-Conference Questionnaire

KnowledgeAdvisors

EMAIL (optional) _____

Check which best describes you: ○ Private Sector ○ Public Sector ○ Academic ○ Vendor (product/service)

SESSIONS

	Strongly Agree	Strongly Disagree
	7 6 5 4 3 2 1 n/a	
1. I was satisfied with the speakers.	○ ○ ○ ○ ○ ○ ○ ○	
2. I was satisfied with the content.	○ ○ ○ ○ ○ ○ ○ ○	

The session I found *most valuable* was:

_____

The session I found *least valuable* was:

_____

Topics and Speakers that should be included in future events:

_____

NETWORKING

	Strongly Agree	Strongly Disagree
	7 6 5 4 3 2 1 n/a	
3. I had adequate time to network:		
a. between sessions	○ ○ ○ ○ ○ ○ ○ ○	
b. in structured discussion groups	○ ○ ○ ○ ○ ○ ○ ○	
c. during evening events	○ ○ ○ ○ ○ ○ ○ ○	
d. overall	○ ○ ○ ○ ○ ○ ○ ○	

CONFERENCE OPERATIONS

	Strongly Agree	Strongly Disagree
	7 6 5 4 3 2 1 n/a	
4. On site registration went smoothly.	○ ○ ○ ○ ○ ○ ○ ○	
5. I was satisfied with the service.	○ ○ ○ ○ ○ ○ ○ ○	
6. I was satisfied with my hotel stay.	○ ○ ○ ○ ○ ○ ○ ○	
7. Conference facility was conducive to learning and networking.	○ ○ ○ ○ ○ ○ ○ ○	

LEARNING EFFECTIVENESS

	Strongly Agree	Strongly Disagree
	7 6 5 4 3 2 1 n/a	
8. I learned new knowledge/skills from this conference.	○ ○ ○ ○ ○ ○ ○ ○	

9. Rate your **INCREASE** in new knowledge/skill learned:
□0% □10% □20%□30% □40% □50%□60%□70% □80% □90%□100%

JOB IMPACT

	Strongly Agree	Strongly Disagree
	7 6 5 4 3 2 1 n/a	
10. I will be able to apply the knowledge skills learned to my job.	○ ○ ○ ○ ○ ○ ○ ○	

11. What percent of new knowledge/skills learned do you estimate you will directly apply to your job?
□0% □10% □20%□30% □40% □50%□60%□70% □80% □90%□100%

12. What percent of your total work time requires the knowledge and skills presented in this event? Check only one.
□0% □10% □20%□30% □40% □50%□60%□70% □80% □90%□100%

JOB IMPACT (continued)

13. On a scale of **0%** (not at all) to **100%** (extremely critical), how critical is applying the content of this event to your job success? Check only one.
□0% □10% □20%□30% □40% □50%□60%□70% □80% □90%□100%

14. When will you be able to use this information on your job?
○ At once   ○ Within 60 days   ○ 3-6 months
○ 6-12 months   ○ Won't use

BUSINESS RESULTS

	Strongly Agree	Strongly Disagree
	7 6 5 4 3 2 1 n/a	
15. Specific business results will be impacted by what I can apply from what I learned here.	○ ○ ○ ○ ○ ○ ○ ○	

16. Given all factors, including this event, estimate how much your job performance and productivity related to the event subject matter will Improve.
□0% □10% □20%□30% □40% □50%□60%□70% □80% □90%□100%

17. Based on your response to the prior question, estimate how much of the improvement will be a direct result of this event. (For example if you feel that half of your improvement is a direct result of the training, enter 50% here.)
□0% □10% □20%□30% □40% □50%□60%□70% □80% □90%□100%

18. This event will have a significant impact on: (check all that apply)
□ increasing quality □ increasing productivity □ increasing employee satisfaction
□ decreasing costs □ increasing sales   □ increasing customer satisfaction
□ decreasing risk   □ decreasing cycle time

RETURN ON INVESTMENT

	Strongly Agree	Strongly Disagree
	7 6 5 4 3 2 1 n/a	
19. This event was a worthwhile investment in my career development.	○ ○ ○ ○ ○ ○ ○	
20. This event was a worthwhile investment for my employer.	○ ○ ○ ○ ○ ○ ○	

OVERALL

	Strongly Agree	Strongly Disagree
	7 6 5 4 3 2 1 n/a	
21. I was satisfied with this conference.	○ ○ ○ ○ ○ ○ ○ ○	
22. I am leaving with actionable ideas.	○ ○ ○ ○ ○ ○ ○ ○	
23. I would recommend this to others.	○ ○ ○ ○ ○ ○ ○ ○	

24. How did you hear about this conference? (check all that apply)
□ website   □ newsletter
□ brochure/mailer □ other? (describe)_____

What about this event was *most* useful to you?

_____

What about this event was *least* useful to you?

_____

How can we improve the event to make it more relevant to your job?

_____

Please feel free to add additional comments on the back of this form.

Figure 2. Knowledge Advisors Follow Up Questionnaire

Follow Up Survey —evaluation to assess training's impact on the job after the training has ended

Course Name   End Date of Training   Learning Provider Name
Our records indicate that you took the above training class. Please answer this brief follow-up survey pertaining to that class so that we may continue to improve the training programs we offer to you and others. Thank you in advance.

LEARNING EFFECTIVENESS

	Strongly Agree						Strongly Disagree	
	7	6	5	4	3	2	1	n/a
1. I learned new knowledge/skills from this training.	○	○	○	○	○	○	○	○

JOB IMPACT

	Strongly Agree						Strongly Disagree	
	7	6	5	4	3	2	1	n/a
2. I have been able to successfully apply the knowledge/skills learned in this class to my job.	○	○	○	○	○	○	○	○

3. What percent of your total work time have you spent on tasks that require the knowledge/skills presented in this training? Check only one.
  □0% □10% □20%□30% □40% □50%□60%□70% □80% □90%□100%
4. On a scale of 0% (not at all) to 100% (extremely critical), how critical was applying the content of this training to your job success? Check only one.
  □0% □10% □20%□30% □40% □50%□60%□70% □80% □90%□100%
5. What percent of new knowledge and skills learned from this training did you directly apply to your job? Check only one.
  □0% □10% □20%□30% □40% □50%□60%□70% □80% □90%□100%
6. I was able to apply the training to my job within:
  ○ 1 week
  ○ 2-4 weeks
  ○ 5-6 weeks
  ○ I haven't applied what I learned yet, but I plan to in the future
  ○ I don't expect to use the knowledge or skills gained
7. If you have NOT been able to successfully apply the knowledge and skills, why not? (check all that apply)
  □ content not practical
  □ prevented or discouraged from using
  □ no opportunity
  □ other higher priorities
  □ other (please specify) _____

BUSINESS RESULTS

	Strongly Agree						Strongly Disagree	
	7	6	5	4	3	2	1	n/a
8. This training has improved my job performance.	○	○	○	○	○	○	○	○

9. Given all factors, including this training, estimate how much your job performance related to the course subject matter has improved since the training.
  □0% □10% □20%□30% □40% □50%□60%□70% □80% □90%□100%
10. Based on your response to the prior question, estimate how much of the improvement was a direct result of this training. For example if you feel that half of your improvement was a direct result of the training, enter 50% here.
  □0% □10% □20%□30% □40% □50%□60%□70% □80%□90%□100%

BUSINESS RESULTS (continued)

11. This training had a significant impact on:(check all that apply)
  □ increasing quality □ increasing productivity □ increasing employee satisfaction
  □ decreasing costs □ increasing sales □ increasing customer satisfaction
  □ decreasing cycle time □ decreasing risk

SUPPORT TOOLS

	Strongly Agree						Strongly Disagree	
	7	6	5	4	3	2	1	n/a
12. The participant materials (manual, presentation handouts, job aids etc.) have been useful on the job.	○	○	○	○	○	○	○	○
	7	6	5	4	3	2	1	n/a
13. My manager and I set expectations for this learning prior to attending training.	○	○	○	○	○	○	○	○
	7	6	5	4	3	2	1	n/a
14. After training, my manager and I determined how I will use the learning on my job.	○	○	○	○	○	○	○	○
	7	6	5	4	3	2	1	n/a
15. I was provided adequate resources (time, money, equipment) to successfully apply this training on my job.	○	○	○	○	○	○	○	○

RETURN ON INVESTMENT

	Strongly Agree						Strongly Disagree	
	7	6	5	4	3	2	1	n/a
16.This training was a worthwhile investment in my career development.	○	○	○	○	○	○	○	○
	7	6	5	4	3	2	1	n/a
17.This training was a worthwhile investment for my employer.	○	○	○	○	○	○	○	○

FEEDBACK

How can we improve the training to make it more relevant to your job?
_____
_____
_____

If you feel you were successful in applying this learning please provide a few tangible examples of how you applied it.
_____
_____
_____

Thank you for completing our survey.

Sixty days following the symposium, a follow-up questionnaire, shown in Figure 2, was sent via email to all attendees who responded to the end-of-conference questionnaire. This questionnaire, which measured the actual results of Levels 3 through 5, included the following categories:

- Learning effectiveness
- Job impact
- Business results
- Return on investment
- Support tools
- Feedback

Data Analysis

The questionnaire results were tabulated automatically through KnowledgeAdvisor's Metrics that Matter® Learning Analytics technology. Scaled questions were averaged on a 7-point scale. Answers to multiple-choice questions were summarized into percentage of total responses, and feedback to open-ended questions were compiled.

Isolation of Symposium Impact

A control group, trend line, or other statistical modeling methods could not be used to isolate the impact of the symposium. Instead, certain questions were asked on both the end-of-conference and follow-up questionnaires so that respondents could estimate their improvement percentage, isolate what percentage of the improvement was a result of the symposium, and indicate what percentage of their work time requires the knowledge and skills learned from the meeting. These questions (shown in Table 1) were included so that the Phillips' Guiding Principles of estimation, isolation, and adjustment were followed:

- Guiding Principle 4. When analyzing data, choose the most conservative among alternatives.
- Guiding Principle 5. At least one method must be used to isolate the effects of the meeting.
- Guiding Principle 7. Estimates of improvement should be adjusted for the potential error of the estimate.

Table 1. Estimation, Isolation, and Adjustment Questions Found on the End-of-Conference Questionnaire

Estimation Question:
Question 16. Given all factors, including this event, estimate how much performance and productivity related to the event subject matter will improve.
☐0% ☐10% ☐20% ☐30% ☐40% ☐50% ☐60% ☐70% ☐80% ☐90% ☐100%

First Isolation Question Used:
Question 17. Based on your response to the prior question, estimate how much of the improvement will be a direct result of this event. (For example, if you feel that half of your improvement is a direct result of the training, enter 50% here.)
☐0% ☐10% ☐20% ☐30% ☐40% ☐50% ☐60% ☐70% ☐80% ☐90% ☐100%

Second Isolation Question Used:
Question 12. What percent of your total work time requires the knowledge and skills presented in this event? Check only one.
☐0% ☐10% ☐20% ☐30% ☐40% ☐50% ☐60% ☐70% ☐80% ☐90% ☐100%

Average responses, standard values, and an adjustment factor were used to calculate the ROI. These results are considered to be a job impact, or Level 3 ROI, and indicate the return relative to human capital rather than specific business results.

This Human Capital ROI model derives the meeting benefit by linking it to the known monetary value that is placed on human capital, an employee salary. The benefits/costs ratio is determined based on the improvement in an employee's job performance, quantified by the employee's salary, relative to the cost of attending the meeting. Simply put, if the employee is worth at least $50,000 to the company, a ten percent increase in that employee's job performance would translate into a business contribution to the company of approximately $5,000.

A series of steps, shown in Table 2, were taken to convert job impact to money and calculate the ROI immediately after the symposium and sixty days later.

KnowledgeAdvisor's research and other meta-analytic studies (statistical approach to comparing and aggregating findings across a large number of studies on the same topic) have shown that post-training surveys that assess the relevance and utility of the training are more likely to correlate with job impact or extent to which the training influenced activities on the job. Therefore, KnowledgeAdvisors has concluded that this methodology is a reasonable way to measure training quality and impact without determining the specific business impacts.

Evaluation Results

The questionnaires have remained the same since the 2004 conference so comparisons can be made among data results on an annual basis. The results presented in this section are from the 2005 symposium, 2006 symposium, and the Metrics

Table 2. Steps Used to Calculate the Attendee ROI

Step 1: Average all responses to Question 16, the estimation question.

- From this questionnaire, the average of attendee responses was 30%.

Step 2: Average all responses to Question 17, the isolation question.

- The average of attendee responses was 70%.

Step 3: Average all responses to Question 12, a second isolation question. Since the monetary benefit will be based on attendee annual salary, this additional isolation question was used. The attendee's full salary cannot be used since the attendee's full work time is not dedicated to the content of the meeting. By having a second isolation question, the portion of the salary not specific to the meeting content is removed.

- The average of attendee responses was 40%.

Step 4: Multiply the averaged responses from Steps 1, 2, and 3.

- 30% x 70% x 40% = 8.4%

Step 5: Multiply the results of Step 4 by an adjustment factor of 35%. Studies conducted by organizations such as the Tennessee Valley Authority and separate studies by KnowledgeAdvisors suggest that respondents tend to over estimate by 35%. Therefore, an adjustment factor of 35% is used against the results from Step 4.

- 8.4% x 35% = 2.94%

The 2.94% is known as the adjusted percent of improvement due to the symposium and indicates that the human capital value of those who came to the meeting increased by 2.94%.

Step 6: Multiply the results of Step 5 by the attendee average salary, which is considered the base economic value of human capital, to yield the average monetary meeting benefit for the attendee.

- 2.94% x $50,000 average annual salary = $1,470. Therefore, $1,470 is considered the attendee's meeting benefit.

Step 7: Determine the cost of the symposium to the attendee. It was estimated that the symposium cost attendees, on average, $1,000 to attend. This meeting cost included a registration fee, travel expenses, and the value of lost work time.

Step 8: Calculate the benefits/costs ratio (BCR) and ROI percentage.

$$\frac{\text{Attendee}}{\text{BCR}} = \frac{\text{Total Benefits}}{\text{Total Coast}} = \frac{\$1,470}{\$1,000} = 1.47$$

$$\frac{\text{Attendee}}{\text{ROI}} = \frac{\text{Meeting Benefits} - \text{Meeting Costs}}{\text{Meeting Costs}} = \frac{\$1,470 - \$1,000}{\$1,000} \times 1000 = 47\%$$

that Matter® benchmark data. The benchmark data come from results of other meetings measured and evaluated using KnowledgeAdvisors' technology. Several hundred organizations have contributed to this benchmark data.

The results shown in this case study are the ones deemed most important by senior management to review and act upon. Other data were captured from the questionnaires but were viewed as less important and not essential for review by the KnowledgeAdvisors senior team. Therefore, the non-essential results were not included.

Level 1, Reaction

The Level 1 data (shown in Table 3) show a slight dip in satisfaction indicators between 2005 and 2006 for the instructor performance category. The data showed the 2006 instructors were a bit too vendor-specific and sales/marketing oriented, even though their content had promise. Based on this feedback, facilitators will be coached to avoid marketing and, rather, present useable content during the 2007 symposium. The benchmark data also indicate some improvement can occur in this area. Although they were not up to benchmark levels, the learning environment and the courseware quality categories did improve from 2005 to 2006.

Table 3. Level 1 Results from the End-of-Conference Questionnaire

Number of Respondents	57	53	780,474
Level 1: Satisfaction	**2005**	**2006**	**Benchmark**
Instructor Performance	6.02	5.92	6.47
Environment Conductive to Learning	5.44	5.79	6.15
Courseware Quality	5.48	5.64	5.99

Level 2, Learning

The key results representing Level 2, Learning, are shown in Table 4. These results reflect responses to the statement "I learned new knowledge/skills from this conference," found on the end-of-conference questionnaire. Since the symposium's nature and environment was not favorable to a more traditional testing option, it was felt that this statement or question was a way to obtain a reasonable indicator for Level 2 data.

Table 4. Level 2 Results from the End-of-Conference Questionnaire

Number of Respondents	57	53	780,474
Level 2: Learning	**2005**	**2006**	**Benchmark**
Effectiveness	5.67	5.96	5.99

These results show that the objective to highlight emerging issues at the 2006 symposium was achieved. The scores for learning effectiveness increased from 2005 and were consistent with the benchmark data.

Level 3, Application and Implementation

The Level 3 indicators were predicted at the end of the symposium on the end-of-conference questionnaire and then confirmed sixty days later on the follow-up questionnaire. Table 5 reflects responses to the following questions on the follow-up questionnaire:

- Question 2. I have been able to successfully apply the knowledge/skills learned in this class to my job. (7-point scale. Strongly Agree or Strongly Disagree)
- Question 3. What percent of new knowledge and skills learned from this training did you directly apply to your job? Check only one. (0% to 100%; 10% point increments)

Table 5. Level 3 Results from Follow-Up Questionnaire

Number of Respondents	13	21	80,569
Level 3 Job Impact	2005	2006	Benchmark
Application of knowledge/skills to the job	5.54	5.09	5.29
Percent of training actually applied to job	38%	38%	39%

Table 5 shows a slight dip in the application of knowledge/skills from the conference to the attendee's job. However, it was decided that the results were reasonable compared to the prior year and to the benchmark database.

Table 6 shows responses to the statement "I was able to apply the training to my job within . . ." The goal was for most attendees to apply what they learned within the first six weeks. Otherwise, knowledge decay would take place. The 2006 data did result in a higher percent of application of the knowledge and skills learned within the first six weeks following the conference, and this data exceeded the benchmark. The increase was attributed to more relevant, action-oriented content in 2006.

Table 6. Timeframe for Job Impact from Follow-Up Questionnaire

Number of Respondents	13	21	80,569
Time to Job Impact	2005	2006	Benchmark
1 Week	53.85	61.9	49.66%
2 – 4 Weeks	30.77	28.57	22.43%
5 – 6 Weeks	7.69	4.76	5.97%
I haven't applied what I learned yet, but I plan to in the future.	7.69	4.76	18.20%
I don't expect to use the knowledge or skills gained.	–	–	3.48%

Level 4, Impact

Because there could have been several business outcomes as a result of the symposium, attendees were asked to identify which business results occurred. Table 7 shows the data collected with the question "This training had a significant impact on: (check all that apply)."

Table 7. Level 4 Business Results from Follow-Up Questionnaire

Number of Respondents	13	21	80,569
Level 4: Business Results	**2005**	**2006**	**Benchmark**
Increasing quality	63.64	61.11	54.94%
Decreasing costs	–	16.67	12.68%
Decreasing cycle time	–	–	34.08%
Increasing productivity	18.18	38.89	52.12%
Increasing sales	9.09	–	7.58%
Increasing customer satisfaction	45.45	44.44	32.04%
Increasing employee satisfaction	27.27	16.67	35.33%

Between 2005 and 2006, the biggest area of improvement was in productivity. This makes sense because some of the symposium's content was geared toward this business measure. Additional business results could have been attained by the use of conditional questions that probed specific results in more detail. However, it was decided that the survey should be concise. In addition, it was not feasible to go into the attendees' organizations and retrieve more precise data. The 'roughly reasonable' indicators were found to be in line with what was needed to make future decisions.

Level 5, ROI

While not an actual ROI based on business impact data, Table 8 illustrates the human capital improvement due to the symposium, as well as the benefits/costs ratio achieved by attendees. In the section on Data Analysis, the questions, rationale, and steps used to calculate ROI were covered. The benefits/costs ratio did increase between 2005 and 2006. This proves that attendee ROI can be improved if

Table 8. Level 5 ROI Results from End-of-Conference Questionnaire

Number of Respondents	57	53	780,474
Level 5: Return on Investment	**2005**	**2006**	**Benchmark**
Adjusted percent improvement due to training	2.97%	3.38%	8.04%
Benefits (using $50,000 US salary)	$1,485	$1,690	$4,020
Costs (standard cost of $1,000 US)	$1,000	$1,000	$1,000
Benefits/Costs	1.485	1.69	4.02

a conference is designed and produced based on a specific goal to achieve greater effectiveness, impact, and results.

For every $1 spent, attendees received $1.69 in benefits from the symposium, or a 69% return on investment, compared to a 48.5% ROI in 2005. However, the benefits/costs ratio fell short of the 4.02 benchmark. KnowledgeAdvisors' analysis shows that single events versus multiple ones within a conference get higher ROIs due to the level of focus on one topic area. Nonetheless, KnowledgeAdvisors has a strong goal to reach the benchmark and feels this can be achieved through improvements in the value proposition. For example, the 2007 symposium will be tactical and focus on the 'how' versus the 'why' of the subject to increase the attendee's ROI.

Communication Strategy

Once the responses to the end-of-conference questionnaire were obtained, the Metrics that Matter analytics system produced a scorecard of all the learning levels and a Learning Levels Card, as shown in Table 9. This Learning Levels Card reveals a combination of the end-of-conference and follow-up results as compared to the goals for the symposium and the benchmark data. The goals, appearing in the column labeled "My Goal," were entered into the system prior to the symposium and were derived based on management's expectations considering past results and the benchmark data.

The goals for satisfaction, learning effectiveness, and business results were not achieved, but the goal for ROI was achieved. The goal for job impact was nearly accomplished, but was short 0.08. These benchmarks can be used to strive for continuous improvement, to recalibrate future goals, and as a motivational data set to serve as an example.

Table 9. Metrics that Matter Learning Levels Card for this Symposium

	My Average	My Average Number of Responses	My Goal	MTM Benchmark	MTM Number of Responses for Benchmark
Level One - Satisfaction	5.67	53	6.5	6.09	660,769
Level Two - Learning Effectiveness	5.88	74	6	5.95	515,654
Level Three - Job Impact	5.42	72	5.5	5.57	354,359
Level Four - Business Results	4.83	69	5	5.71	529,627
Level Five - ROI	5.64	74	5.5	5.82	418,783

During a conference debrief meeting, this information, along with the qualitative comments, was presented to the senior executive team which consisted of the CEO and members from marketing, technology, sales, and services. Each track within the conference and each speaker were assessed. Attendees decided if the speaker should be invited back the next year, based on the team's opinions and the evaluation results.

While results were not shared automatically with all participants, attendees or their organizations could request and receive the scorecard analysis of Levels 1 to 5 from the end-of-conference and/or follow-up questionnaires. Since this data was easily available from the Metrics that Matter system, it was an easily-fulfilled request.

Lessons Learned

The evaluation process and results have allowed KnowledgeAdvisors to continuously modify and improve the annual symposium. Since many attendees return each year, evolving and changing the symposium is necessary.

KnowledgeAdvisors has learned several lessons that can be helpful to others. First, try not to over-analyze data. Use the data as a guide for improvement, not for blame. Also, it is easy to make measurement a nice-to-have or a do-it-if-you-have-time exercise. Instead, evaluation should be a regular process that is incorporated into the larger meeting planning process. Other lessons learned, along with the best practices are listed below:

- Use consistent surveys year after year so that the data can be compared over time.
- Use surveys that can be benchmarked against industry data so that results can be compared against external indicators.
- Ensure that the end-of-conference questionnaire gathers all levels of indicators (Level 1 – Level 5) so that Levels 1 – 2 can be evaluated and Levels 3 – 5 can be forecasted.
- Use a practical ROI approach by building estimation, isolation, and adjustment into the evaluation process.
- Use technology to collect data and eliminate paper so more time can be spent analyzing the data for improvement, not processing data.
- Use technology and templates to auto calculate the Level 1 through Level 5 indicators.
- Discuss the questionnaire results within a week of the meeting and assign action items to make decisions on the data.

- Conduct a sixty-day follow-up to gather on-the-job feedback.
- Use the results to market future programs.

Recommendations and Use of Results

The results from this symposium will be reviewed prior to setting goals for the next symposium. Also, both the quantitative and qualitative results will be used to market the symposium next year. The qualitative comments or intangibles were deemed just as powerful as the quantitative data. Sharing these results in marketing materials has proven effective in illustrating to potential attendees the value of the symposium. It has also helped potential attendees convince their management of the symposium's value.

The data have resulted in the following changes:
- The results indicated that presenters were a bit too vendor-specific and sales/marketing oriented, even though their content had promise. For the coming year, presenters will be coached so that these mistakes are not repeated.
- Creation of a policy that restricts speakers from over-promoting their products and services.
- Speaker evaluation results will be used as one criterion (not the only one) for a possible return the following year.
- Pre-conference workshops will be added to the symposium to allow more focused time on a single topic, generating a higher attendee ROI.
- Specific content during the next symposium will be included to ensure that desired business results are achieved.

Resources

Phillips, J. J. *Return on Investment in Training and Performance Improvement Programs* (Burlington, MA: Butterworth-Heinemann, 1997)

Kirkpatrick, D., *Evaluating Training Programs: The Four Levels, 2nd Edition*, (San Francisco, CA: Berrett-Koehler Publishers, 1998)

KnowledgeAdvisors Metrics that Matter® Learning Analytics technology

KnowledgeAdvisors, *Validating the Human Capital ROI Score Card: A Comparison of Results from Three Impact Methods* whitepaper.

Questions for Discussion

1. Was the data collection approach sufficient for capturing attendee feedback?
2. Is the process for calculating an attendee ROI based on the monetary value of job impact (value of human capital) credible?
3. What attendee costs should be included in the fully-loaded cost of a three-day symposium?
4. Is the industry benchmark data helpful in assessing the results?

5. Would you be able to apply a similar process at your organization? What challenges would you face?

About the Author

Jeffrey Berk is Vice President of Products and Strategy for KnowledgeAdvisors. Mr. Berk, the author behind the company's proprietary learning measurement methodologies, works closely with clients to implement the Metrics that Matter technology and devise appropriate learning measurement strategies. Prior to joining KnowledgeAdvisors, Mr. Berk worked with Andersen for nearly a decade where he was the Manager of Benchmarking Services. Mr. Berk is also an adjunct professor of management at Northwestern's Kellogg School and Loyola University's MBA program, where he teaches a graduate school course on performance improvement. He is the author of the book *Champions of Change: The Managers Guide to Sustainable Process Improvement*. He has an MBA from the University of Chicago and degrees in business and accounting from the University of Kansas.

Editor's Notes

The methodology and process used in this case study to calculate the attendee's ROI can be easily replicated by many organizations. The key, however, will be to ensure that meeting stakeholders view an increase in the value of human capital as a credible way to calculate the monetary meeting benefits.

There is some question as to whether a standard value of $1,000 would cover all the costs incurred by an individual attending this symposium. Higher attendee costs would result in a decreased ROI. Allowing attendees to provide their own fully-loaded costs would result in a more accurate ROI for this symposium; however, guidelines would be necessary to ensure consistency.

Case Study
Measuring ROI in Preventing Sexual Harassment
Faith Hospitals

By Patti Phillips, Ph.D, CEO, ROI Institute

This case was prepared to serve as a basis for discussion rather than an illustration of either effective or ineffective administrative and management practices. All names, dates, places, and organizations have been disguised at the request of the author or organization.

Abstract

Most organizations have sexual harassment prevention programs, but few are subjected to accountability up to and including an ROI analysis. In this case study, a large health care chain conducted sexual harassment prevention meetings with all 7,500 employees. Several unique issues are involved in the evaluation of these meetings, including the techniques used to isolate the effects of the meeting and convert data to monetary values. The analysis used a traditional ROI model. The results surprised the meeting planners, HR staff, and senior managers.

Background

Faith Hospitals (FH) is a regional provider of a variety of health care services through hospitals, HMOs, and clinics in a large, metro area. FH has grown steadily in the last few years and has earned a reputation as a progressive and financially sound company. The non-supervisory employment level is at 6,844. First- and second-level managers number 655, while the senior management team numbers 41.

In the United States, sexual harassment continues to grow as an important employee relation's issue. Sexual harassment claims throughout the United States and in the health care industry continue to grow, sparked in part by increased public awareness of the issue and the willingness of the victims to register harassment complaints. FH has experienced an increasing number of sexual harassment complaints, with some of them converting to charges and lawsuits. The complaint record was considered excessive by executives and represented a persistent and irritating problem. In addition, FH was experiencing an unusually high level of turnover, which appeared to be linked to sexual harassment.

Senior management, concerned about the stigma of continued sexual harassment complaints and the increasing cost of defending the company against claims, instructed the Human Resources (HR) Vice President to take corrective and preventive action to reduce complaints and ultimately rid the workplace of any signs of harassment. The HR Vice President asked the corporate meeting and events department to schedule and conduct a series of meetings with all employees, but only if there was a lack of understanding and knowledge of the issue.

Initial Needs Assessment

In response to the request, the meeting planning staff conducted interviews with the entire EEO and Affirmative Action staff during which the magnitude of the problem and the potential causes were explored. Most of the staff indicated there appeared to be a significant lack of understanding of the company's policy on sexual harassment and what actually constitutes inappropriate or illegal behavior.

In addition to interviews, the complaints for the last year were examined by the EEO/AA representatives for issues and patterns. From an analysis of complaints, the typical person accused of sexual harassment was a supervisor and usually male. The typical victim of harassment was non-supervisory and female. The analysis also revealed that the type of sexual harassment typically experienced at FH was defined by the EEOC as "an individual making unwelcome sexual advances or other verbal or physical conduct of a sexual nature with the purpose of, or that creates the effect of, unreasonably interfering with an individual's work performance or creating an intimidating, hostile, or offensive working environment." This type of harassment should be minimized by developing a clear understanding of FH's policy regarding harassment, and by teaching managers to identify illegal and inappropriate activity.

Exit interviews of terminating employees for the last year were reviewed by the HR staff to see if there was a link to sexual harassment. Approximately 11% of those departing employees identified sexual harassment as a factor in their decision to leave FH. Exit interview data was computerized and readily available. Because of the request to proceed with this project, the HR staff did not conduct a full-scale needs assessment. Instead, they augmented the input from the EEO/AA staff and exit interviews with ten randomly selected interviews with first-level supervisors to explore the level of understanding of the policy, inappropriate and illegal behavior, and the perceived causes of the increased complaint activity.

The Meeting

Armed with input from ten supervisor interviews, detailed input from the EEO/AA staff, and information from company records, the major causes of the problem were identified. There was an apparent lack of understanding of (1) the company's sexual harassment policy and (2) what constitutes inappropriate and illegal behavior. In addition, there was an apparent insensitivity to the issue. As a result, a half-day meeting was designed for all employees and managers, in separate sessions. The objectives of the meetings were to enable participants to:

- Understand and administer the company's policy on sexual harassment
- Identify inappropriate and illegal behavior related to sexual harassment
- Ensure that the workplace is free from sexual harassment
- Reduce the number of sexual harassment complaints

Because of the implications of this issue, it was important for the information to be discussed with all employees so that there would be no misunderstanding about the policy or inappropriate behavior. The meeting design was typical, using a combination of purchased and internally developed materials. The half-day meetings were conducted over a 45-day period with seventeen sessions, involving all employees. Managers attended a separate meeting, with two of the seventeen sessions devoted to them. HR managers and coordinators served as meeting facilitators.

Why ROI?

The meetings usually targeted for an ROI calculation are those perceived to be adding significant value to the company and closely linked to the organizational goals and strategic objectives. The ROI calculation is pursued to confirm the added value. Based on the results of the ROI analysis, programs may be enhanced, redesigned, or eliminated if the ROI is less than desired. Sexual harassment prevention is usually different. The ROI (negative or otherwise) does not dictate the future of the meeting. Data collected through the evaluation may drive session changes for the future, however.

At FH, this meeting was chosen for an ROI calculation for two reasons. First, the HR department was interested in the accountability of all major projects, including sexual harassment. Second, a positive ROI would clearly show management that these types of issues, which are preventive in nature, can significantly influence the bottom line.

Planning for Evaluation

Figure 1 shows the completed data collection plan for the sexual harassment prevention meeting. A pre- and post-test was administered (before and after the meeting) to measure knowledge of the FH's sexual harassment policy and inappropriate and illegal behavior. The simple, twenty-item questionnaire was evenly split on policy and behavior issues.

Figure 1. Data Collection Plan

Meeting: Preventing Sexual Harassment **Responsibility:** Patti Phillips   **Date:** ___   Evaluation Purpose: Show the Impact of Compliance issues

Level	Broad Meeting Objective(s)	Measures	Data Collection Method/Instruments	Data Sources	Timing	Responsibilities
1	**REACTION/SATISFACTION & PLANNED ACTIONS** • Obtain a positive reaction to meeting and materials • Obtain input for suggestions for improving meeting	• Average rating of at least 4 on 5 scale on quality, usefulness, and achievement of objectives.	• Reaction feedback questionnaire	• Participant	• End of meetings	• Meeting Planner
	• Identify planned actions (Managers Only)	• 90% submit planned actions (check off)	• Action plan	• Manager (Participants)	• End of meetings	• Meeting Planner
2	**LEARNING** • Knowledge of policy on sexual harassment • Knowledge of inappropriate and illegal behavior	• Ability to identify 7 of 10 policy issues • From a list of actions, and lack of actions, be able to identify 7 of 10 that constitute sexual harassment	• Pre- and Post-test	• Participant	• Beginning of meetings	• Meeting Planner
3	**APPLICATION/IMPLEMENTATION** • Administer policy appropriately • Ensure that workplace is free of sexual harassment	• At least 4 on 5 scale on appropriate application of policy and removal of SH activity	• Employee Survey (25% sample)	• Sample of Participant	• 6 months after meeting	• HR Staff
	• Complete action plan	• Actions taken to eliminate sexual harassment (checklist) • Isolation estimates	• Action plan	• Managers	• 6 months after meetings	• Meeting Planner
4	**BUSINESS IMPACT** • Reduce internal complaints • Reduce voluntary employee turnover	• Formal internal complaints related to sexual harassment • Voluntary turnover	• Performance Records Monitoring	• Human Resources complaint records • Human Resources exit records • Managers	• Monthly for one Year before and after meetings • 6 Months after meeting	• Meeting Planner and HR staff
5	**ROI** Target ROI – 20%	Comments: _Managers attend separate session, same content._				

To measure the successful application of the meeting, two data collection methods were used. The first data collection method was a survey of the non-supervisory employees. Although all employees could have been surveyed, it was felt that it was more important to examine behavior change from a sample of those who were more likely to be victims of harassment. The survey was planned for administration six months after the meetings were conducted. It provided post-meeting data only, and therefore, each questionnaire had to be worded to measure behavior change since the meeting was conducted. The fifteen-item survey examined specific behavior changes and environmental changes related to harassment activity, including actions that might be considered inappropriate or offensive. Table 1 presents some typical questions.

Table 1. Sample of Follow-Up Questions

In the Last Six Months	Strongly Disagree	Disagree	Neutral	Agree	Strongly Agree
I have noticed less offensive language at work.	☐	☐	☐	☐	☐
The company is more likely to take swift action against those who are found guilty of sexual harassment.	☐	☐	☐	☐	☐

The second data collection method was the action plans completed by supervisors and managers. These plans captured actions and results linked to the meetings. While there were a variety of other data collection possibilities, including focus groups, interviews, and third party observation, it was felt that, given the time and cost considerations, these two methods provided sufficient data to capture behavior change and show that the meeting had been successful.

Business results measures included two items. The first measure was internal complaints. These were lodged formally with the Human Resources Division and were monitored for the evaluation. Because of the lag time between changes in behavior and a reduction in complaints, data would be collected for one year after the meetings and compared to one year before the meetings to determine specific improvements. Because of the perceived link between sexual harassment and turnover, annual employee turnover was selected as the second measure. This measure would be examined for the same time period as complaints.

Figure 2 shows the completed ROI analysis plan. Because of the relatively short time frame required to conduct the meetings and the desire from top management to implement it throughout the organization quickly, a control group arrangement was not feasible to isolate the effects of the meetings. However, because historical data were available on complaint measures, a trend line analysis was initially planned. Complaint activity would be projected based on twelve months of data prior to the meetings. Actual performance would be compared to the projected data and the difference would reflect the actual impact of the meetings on that measure. In addition to trend line analysis, participants' estimation was planned to compare with trend line data. In this situation, supervisors and managers (participants) are asked to indicate the extent to which the meetings influenced the changes in the number of complaints.

To isolate improvement in turnover to the meetings, trend line analysis could not be used because of the other initiatives that were planned to reduce turnover. For the trend line analysis to be used, no additional influences should enter the process during the post-meeting evaluation period. Consequently, a type of forecasting (or projection) was used. The percentage of turnover related to sexual harassment was developed for the twelve-month period prior to the program. The same percentage is projected (forecasted) for the post-meeting period. Difference in actual vs. forecast could be attributed to the meeting.

In regard to converting the data to monetary values, the cost of complaints would be derived from both historical data when available, and with estimates for other factors, such as the actual time used on harassment complaints. The estimates would be developed with input from the EEO/AA staff. For turnover, industry data would be used since FH had not calculated the actual cost of turnover for any employee groups. The specific cost items, intangible benefits, other influences, and communication targets were all identified and are presented in Figure 2.

Results: Reaction and Learning Data

A typical end-of-meeting questionnaire was used to capture reaction data. Overall, the participants had a positive reaction to the meeting and perceived it to be timely and useful. A composite rating of 4.11 out of a possible 5 was achieved. This exceeded the target of 4 out of 5. The vast majority of the managers (93%) provided a list of action items planned as a result of the meeting.

For learning evaluation, the pre-meeting test scores averaged 51 and the post meeting scores averaged 84, representing a dramatic increase of 65%. These results were significant and exceeded the expectations of meeting planners. Two important points were underscored with the learning assessment. First, the low scores on pre-meeting tests provided evidence that the project was necessary, validating the needs assessment. The participants did not understand the organization's policy, nor did they recognize what constituted inappropriate and illegal behavior. Second, the dramatic improvement in scores provided assurance that the content of the meeting was appropriate for both key issues as the participants learned much about policy and behavior.

Figure 2. ROI Analysis Plan

Meeting: Preventing Sexual Harassment **Responsibility:** Patti Phillips   **Date:** _____

Data Items (Usually Level 4)	Methods for Isolating the Effects of the Meeting	Methods of Converting Data to Monetary Values	Cost Categories	Intangible Benefits	Communication Targets for Final Report	Other Influences/ Issues During Application	Comments
1. Formal internal complaints of sexual harassment 2. Voluntary employee turnover	1. Trendline Analysis 2. Participant estimation (for back up) 2. Forecasting using percent of turnover related to sexual harassment	1. Historical costs with estimation from EEO/AA Staff (standard values and expert input) 2. External turnover cost studies within industry	• Needs assessment • Meeting development • Coordination, speaker time • Program materials • Food/ refreshments • Facilities/ travel • Participant salaries and benefits (for the meeting time) • Evaluation (time and materials)	• Job satisfaction • Absenteeism * Stress reduction • Image of FH • Recruiting	• All employees (condensed info.) • Senior executives (summary of report with detailed backup) * All supervisors and managers (brief report) • All HR Staff (full report) • All Meeting and Events Staff	• Several initiatives to reduce turnover implemented during the time period	Complaints of sexual harassment is a significant issue with management

Results: Application Data

Six months after the meetings were conducted, an anonymous survey was conducted with a 25% sample of non-supervisory employees. A total of 1,720 surveys were distributed and 1,100 were returned for a response rate of 64%. The survey yielded an average score of 4.1 on a scale of 1 to 5. The rating represents the extent to which the behavior has changed in the six months since the meetings were conducted. Overall, the survey results indicated that significant behavior change had occurred, and the work environment was largely free of harassment.

Action plans were collected from managers six months after the meetings were conducted. A total of 571 plans were returned representing a response rate of 87%. The plans provided details about the extent to which meeting materials were used and specific behavior changes had been realized. In addition, managers estimated the amount of improvement in sexual harassment complaints that was directly attributable to this meeting. Although the input from managers and supervisors may be biased, significant changes were reported. In regard to actions completed, 92% reported that some actions were completed, while 68% reported that all actions were completed.

Results: Business Impact

Table 2 shows the one year of complaint and turnover data prior to the meetings and one year after the meetings. The total cost value includes the cost of all activities and direct expenses related to sexual harassment. Theoretically, if there were no complaints, this value would be zero. When collecting action plans, managers were provided the six-months average before and after the meeting, and were asked to estimate the percent of improvement that was actually caused by these meetings. The average percent of managers, included in the right column, is 74% after adjustment for confidence.

Table 2. Performance Measures Related to Sexual Harassment

Business Performance Measure	One Year Prior to Meeting	One Year After Meeting	Factor for Isolating the Effects of Meeting
Internal Complaints of Harassment	55	35	74%
Total Cost of Sexual Harassment Prevention, Investigation, and Defense*	$1,655,000	$852,000	
Turnover (Non-Supervisory) Annualized	24.2%	19.9%	54%

*Includes legal fees, settlement/losses, portion of EEO/AA staff assigned to sexual harassment, management time for this activity, printed materials, and miscellaneous expenses.

The exhibit also shows the turnover rate for the non-supervisory employees for the twelve months preceding the meeting and the twelve months after the meeting. Manager estimates of the impact of these meetings on turnover were collected when considering the various factors influencing turnover. This estimated was 54%, after adjustment for confidence.

For sexual harassment complaints, the pre/post difference was 55-35=20. Figure 3 shows the trend line projections for the internal complaint data. The trend, established prior to the meeting, was projected for the one year post-evaluation period. As the projection shows, the impact of the meeting was even more dramatic than illustrated in the pre/post difference, because of the upward trend of the data. An estimated monthly difference yielded an annual improvement value of about thirty-two complaints, instead of twenty. Since the impact was more conservative using the pre/post difference from the managers' estimates, this figure was used in the analysis. Consequently, the actual calculations represented an understatement of actual performance. The trend line results were credible and could have been used in the analysis. However, the ROI value (presented later) was already larger than most expected. A conservative approach was needed to build credibility.

Figure 3. Formal Internal Complaints of Sexual Harassment

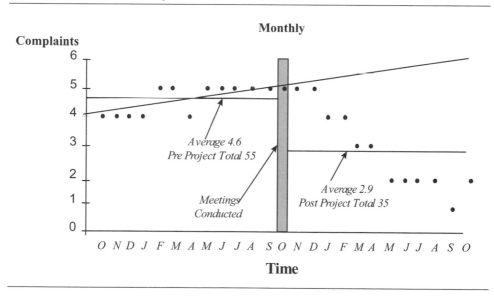

The turnover rate showed improvement during this same time frame, although the employment grew. On a pre-meeting basis, the non-supervisory employees averaged 6,651 compared to 6,844, post-meeting. Because of the excessive levels of turnover, other initiatives were undertaken to help reduce the departure rate of employees. Recruiting processes were enhanced, entry-level salaries were increased, and more effective selection techniques were employed during the same time period. All these actions were initiated to develop a better match between the employees and the culture at FH. Therefore, the trend line forecast for the turnover rate would not be appropriate because of the influence of these factors on the turnover rate.

To estimate the percent of turnover reduction directly related to these meetings, a forecasting process was used. During the needs assessment, exit interview data were reviewed for evidence of sexual harassment as a factor in the decision to leave. In these cases, 11% of the voluntary turnover had mentioned sexual harassment as a reason for departure. Employees are often reluctant to indicate the presence of sexual harassment, although the issue may be the reason for their departure. Therefore, it was felt that this 11% figure was a conservative estimate of the number of terminations related to sexual harassment activity. Because of this, the 11% figure was "forecasted" to continue in the next year. However, a twelve-month review of exit interviews, on a post-meeting basis, revealed that only 3% of the departing employees mentioned sexual harassment among the reasons for their departure. Therefore, the percent of employees leaving because of sexual harassment dropped from 11% to 3% of terminations.

Costs

Table 3 shows the meeting costs. The costs were fully-loaded and included the cost of the needs assessment ($9,000), design and development of the meeting ($15,000), and evaluation ($11,000). The needs assessment cost was an estimate based on the direct time and expenses involved in the process. The development costs were low because of the use of purchased materials. Evaluation costs included an estimate of all internal and external costs associated with the follow-up evaluation, including developing the ROI. Participants' salaries and benefits were included for the time of the meeting, although it was not FH's policy to include participant salaries and benefits as an expense for a half-day meeting. In all, 7,421 people attended. The average hourly salary of all participants was estimated to be $31. The meeting lasted four hours. The employee benefits factor was 39%. Total cost of participant time in the meeting was $1,279,084. The time necessary for coordination was estimated along with the time for facilitator preparation and delivery. When considering the average salaries plus benefits for individuals coordinating and facilitating the meetings, a value of $19,400 was estimated. Travel and lodging for coordination and facilitation was a minor factor, estimated to be $1,520. Meeting materials were $6 per participant, and food and refreshments during the meeting were $10 per participant for a total of $44,526 and $74,210, respectively. A ballroom of the local hotel was used for each meeting with an average cost of $2,500 per session for seventeen sessions, totaling $42,500. Most participants arranged their own travel, and reimbursement was required. Some participants had to travel longer distances and were reimbursed. Still others were provided transportation in buses. Total travel costs were estimated to be $98,500. The fully-loaded costs for the meeting came to $1,594,740.

Table 3. Program Costs

Cost Category	Total Cost
Needs Assessment (Estimated Cost of Time)	$9,000
Development/Acquisition	15,000
Coordination/Facilitation Time	19,400
Travel and Lodging for Facilitation and Coordinators	1,520
Travel and Lodging for Participants 1,520	98,500
Program Materials (7,421 @ $6)	44,526
Food/Refreshments (7,421 @ $10)	74,210
Facilities (17 @ $2,500)	42,500
Participant Salaries and Benefits ($31 x 4 x 7,421 x 1.39)	1,279,084
Evaluation (Estimated)	11,000
	$1,594,740

Monetary Benefits of the Meetings

Table 4 shows the calculation for the monetary benefits from the sexual harassment complaint. For the reduction of complaints, the value was based on reducing internal complaints. The value for this measure is shown in the table. The values were developed by taking the total cost of sexual harassment prevention, investigation, and defense (from Table 2), and dividing it by the number of complaints. Pre- and post-meeting values are shown in Table 4. The lower value was used to be conservative, and it represented the most recent. Not only did the complaints reduce, but the cost of a complaint also was reduced. Consequently, the value of one internal complaint was placed at $24,343 (i.e. if one complaint could be avoided, FH would save that amount in one year).

Table 4. Monetary Benefits form Complaint Reduction

	Pre-Meeting	Post-Meeting
Average Cost of an Internal Complaint	$30,090	$24,343

Unit of Improvement = One Internal Complaint
Value of One Internal Complaint = $24,343
Total Improvement: 55 - 35 = 20
Improvement Related to Meetings: 20 x 74% = 14.8 (Based on manager estimates)
Value of Improvement = 14.8 x $24,343 = $360,276

Another approach is to examine the total cost of sexual harassment, including prevention, investigation, and defense and use a value equal to the reduction in cost. However, because there was a lag between measures of complaints and actual losses and legal expenses, the total costs from one year compared to the next may not reflect the actual cost savings.

While the total annual improvement was twenty internal complaints (pre/post differences), the improvement related directly to the meeting was 74% of that figure, or 14.8 complaints. The 74% was an estimate from the managers taken directly from the action plan, as they were asked to indicate the extent to which the reduction in complaints was related directly to the meeting. The value of the improvement was $360,276. Table 4 shows these calculations.

The value for the turnover reduction was developed in a similar manner as illustrated in Table 5. The unit of improvement was one turnover statistic. The target group for the turnover reduction was non-supervisory employees which represented an average of 6,844 on a post-meeting basis and 6,651 on a pre-meeting basis. Prior to the meetings, the 24.2% turnover rate represented 1,610 employees who left voluntarily. According to the exit interviews, 11% of those were related to sexual harassment. Therefore, 177 departures were related to sexual harassment. On a post-meeting basis, the 19.9% turnover represented 1,362 employees. Post-meeting exit interviews revealed that 3% were related to sexual harassment. Therefore, forty-one employees left because of this issue. The improvement related directly to the meetings was 136 terminations, a significant number when the cost of turnover was included.

Table 5. Monetary Benefits from Turnover Reduction

Unit of Improvement = One Voluntary Turnover Statistic (Termination)
Turnover Pre-Meeting = 6,651 x 24.2% = 1,610
Turnover, Pre-Meeting Related to Sexual Harassment: 1,610 x 11% = 177
Turnover, Post Meeting: 6,844 x 19.9% = 1,362
Turnover Post Meeting Related to Sexual Harassment: 1,362 x 3% = 41
Improvement Related to Meeting: 177 - 41 = 136
Cost of One Turnover: 75% of Annual Salary = $37,500 x 0.75 = $28,125
Value of Improvement: 136 x $28,125 = $3,825,000

Several industry studies on the cost of turnover were briefly discussed, which revealed ranges from 110% to 150% of annual salaries. The average non-supervisory salaries for the post-meeting period were $37,500. Although there was sufficient evidence to use the 110% of annual salary as a cost of turnover, to be conservative—and at the request of the HR executive—the team used 75% of the annual salaries, representing $28,125 as a cost of one turnover statistic. Consequently, the 136 terminations avoided as a result of the sexual harassment prevention meetings yielded a staggering $3,825,000 in savings.

ROI Calculation

Figure 4 shows the benefits/costs ratio and ROI calculations for these values. Benefits based entirely on complaint reduction and turnover reduction was used in the benefits/costs ratio to yield 2.62:1. Therefore, for each $1 spent on the meeting, $2.62 was realized in benefits. The ROI calculation, which uses net benefits, shows an ROI of 162%, an impressive amount. The results were greater than expected by the evaluation team and senior management.

Figure 4. ROI Calculation

$$BCR = \frac{Benefits}{Costs} = \frac{\$360,276 + \$3,825,000}{\$1,594,740} = \frac{\$4,185,276}{\$1,594,740} = 2.62{:}1$$

$$ROI = \frac{Net\ Benefits}{Costs} = \frac{\$4,185,276 - \$1,594,740}{\$1,594,740} \times 100 = 162\%$$

Communication Strategy

To communicate appropriately with the target audiences outlined in the ROI analysis plan, the meetings and events team produced three specific documents. The first report was a detailed impact study showing the approach, assumptions, methodology, and results using all six data categories. In addition, barriers and enablers were included in the study, along with conclusions and recommendations. The second report was an eight-page executive summary of the key points, including a one-page overview of the methodology. The third report was a brief, five-page summary of the process and results. These documents were presented to the different groups according to the plan presented in Table 6. An article was prepared by the internal communication staff using these three documents, but was presented in a general basis without the actual ROI.

Table 6. Plan for Communicating Results

Audience	Document
All participants	Brief Article
Managers	Brief Summary
Senior executives	Complete study, executive summary
HR Staff	Complete study
Meetings and Events Staff	Complete study, executive summary

Questions for Discussion

1. Was the needs assessment appropriate for this situation? Please explain.
2. Should this project be evaluated at Levels 4 and 5? Please explain.
3. Critique the Level 2 and Level 3 results. Was the employee survey necessary? Explain.
4. To isolate the effects the meeting on complaints which of the methods of isolation would you use? Why? (Trend line analysis or Manager estimates)
5. How could this process be improved?
6. How would you present these data to management? To all employees?

About the Author

Patti Phillips, Ph.D., is President of the ROI Institute, Inc., the leading source of ROI competency building, implementation support, networking, and research. She has twenty-five years of corporate and consulting experience. Dr. Phillips helps organizations implement the ROI Methodology in countries around the world including South Africa, Singapore, Japan, New Zealand, Australia, Italy, Turkey, France, Germany, Canada, and the United States.

Dr. Phillips' academic accomplishments include a Ph.D. in International Development and a Master of Arts Degree in Public and Private Management. She has authored several publications on accountability and ROI. Dr. Phillips' most recent publications include *ROI Basics*, ASTD (2005); *Proving the Value of HR: How and Why to Measure ROI*, SHRM (2005); *Make Evaluation Work*, ASTD (2004); *The Bottom Line on ROI*, Center for Effective Performance (2002), which won the 2003 ISPI Award of Excellence; *ROI at Work*, ASTD (2005); the ASTD *In Action* casebooks, *Measuring Return on Investment Volume 3* (2001), and *Measuring ROI in the Public Sector* (2002).

She can be reached at patti@roiinstitute.net.

Editor's Notes

This study is a good example of how significant value can be added using a compliance-related, prevention meeting—in this case, on the topic of sexual harassment complaints. It also shows the contribution of the meetings and events staff members and how they maintain independence by having the HR staff be the actual client.

Case Study
Measuring the ROI in a Pro-AM Golf Tournament
ComCo

By Ed Jones, President, Constellation Communication Corporation

This case study is derived from the basic measurement programs and results for multiple pro-am events and multiple companies. All names, dates, amounts, and other data are fictional to protect the confidentiality of the host companies.

Abstract

Measuring the value of a group of executives playing golf has been compared to "nailing Jell-O to a tree." It is difficult to accomplish and troublesome to determine the results. However, in today's environment of extreme focus on corporate ethics and responsibility, there are few alternatives. This case study demonstrates how the value of an executive hospitality event (or any other event) can be assessed by applying a simple structure of how value is achieved with some forthright investigation.

Background

Imagine you are hosting the annual stockholders meeting of your multibillion-dollar global enterprise, and this question comes from a stockholder, "Chairman Smith, would you tell me why it was beneficial to the stockholders that this company spends hundreds of thousands of dollars entertaining you and your golfing buddies at the ComCo Classic Executive Pro-AM every year?" His only response was simply, "Gulp!"

That actually happened to the CEO of a company we all know.

(Note: Pro-AM is an acronym for Professional – Amateur pairings on the last practice round before tournament play begins. The slots are part of the tournament cost to the sponsor and are used to pair customers, executives, and professional golfers for executive hospitality.)

The next time a question was posed about the company's executive hospitality events, he was ready. Using a briefing card, prepared by the corporate PR team from the ROI analysis conducted on every executive hospitality event thereafter, his answer went something like this:

"That is a very good question. We formally assess our return on investment in these

types of events. Let's take the ComCo Classic Pro-AM tournament, for example. Forty-one executives, representing thirty-eight companies of the greatest importance to ComCo, participated in our annual Pro-AM tournament. Those executives represented $2.2 billion of recurring revenue to our company and $360 million in proposed new revenue within six months of the event. The event was purposefully planned and executed to facilitate interaction between the key executives of our largest customer base and our leadership team.

"*...Any questions?*"

Good answer!

The additional details to convey, as needed, were:

- The event was purposefully designed to allow ComCo to exchange information, ideas, and most importantly, to gain and make commitments with the high-level, key customers.
- For that event, 87% of the guest executives indicated their interactions with ComCo executives and sales personnel had a direct and positive impact on the probability of continuation of their existing business and current proposed projects.
- The internal estimate of the event's value, based upon ROI analysis of that event, was approximately $3 (net) for every dollar spent.

   This value was determined by an equation that took a 5% cost of retention (agreed upon by company management) and a 1% weight for the executive inter-action verses all the other customer relationship management (CRM) activities for the year (again agreed by management), to produce a factored value of the CRM activity accomplished through the event. Since the equation dealt with a cost, it was "net" by definition. The other event benefit factor was to estimate how much expense avoidance was associated with having "C" level executives meet with each other and with other host company management in mass at the event, eliminating expensive executive time and travel, plus costs for staff and facilities to support those events in the future.

- ComCo used this analysis to determine how to improve effectiveness on future executive hospitality events.

Like many corporate executive hospitality events, the Pro-AM events were held because the company leadership knew, if only intuitively, that business was facilitated by interaction and trust developed through relationship-oriented activities. This is especially true where achievement-oriented team activities are involved, such as golf.

Most companies have no idea how to quantify the value of executive hospitality events, even in simple terms, or how to focus the execution of the event on tangible results. The following details provide more insight into where to find the value and how to describe it.

Objectives

ComCo was concerned that executive hospitality programs and other customer and prospect hospitality events would actually deliver tangible value to the company. To understand the value of those programs, ComCo had to understand:

- How those events influenced and impacted the business decisions of the executives attending the events.
- How to measure the potential value.
- How to state (report) the value.
- How to use the results to improve value the next time.

The ROI studies focused on the following:

- Assess the impact of executive participation at the event on the relationship and level of business with ComCo.
- Determine the types and mix of customer executive activities that are most effective for the future.
- Assess the guest executives' level of satisfaction with the event, gain their suggestions regarding the event, and identify continuous improvement targets for this and similar events in the future.

Evaluation Methodology

The event ROI consultants (Constellation Communication Corporation, hereinafter "the consultants") developed a qualitative survey addressing the study objectives. The survey was implemented through a voluntary telephone interview with executives who attended the Classic. Twenty-two out of forty-one participants, approximately 54%, were surveyed. Some executives were not reachable in the period allotted for the study. Others were interviewed for previous events and were not repeated. Those participants' intentions and value were assessed based upon prior feedback. All participants were included in the account profiling and valuation data. The study and report were a combination of quantitative and qualitative findings, and the report highlighted the qualitative nature of some of the findings and conclusions.

Data Collection and Data Analysis

The consultants designed an account profile format that would provide the information necessary to value the event. The ComCo Event Marketing staff developed the account profiles on each executive and his company for use in final selection of participants and the briefing of ComCo event personnel. The profile information included the dollar amounts of current billed revenue and the amounts of pending revenue opportunities, providing the basis for the revenue-related analysis in the study. The consultant staff observed the event activities and, after the event, conducted the executive interviews by telephone.

Responses to survey questions were reported verbatim, or in close paraphrase, of the actual responses. The consultants made observations regarding those responses and provided interpretive comments in clearly-marked sections immediately following the tables of actual responses. In some cases, the consultants assessed the responses and assigned them to categories, making it easier to interpret the overall findings. The consultants provided a series of conclusions and recommendations in the final section of the report, based upon the qualitative and quantitative analysis.

Follow-up investigations with account teams were conducted at year's end to determine results against the forecasts used in the invitation and profiling process.

Evaluation Results

The following is derived from the executive summary of the report for the 2006 event.

The event created an opportunity for ComCo executives and account teams to directly influence the retention of approximately $2.02 billion in contracted revenue and influence the sale of $367.5 million in identified near-term revenue opportunities for the company. (For example, near term was defined as before year end for an event held in April, and within one year for an event held in October.) The combined total of retainable and potential revenue at this event, accessible through customer executives was more than $2.7 billion. The average addressable ComCo revenue per guest was more than $65.85 million. The event cost per dollar of total revenue represented by the executives in attendance was just over 1.6/100 of a cent per revenue dollar ($0.0001625/1) or 0.016%.

This study demonstrates the tangible impact on both retention of current revenue and probability of sale for pending opportunities through interaction with the executives represented at the event. The targeting and invitation process for the Classic was effective, with 95% of the guests having pending, near-term proposals. Pending proposals for this group of executives represented an average increase of 15.6% over the current billed revenue amounts. Many of the pending proposals represented significant increases in total revenue for ComCo, as much as 800+ percent for one account. Nine of the executives represented accounts for which the pending revenue increase was in excess of 100% of the current billed revenue. Twenty-six executives, or approximately 64%, represented accounts for which the pending revenue increase was 25% or more of the current billed revenue. See Table 1 for an example of how this data is reported.

Table 1. An Example Analysis Sheet Correlating Qualitative and Quantitative Findings

Investment in Retention and Revenue Development

Definitely Impacts the Level of Business

Name	Company	Impact on Business (D)efinite, (R)einforces Business Relationship, (G)enerally Positive, (N)eutral, (No)ne	Current Billed Revenue	Pending Business	Proposed Revenue	Proposed Revenue as % of Current Billed Revenue
Walker, Walter	American National Bank	D - It raises the level of trustl It s important in business to trust who you are dealing with, especially when things go wrong you can trust they will be taken care of accurately and thirgs dc go wrong	$553,200,000	Yes	$22,850,000	4.1%
Manville, Gregory	Cola Enterprises, Inc.	D - Had a direct effect on it.	$67,200,000	Yes	$12,000,000	17.9%
Walker, Harry	IMC GAMMANET	D - Definitely enhances the ability to negotiate whatever deal it is you are working on/with due to the enhancement of the relationship that you have built with executives.	$806,000,000	Yes	$32,780,000	3.9%
Simpson, John	Medical Services of America, Inc.	D - Gives sense of who, people are, in charge. Learn they are completent and know if I want to maintain or grow business with them in the future. Really important to me	$2,168,712	Yes	$19,400,000	818%
Domaway, Don	Greenmont Health System/CIO	D - Increases business, finds solutions, meeting with others who share the same products anc concerns.	$13,000,000	Yes	$2,000,000	15.38%

Every executive interviewed cited a business purpose as the basis for his or her participation. A common finding among three consecutive event surveys was guest executives prefer, if not require, a legitimate business reason for attending events of this type. They felt the structure of the account team and executive interactions built into the event activities were productive, made the investment of time in the event productive, and most importantly, deemed it justifiable to their companies and investors.

A customer executive marketing event such as the Classic is rarely the only factor in a company's decision to buy or continue doing business with ComCo. However, this event places top ComCo executive management and account management in direct, personal association with top executives of key customer organizations. The customer executives detailed, through their answers presented in this report, what was accomplished as a result of this event. The findings of this study support the conclusion that the event had definite impact on ComCo profitability. A representative comment from a top-tier account executive:

"We already have a lot of eggs in the basket with ComCo. Keeping this support secure is important to us. The bulk of our business is with ComCo. At the end of the day, price and performance matter the most. ComCo needs to know what is required by us and we need commitments from the top. These events help tip the scale as far as decision making goes."

This study shows the Classic was a superior event by comparison to the other events these executives were invited to attend. The satisfaction level with the event among the executives surveyed was 100%. These customer executives attend only one to three events of this type each year and competition for their participation is keen. The accomplishments cited by the customer executives attending the event continued to focus on meeting and interacting with ComCo executives and account teams, and increased confidence in their business relationship, with ComCo as a direct result of the interaction.

The event delivered approximately $780,000 in equivalent value of sales support and CRM impact, per dollar expended. This value estimate was based upon the conservative assumption that the event represented only 1/100 (1%) of the amount ComCo account teams expend annually in retention efforts (CRM) and for new revenue development (sales) with these accounts represented at the event.

The ComCo Event Marketing team delivered this event at a lower cost per participant, compared to 2005. The cost per executive dropped to $8,717 for 2006, compared to $11,975 for 2005. As a result, the estimated payback or benefits/costs ratio on this event increased from $1.81/$1 in 2005 to $2.97/$1 in 2006 when all benefits of the event (profit on estimated net sales impact, cost savings, and promotion value) were divided by the event's budget.

Communication Strategy

In addition to equipping the corporate PR team with data to justify executive hospitality events, these findings were used to help determine the "hurdle" requirements for inviting future accounts to the top level Pro-AM, and for a lower tier Pro-AM. The results were shared with the business development teams, who participated in tracking and reporting associated results. Reported results were compared to the forecast developed before and refined after the event. The account profiles were used to prepare briefing packages for the executives and account team members at the event.

Lessons Learned

Executive hospitality events deliver real value. However, most companies do not have a yardstick for determining who to invite to expensive events and often, when scrutinized, the expense of entertaining some guests exceeds their profit value to the host. Invitations are often based upon "the good old boy" network and not on value.

Most companies do not have an effective way to predict or determine value for a hospitality event. When a value-focused approach is implemented, the value of the guest list increases dramatically.

Guest executives are under more pressure to demonstrate a business reason for participating in these events. These guests expect to accomplish business-related objectives at hospitality events.

Simple approaches to determining and reporting value work, primarily because they are easily understood and the need for supporting data is so great. Complex approaches are more difficult to produce and can be prone to communication failure.

Recommendations and Use of Results

The invitation processes for these companies, and therefore the value of the events, were radically modified over the course of these evaluations. Account profiling became a requirement for nomination for an event invitation. All events, including hospitality "Sky Boxes" at sports venues, received the same level of investigation.

Appropriate levels of spending on these and other types of events can be determined using the same techniques. Companies are often over-spending or under-spending on these events.

Performance information is the best tool for convincing the company to invite guests to events based upon potential and not simply prior relationships.

Resources

Client executive hospitality event evaluations.
Constellation Communication Corp. Return on Investment in Events ROI Model and Database
Constellation Event Critical Success Factors and Communication Action Value Chain models

Questions for Discussion

1. As a ComCo shareholder, would you have been satisfied with the data in this study about the event ROI?
2. Can executive hospitality events be measured? Should they?
3. Are additional data categories and information needed to convince you of the success of this event? If so, what are they?
4. Is the measurement, as presented here, quantitative enough to make decisions about future events?
5. Should the total potential revenue or the total potential profit be used for the value calculations?

About the Author

Ed Jones is President of Constellation Communication Corporation. His experience is in equal parts finance, marketing, sales, and creative. His consulting firm researches and analyzes all types of communications projects and events. It provides guidance for choosing the best mix and appropriate investment in events to reach marketing goals. Clients include companies, show and event organizers, and associations.

Mr. Jones is a well-known speaker and author on topics of interest to meetings and events professionals. He co-authored *How to Measure the Value of Trade Shows* and *How to Measure the Value of Events,* required for Certified Trade Show Manager certification. He can be reached at edjones@constellationcc.com or at 770.391.0015.

Editor's Notes

This case study shows that the current and potential revenue values of companies represented at an executive hospitality event can be developed through careful planning and assistance from the sales and business development department. This data is particularly useful in determining who should be invited to these types of events, and why.

It is important to determine the event's actual return on investment to see how the forecasted and actual results compared and to link the success to the event. Often, a timely and complete picture of an event's monetary benefits are difficult to ascertain due to lack of data and a lengthy sales cycle.

Case Study
Measuring the ROI in the Annual Agents Conference Neighborhood Insurance Company

By Monica Myhill, CMP, President, Meeting Returns

This case was prepared to serve as a basis for discussion rather than an illustration of either effective or ineffective administrative and management practices. All names, dates, places, and organizations have been disguised at the request of the author or organization.

Abstract

Setting clear and measurable meeting objectives is critical to the design of a successful and results-based meeting that can be evaluated at the ROI level. In the case of Neighborhood Insurance Company, a needs assessment was conducted to create objectives and define the content for its annual agents conference. These objectives were then used as the basis for the evaluation plan used to measure the conference. This case study demonstrates how the Phillips ROI Methodology can be applied to a sales conference.

Background

Neighborhood Insurance Company (NIC) operates in most major communities in the Midwestern United States, offering life, homeowners, and automobile insurance to consumers. NIC does not serve corporate clients or offer health insurance. NIC operates through local agents who provide service and support to policyholders.

Although the company conducts some national advertising and promotion, each agent has a budget for local advertising. However, agents obtain much of their business through customer referrals, following up on contacts, and presenting the business case for switching insurance providers to NIC. Therefore, much of the hard work to grow the business is through the agents' sales efforts and reputation in their own community.

Each year, NIC conducts an annual agents conference. The purpose is to obtain updates on the company, network with other agents, review changes in products and processes, and most important, develop and refine marketing and business development tools and processes. Approximately 60% of the 1,000 agents, the company's CEO, and senior staff attend. The agents conference and attendance expenses are entirely paid from each agent's advertising and promotion budget. Because of this, some agents do not attend, choosing to spend their advertising money in other ways.

Why ROI?

From the perspective of top management, this is one of the most important company meetings. However, due to increased costs of conducting the meeting, the CEO questioned the value of this conference in its present form. Among other things, the CEO wanted to know if it would be more cost effective to conduct the meeting in some other format, such as a series of live teleconferences, or perhaps the meeting could be eliminated altogether in favor of more direct communications and visits by regional executives. As a starting point, the CEO wanted to know the value that NIC received from this conference, essentially addressing this question: What impact does this meeting have on NIC's revenue, market share, profits, and other important measures? Does the monetary value offset the costs?

Evaluation Methodology

The Phillips ROI Methodology was adopted as the evaluation method to be used. This approach was expected to produce six types of data: reaction and satisfaction, learning, application and implementation, business impact, ROI, and intangible measures.

This methodology was selected based on its proven and documented use. Key members of the meetings and events team attended five-day certification workshops on this methodology before conducting the impact study.

Evaluation Planning

To better understand the desired impact of the conference, the Director of Meetings and Events facilitated a meeting with the CEO and other senior executives to determine their expectations from the conference and desired impact measures, such as revenue, market share, profits, efficiencies, and customer satisfaction. They explored the specific actions expected of the agents when they returned to work after the conference, detailing as much as possible the steps, tasks, contacts, follow-up, and even behavior changes expected. This became difficult for the executives because they had not thought through those issues clearly.

Based on the above information, the Director of Meetings and Events then probed for specific learning that should take place, contacts that should be made and desired takeaways from the meeting. This issue became even more difficult for executives to discuss. They deferred to others who might be able to provide these answers.

Finally, details about the expected reaction from the agents were clarified. These included whether the conference would be perceived as useful and/or valuable, how the agents should feel when they leave, whether the conference would be important to the agents' success, and whether the agents would be motivated at the end of the conference. Based on these discussions, the desired agent reactions to the conference were identified.

The Director of Meetings and Events also met with some regional managers and agents to clarify some of these issues, their conference expectations, their challenges, and their annual performance goals. Their feedback, along with that of the executives, was invaluable in determining the objectives of the meeting.

Meeting Objectives

Specific and measurable objectives at each level of measurement were created and agreed upon by all key meeting stakeholders.

Reaction Objectives

After attending this conference, attendees will perceive it to be:
- Organized and efficient
- Conducted by effective speakers
- Valuable for business development
- Important to their success
- Motivating
- Challenging
- An excellent use of their time
- Full of new information
- Action-oriented—they intend to use the material

Learning Objectives

At the end of the conference, attendees should be able to:
- Identify the five steps of the business development strategy
- Develop a business development plan
- Select the best community service organization to join for business development
- Explain the changes in three products
- Identify the five most effective ways to turn a contact into a sale
- Identify at least five agents to call for suggestions and advice

Application Objectives

Within six months of the conference, each attendee should:

- Implement a business development plan
- Implement at least two new business development strategies
- Contact at least ten percent of the current customer base to offer them the new changes in auto insurance coverage
- Make a random five percent customer service check with current clients
- Follow-up with at least three agents to discuss successes, concerns, or issues
- Join at least one additional community service group targeted for a potential customer base
- Use selling skills to turn a contact into a sale

Impact Objectives

Six months following the conference, the following should occur:
- New policies for automobile insurance should increase 10%
- Revenue of all other products should increase 5%
- New customers should increase by 5%
- Market share should increase
- Customer Satisfaction

ROI Objective

Within one year of the conference, a 20% return on the investment in the conference should be achieved.

Conference Marketing and Pre-Work

A marketing brochure was sent out to all attendees to promote the conference and link the conference directly to NIC's business drivers. The brochure contained details on the agenda, the meeting objectives, speakers, session topics, issues to be addressed, and expectations from attendance. After reviewing this conference material, each agent was asked to pick two or more business impact measures prior to the conference that they could improve based on the conference content. It was hoped that attendees would attempt to improve all five measures listed in the business impact objectives.

Data Collection and Data Analysis

Figure 1 shows the Data Collection Plan that identifies objectives at each level of measurement, the data collection method used, the data sources, the timing of data collection, and who within NIC was responsible for data collection. Questionnaires were used to collect feedback and data from the conference attendees.

The end-of-conference questionnaire (shown in Figure 2), focusing on Level 1 and 2 measures, contained sixteen feedback items, with an open-ended question for improvement recommendations. A Web link to the follow-up questionnaire (shown in Figure 3) was emailed to the agents six months after the conference. This timeframe was selected because six months was needed for the business impact results to materialize. This questionnaire explored application of conference content, chain of impact data, barriers to application, enablers to application, and suggestions for improvement.

A variety of techniques were used to increase response rates to the questionnaires. One of the most important techniques was a review of the questionnaires with attendees—question by question—at the end of the conference. This allowed NIC to clarify the issues, create expectations, and gain commitment to provide data. The following additional techniques were used to increase response rates:

- Marketing packet cover letter, which mentioned the evaluation study, signed by the CEO
- Advance communication about the questionnaires
- Reason for evaluation and questionnaires communicated
- Info on who would see the results and how the results would be used
- Reminder to attendees that a follow-up questionnaire was coming
- Response deadline communicated
- Emphasis on anonymous and confidential responses
- Two follow-up reminders sent to non-respondents using a different medium other than email
- Giveaway item enclosed with the questionnaire

Figure 1. Completed Data Collection Plan

		Data Collection Plan				
Level	Objective(s)	Measures/Data	Data Collection Method	Data Sources	Timing	Responsibilities
1	**Reaction/Satisfaction** • Effective speakers • Valuable for business development • Organized and efficient • Important to attendees' success • Motivating • Challenging • Excellent use of time • New information • Action oriented	4 out of 5 on a 5 point scale	Questionnaire	Attendees /Agents	During General Session at End of Conference	Meetings Department
2	**Learning** • Identify the five steps of the business development strategy. • Develop a business development plan. • Select the best community service organization to join for business development. • Explain the changes in three products. • Identify the five most effective ways to turn a contact into a sale. • Identify at least five agents to call for suggestions and advice.	4 out of 5 on a 5 point scale	Questionnaire	Attendees/ /Agents	During General Session at End of Conference	Meetings Department

#						
3	**Application/Implementation** • Implement a business development plan. • Use two new business development strategies. • Contact at least 10% of the current customer base to offer new changes in auto insurance coverage. • Make a random 5% customer service check with current clients. • Follow-up with at least three agents to discuss successes, concerns, or issues. • Join at least one additional community service group targeted for a potential customer base. • Use selling skills.	4 out of 5 on a 5 point scale	Questionnaire	Attendees/ /Agents	6 months following conference	Meetings Department
4	**Business Impact** • New policies for automobile insurance • Revenue (excluding auto and new customers) • Increase in new customers	• 10% increase in new auto policies • 5% increase in revenue of all other products • 5% increase in completely new customers	Questionnaire	Attendees/ Agents	6 months following conference	Meetings Department
5	**ROI** • Achieve a 20% ROI					

Figure 2. End of Conference Questionnaire

END OF CONFERENCE QUESTIONNAIRE

Please take a few minutes to provide the following information. This feedback will be helpful to understand the value of this conference and for planning future conferences. Please indicate your level of agreement/disagreement with each of the following:

REACTION

	Strongly Disagree			Strongly Agree		
	1	2	3	4	5	n/a
1. The meeting was organized and efficient.	O	O	O	O	O	O
2. The speakers were effective.	O	O	O	O	O	O
3. The meeting was valuable for business development.	O	O	O	O	O	O
4. The meeting content was important to my success.	O	O	O	O	O	O
5. The meeting was motivating.	O	O	O	O	O	O
6. The meeting was challenging.	O	O	O	O	O	O
7. The meeting contained new information.	O	O	O	O	O	O
8. The meeting represented an excellent use of my time.	O	O	O	O	O	O
9. I will use the material from this conference.	O	O	O	O	O	O
10. I can identify the five steps for business development strategy.	O	O	O	O	O	O
11. I can develop a business development plan.	O	O	O	O	O	O
12. I can select the best community service group to join for business development.	O	O	O	O	O	O
13. I can explain the changes in products.	O	O	O	O	O	O
14. I can identify the five most effective ways to turn a contact into a sale.	O	O	O	O	O	O
15. I can identify at least five agents to call for suggestions and advice.	O	O	O	O	O	O
16. What suggestions do you have for improving this conference?						

Figure 3. Follow-Up Questionnaire

FOLLOW UP QUESTIONNAIRE

Our records indicate that you participated in the NIC Annual Agents Conference. Your participation in this follow-up survey is important to the continuous improvement of the conference. Completion of this survey may take 45 to 60 minutes. Thank you in advance for your input.

APPLICATION

	Strongly Disagree				Strongly Agree	
	1	2	3	4	5	n/a
1. I implemented the business development plan.	O	O	O	O	O	O
2. I applied at least two new business development strategies.	O	O	O	O	O	O
3. I contacted at least 10% of current customers to offer new changes in auto insurance coverage.	O	O	O	O	O	O
4. I made a random 5% customer service check for existing clients.	O	O	O	O	O	O
5. I followed-up with at least three agents to discuss successes, concerns, or issues.	O	O	O	O	O	O
6. I joined at least one additional community service group targeted to our potential customer base.	O	O	O	O	O	O
7. I have used selling skills to turn a contact into a sale.	O	O	O	O	O	O

BARRIERS/ENABLERS TO APPLICATION

8. Which of the following deterred or prevented you from applying the concepts and materials from the conference? (Check all that apply.)
   - ☐ no opportunity to use the material
   - ☐ lack of support from regional managers
   - ☐ not enough time
   - ☐ insufficient knowledge and understanding
   - ☐ lack of confidence to do it
   - ☐ lack of resources
   - ☐ other

9. Which of the following supported you in applying the concepts and materials? (Check all that apply.)
   - ☐ tools and templates provided
   - ☐ my regional manager
   - ☐ support from colleagues and peers
   - ☐ disciplined approach
   - ☐ confidence to apply the materials
   - ☐ support from marketing
   - ☐ other

10. If you selected "other" above, please describe here.
    Barriers: Enablers:

RESULTS – 1st Measure

11. Which of the following measures were you able to most improve?
    - ☐ Increase in new policies for automobile insurance.
    - ☐ Increase revenue for all other products.
    - ☐ Increase new customers.

☐ Improve market share.
☐ Improve customer satisfaction.

12. What is this measure's single unit of value?

_____

_____

13. For this measure, what is the monetary value of improvement for one unit of this measure?

_____

_____

14. Please state your basis for the value of the unit of improvement you indicated above. If it is an estimate, show details.

_____

_____

15. How much has this measure improved since the conference?

_____

_____

16. Indicate the frequency base for the improvement listed above (question 15).
    ☐ daily   ☐ weekly   ☐ monthly   ☐ quarterly

RETURN ON INVESTMENT – 1st Measure

17. What is the annual value of improvement in the measure you selected above? Multiply the increase (question 15) by the frequency (question 16) times the unit of value (question 13).

_____

18. List the other factors that could have influenced these results.

_____

19. Recognizing that the other factors could have influenced this annual value of improvement, please estimate the percent of improvement that is attributable (i.e. isolated) to the conference. Express as a percentage out of 100%.
_____%

20. What confidence do you place in the estimates you have provided in the questions above? A 0% is no confidence; a 100% is certainty.
_____%

RESULTS – 2nd Measure

21. Which of the following measures was your second most improved and selected measure?
☐ Increase in new policies for automobile insurance.
☐ Increase revenue for all other products.
☐ Increase new customers.
☐ Improve market share.
☐ Improve customer satisfaction

22. What is this measure's single unit of value?

_____

_____

23. For this measure, what is the monetary value of improvement for one unit of this measure?

_____
_____

24. Please state your basis for the value of the unit of improvement you indicated above. If it is an estimate, show details.

_____
_____

25. How much has this measure improved since the conference?

_____
_____

26. Indicate the frequency base for the improvement listed above (question 25).

☐ daily ☐ weekly ☐ monthly ☐ quarterly

RETURN ON INVESTMENT – 2nd Measure

27. What is the annual value of improvement in the measure you selected above? Multiply the increase (question 25) by the frequency (question 26) times the unit of value (question 22).

_____
_____

28. List the other factors that could have influenced these results.

_____
_____

29. Recognizing that the other factors could have influenced this annual value of improvement, please estimate the percent of improvement that is attributable (i.e. isolated) to the conference. Express as a percentage out of 100%.

_____%

30. What confidence do you place in the estimates you have provided in the questions above? A 0% is no confidence; a 100% is certainty.

_____%

OVERALL

31. Indicate the extent to which you think this conference had a positive influence on the following business measures in your agency. Please check the appropriate response beside each measure.

Business Measure	Not Applicable	Applies but no	Some Influence	Moderate Influence	Significant Influence	Very Significant Influence
Customer Satisfaction	○	○	○	○	○	○
Market Share	○	○	○	○	○	○
Teamwork	○	○	○	○	○	○
Communication	○	○	○	○	○	○
Agent Job Satisfaction	○	○	○	○	○	○
Other	○	○	○	○	○	○

32. What other benefits have been realized from this conference?

_____
_____

ROI Analysis Plan

Figure 4 shows the completed ROI Analysis Plan, which details the business measures converted to monetary value, methods used to isolate the impact of the conference, anticipated meeting costs, expected intangible benefits, communication targets for the results and issues that could affect the study.

Isolation Method

NIC considered using a control group to isolate the impact of the conference. However, it was deemed too difficult because all agents were invited. Given this factor, it was determined that the attending agents were the most credible source of data about how they had driven their business and would be able to isolate the impact of the conference on their improvement.

Converting Data to Monetary Value

Converting measures to a monetary value was relatively easy because most monetary values were readily available. Agent sales reports contained information on their generated revenues from new auto policies, revenues from all other types of products, as well as number of new customers. Agents were aware of the 30% profit margin established by NIC and the standard lifetime profit value for new customers, but the value varied according to the type of new customer. However, agents were asked to contact the actuarial department (considered to be the experts) to confirm these standard values.

Figure 4. ROI Analysis Plan

ROI Analysis Plan

Data Items (Usually Level 4)	Methods for Isolating the Effects of the Meeting	Methods of Converting Data to Monetary Values	Cost Categories	Intangible Benefits	Communication Targets for Final Report	Other Influences/ Issues During Application	Comments
New policies for auto insurance coverage	Participant estimate	Standard value	• Needs assessment • Conference development • Planning • Speaker fees and expenses • Conference materials • Coordination • Travel, food and beverages • Meeting space rental • Agent salaries & benefits - for time away from work • Manager salaries & benefits - for time involved in conference • CLARIFY • Cost of overhead (allocated) • Evaluation	• Increase in customer satisfaction • Increase in market share • Increase in agent job satisfaction • Improved teamwork • Improved communicaton	• Agents • Senior executives • Regional managers • Meetings and marketing departments • Prospective attendees	Several process improvement initiatives are on-going during this conference time frame.	• Must gain commitment from attendees to provide data. • A high response rate is needed.
Revenue on all products except for auto insurance	Participant estimate	Standard value					
New customers	Participant estimate	• Standard value • Expert input					

Results: Reaction and Learning

Eighty-six percent of attending agents returned a completed an end-of-conference questionnaire during a general session held at the end of the conference. This questionnaire covered attendee's feedback on Level 1 and 2 indicators. Table 1 shows the attendee reaction and satisfaction level from the end-of-conference questionnaire. Each of the reaction measures exceeded the goal of 4.0, except for the issue about the amount of new information, which was slightly less than the desired level.

Table 1. Reaction Data from Attendees

ISSUE	RATING*
Organization	4.3
Speakers	4.1
Worthwhile Investment	4.1
Good Use of My Time	4.6
Motivating	4.3
Challenging	4.2
Important to My Success	4.2
Provided Me with New Information	3.9
Intend to Use Material	4.7

*Rating scale: 1 = Strongly Disagree; 5 = Strongly Agree

As shown in Table 2, the learning measures met or exceeded the 4.0 goal and expectations in terms of the level of new skills and knowledge gained and confidence in using them.

Table 2. Learning Data from Attendees

ISSUE	RATING*
Five Steps of Business Development Strategy	4.6
Develop a Business Development Plan	4.3
Select Community Service Group	4.1
Changes in Products	4.7
Five Ways to Turn Contact into Sale	4.3
Know At Least Five Agents to Call for Suggestions	4.1

*Rating Scale: 1 = Strongly Disagree; 5 = Strongly Agree

Results: Application and Implementation

Seventy-four percent of attendees completed the on-line, follow-up questionnaire. This questionnaire covered Levels 3, 4, and 5 feedback.

Table 3 shows that application exceeded expectations on two items but fell short of the expectations on the other five. Some agents had only partially implemented the business development plan, applied business development strategies, made customer service calls, and joined community service groups. While five of the issues fell just short of the 4.0 target, the applications were deemed successful based on the sheer number of responses.

Table 3. Application Data from Attendees

ISSUE	RATING*
Implemented Business Development Plan	3.7
Applied at Least Two Business Development Strategies	3.8
Contacted at Least 10% of Customers for Auto Insurance	3.9
Conducted Random 5% Customer Service Check	3.6
Follow up with at Least Three Agents	4.3
Joined at Least One Community Service Group	3.8
Used Selling Skills	4.3

*Rating Scale: 1 = Lowest; 5 = Highest

The barriers were minimal in terms of application with "not enough time" and "lack of resources" capturing the top two, as expected. The remaining top three barriers were almost insignificant. However, 11% indicated that a lack of support from regional managers was a concern, because regional manager support was expected to be quite high. This point was validated in Table 4, where 59% of agents said regional manager support was an enabler for success. Other strong enablers were "tools and templates" and "following a disciplined approach" rounding out the top three.

Table 4. Top 5 Barriers and Enablers Identified by Agents

BARRIERS	FREQUENCY
Not Enough Time	34%
Lack of Resources	23%
Insufficient Knowledge and Understanding	16%
Lack of Support from Regional Managers	11%
Lack of Confidence to Apply Learning	6%

ENABLERS	FREQUENCY
Regional Manager Support	59%
Tools and Templates	53%
Disciplined Approach	39%
Support from Colleagues and Peers	23%
Support from Marketing	18%

Level 4: Business Impact

Table 5 shows the business impact data for the business measures that could be converted to monetary values: new auto policies, revenue of all products (excluding new auto policies and new customers), and new customers. The total number of new auto policies and new customers is illustrated along with the annual value of these measures. Only the annual value is shown for revenue from all products (except for auto insurance). Only the first year value was used for the new auto policy and other product revenue, but a lifetime value was used for new customers.

Table 5. Business Impact

Business Measure	Total Number	Annual Value	Profit (30%)	Impact of Conference on Business Measure	Average Number of Other Factors	Average Confidence Level	Adjusted Value
New Auto Policies	2,465	$3,056,600 Revenue	$916,980 Profit	32%	2.3	82%	$240,616
Revenue - All Products (excluding new auto and new customers)	N/A	$8,955,320 Revenue	$2,686,596 Profit	33%	3.1	86%	$762,456
New Customers	4,068	$6,427,440	$6,427,440	22%	3.7	77%	$1,088,808
						Total	$2,091,880

A 30% operating (regional level) profit margin was used to calculate NIC's profit from these business measures. The column titled "Impact of Conference on Business Measure" shows the average of all respondent answers to questions involving percent of improvement that is attributable (i.e., isolated) to the conference. The average number of other identified factors that have influenced these results is shown next. The column titled "Average Confidence" illustrates the average of responses to the question regarding confidence placed on the estimates provided. Here is how the conservative "Adjusted Value" was calculated:

$$\text{Profit of Business Measure} \quad X \quad \text{Impact of Conference on Business Measure} \quad X \quad \text{Average Confidence Level} \quad = \quad \text{Adjusted Value}$$

The business impact showed some surprises for the group. The total number of new automobile policies was captured and extrapolated for a full year yielding 2,465 new policies. On average, the standard first-year revenue value for an automobile policy was $1,240. Therefore, an annual revenue value of $3,056,600 was obtained. Using a 30% profit margin, this yielded a $916,980 profit. When adjustments were made for the conference's percentage of impact and the average confidence level, the conference contributed $240,616.

Revenue from all products, except for auto polices, was impressive. An annual total of $8,955,320 was calculated by taking the revenues generated from the time of the conference to the follow-up period six months later and annualizing this amount. The revenue from new auto policies and new customers was excluded to avoid overlap between measures. Applying the profit margin, percentage of conference impact, and average confidence level, the revenue from all products, except auto policies, yielded $762,476.

For every new customer obtained, there was a monetary life-time value of $1,580 in profit. The number of new customers was impressive, representing 4,068 when annualized, for a $6,427,440 value. Applying the various adjustments yielded the total of $1,088,808.

When the adjusted value of all business measures were combined, the conference resulted in $2,091,880 in meeting benefits. While this does seem substantial, it is necessary to compare the meeting benefits with the fully-loaded costs of the conference to get a true picture of the ROI.

Costs

The total cost of the conference, using a fully-loaded analysis, is shown in Table 6. The needs assessment was estimated at $1,500 and represented the effort to ensure that business needs were fully aligned with the conference. Development of conference materials was estimated to be $2,000, and the conference planning costs were $9,000. The speaker fees and expenses were $24,000, considered low because most of the speakers were internal to NIC. Travel fees were by far the largest with travel, meals, and lodging totaling $1,478 per participant. Coordination expenses covered the overall registration and coordination of the conference with part of the meeting planning expenses included. Hotel charges were $169,500. The attendees' salaries were based on individuals missing an average of one-and-one-half days of work. (Since the conference was on Friday, Saturday, and Sunday, the consensus was that approximately one-and-one-half days of time were actually lost due to the conference. Each attendee's salary was calculated at $300 per day; therefore, one-and-one-half days were calculated at $450 per participant. The overhead allocated was estimated to be $3,000 and the ROI evaluation $5,000. This yielded a total of $1,369,745 in fully-loaded costs of the conference.

Table 6. Fully-Loaded Costs

Conference Cost Summary
(565 Attendees)

Cost of Item	Cost
Needs Assessment	$1,500
Conference Development	$2,000
Planning	$9,000
Speaker Fee/Expenses	$24,000
Conference Materials ($25/participant)	$14,125
Travel, Meals, and Lodging ($1,478/participant)	$835,070
Coordination	$52,300
Hotel Charges	$169,500
Attendees Salaries (Plus Benefits) for Time ($450/Participant)	$254,250
Overhead (Allocated)	$3,000
ROI Evaluation	$5,000
TOTAL:	$1,369,745

Intangible Benefits

Table 7 lists the intangible benefits taken directly from the follow-up questionnaire. Agents were asked to indicate the degree to which this conference influenced each measure listed on the questionnaire. The measures that obtained at least an average of 3 or more on a 5-point scale are listed (in the order of ranking), after a 5% threshold. The attendees indicated several other intangible measures, but none were listed unless at least 5% listed them—the requirement to be included on the list.

Table 7. Intangible Benefits

Intangibles	Percent Indicating
Increased Customer Satisfaction	77%
Increased Market Share	64%
Improved Teamwork	31%
Improved Communication	13%
Increased Agent Job Satisfaction	5%

Analysis

The benefits/costs ratio (BCR) is calculated as follows:

$$\text{BCR} = \frac{\text{Total Benefits}}{\text{Total Costs}} = \frac{\$2,091,880}{\$1,369,745} = 1.53$$

Therefore, for every dollar spent by NIC for this conference, $1.53 was returned. The return on investment is calculated as follows:

$$\text{ROI} = \frac{\text{Meeting Benefits} - \text{Meeting Costs}}{\text{Meeting Costs}} = \frac{\$2,091,880 - \$1,369,745}{\$1,369,745} = 53\%$$

The NIC Annual Agents Conference generated a 53% return on investment.

Credibility of Results

The data were perceived to be credible by both the meetings and events staff and senior management. Credibility rested on eight major issues:

1. The information for the analysis was provided directly from the agents. The agents had no reason to be biased in their input.
2. The data was provided by the agents but based on company reports and standard values. Since the data could be audited, it was unlikely that the agents would be inaccurate in their reporting.
3. The data collection process was conservative, with the assumption that an unresponsive individual had realized no improvement. This concept—no data, no improvement—was ultra-conservative in the data collection.
4. The meetings and events staff did not assign complete credit for results to this conference. The agents isolated a portion of the data that should be credited directly to this conference.
5. The data were adjusted for the potential error of the estimate, because estimates were used to isolate the effects of the conference on the impact data.
6. The costs of the conference were fully-loaded. All direct and indirect costs were incorporated, including time away from work for the agents and managers.
7. The data represented a balanced profile of success showing a clear chain of impact. Favorable reaction, learning, and application data were presented along with business impact, ROI, and intangibles.

Communication Strategy

To communicate appropriately with the target audiences outlined in the ROI analysis plan, four specific documents were produced. The first report was a detailed impact study showing the approach, assumptions, methodology, and results using all data categories. In addition, barriers and enablers were included in the study, along with conclusions and recommendations. The second report was a six-page executive summary of key points, including a one-page overview of the methodology. The third report was a five-page brief summary of the process and results. The fourth was a two-page general interest article. These documents were communicated and presented to the different stakeholder groups in various manners shown in Table 8.

Table 8. Communication Methods Used

Audience	Document Given
Agents	Brief summary
Regional manager	Brief summary
Senior executives	Executive summary and complete impact study
Meetings and events and marketing team	Complete impact study
All employees	General interest article
Prospective attendees	Brief summary

Because this was the first ROI study conducted within NIC, face-to-face meetings were conducted with the executives. The purpose was to ensure that executives understood the methodology, the conservative assumptions, and each level of data. The barriers, enablers, conclusions, and recommendations were an important part of the conference. In the future, after two or three studies have been conducted, this group will receive only a one-page summary of key data items. A face-to-face meeting was also held with key marketing staff in which the complete impact study was described and used as a learning tool.

Lessons Learned and Recommendations

Conducting the needs assessment with senior executives, regional managers, and agents was valuable and made the creation of measurable conference objectives easier than in past years. However, it might be advantageous to survey all potential attendees electronically in advance of next year's conference to better clarify conference expectations, desires for learning, challenges faced, and feelings about the company and its state of affairs.

Conference attendance was not mandatory. Considering these results, this policy should be re-examined for the next conference. The conference ROI would possibly increase next year if all agents were required to attend.

Asking the pre-registered agents to analyze the conference materials in advance of the meeting and consider how the content could be used was a good way of focusing the conference. Most agents came prepared to learn and network. However, attendees may have more success in applying the knowledge and skills from the conference if a performance contract is created between the agent and regional manager in advance of the conference. Based on the principle of mutual goal setting, a performance contract is a written agreement between the meeting attendee and his/her supervisor. A performance contract is created when the attendee and his/her supervisor agree on and document how the attendee will apply the meeting content on the job and the subsequent business impacts due to application. The performance contract outlines what is to be accomplished, when, and with what results.

Having attendees complete the end-of-conference paper questionnaire during the closing general session resulted in a high response rate. However, it was time consuming for staff to tabulate the results. NIC is exploring the use of audience response equipment for this same purpose at next year's conference.

While this impact study was time consuming, it did result in the necessary, requested information for the CEO and caused key stakeholders to work more closely together toward the success of the conference. The CEO has since requested that the meetings department develop an overall evaluation strategy for NIC's meetings and events.

Use of Results

The results of this impact study were used in the marketing of the following year's conference and were used to refine the content of the next conference. Perceived areas of weakness in the conference's content, skill building workshops, and key messaging will be targeted and strengthened for the next conference.

These results also provide a benchmark for which to compare and contrast other NIC meeting results. Over time, this benchmark data will help NIC eliminate or restructure less than successful meetings and justify increased meeting budgets.

Resources
Phillips, J.J. *Return on Investment in Training and Performance Improvement Programs*, 2nd Edition (Burlington, MA: Butterworth-Heinemann, 2003).

Questions for Discussion
1. Was this conference an ideal target for an ROI study? Please explain.
2. Discuss the ways in which this conference was aligned to the specific needs of the organization.
3. How could the needs assessment be made more comprehensive and useful to the conference development?
4. How could this ROI impact study be made more credible?
5. Could a control group have been used to isolate the effects of the conference? If so, please explain.
6. Could an agent's ROI be developed? Explain.

About the Author

Monica Myhill, CMP, serves as President of Meeting Returns, an organization partnering with the ROI Institute, Inc., to provide return on investment (ROI) impact and evaluation studies for meetings and events through the use of the ROI Methodology developed by Dr. Jack J. Phillips. Ms. Myhill is well known as a meeting industry ROI and evaluation expert, consultant, industry speaker, and author. She has more than twelve years' experience in developing, marketing, managing, and evaluating education programs, conferences, and special events in North America and Europe. She can be contacted by phone at 303.220.1920 or by email at Monica@meetingreturms.com.

Editor's Notes

This case study provides a good example of how a sales training meeting or annual sales conference can be evaluated using the Phillips Methodology through the use of questionnaires. Ideally, Level 4 business impacts from sales and new customers would come directly from the organization's sales records instead of the meeting attendees. Also, post-conference sales and the number of new customers were included as meeting benefits.

Case Study
Measuring ROI in the Better Buildings,
Better Business Conference
Energy Center of Wisconsin

By Marge Anderson, Associate Director, Energy Center of Wisconsin;
Ingo Bensch, Senior Project Manager, Energy Center of Wisconsin; and
Scott Pigg, Senior Project Manager, Energy Center of Wisconsin

Portions of this study were published in the proceedings of the 2006 American Council for an Energy Efficient Economy Summer Study on Energy Efficiency in Buildings and are used with permission of the publisher. This case was prepared to serve as a basis for discussion rather than an illustration of either effective or ineffective administrative and management practices. Names, dates, places, and data may have been disguised at the request of the author or organization.

Abstract

This case study evaluates a conference designed to change the way homes are built, the way they use energy, and to quantify return on investment for public sponsors. A secondary goal of the study was to identify specific practices and technologies that changed because of the conference and to demonstrate to product manufacturers that sponsorships and exhibit funding would drive product sales. With better quantification of the impacts of this training, the Energy Center would be better prepared to secure funding for future training programs.

Background

Since 1999, the Energy Center of Wisconsin has annually produced a technical training conference for cold-climate residential builders. It is currently known as the "Better Buildings: Better Business Conference." Its primary objective is to increase the energy efficiency of homes in Wisconsin. The conference uses many methods to achieve this objective:
- Skills-based, hands-on workshops on a variety of best practices in energy-efficient home construction, including insulation, framing, and ventilation.
- Focused training in building science concepts.
- Prominent integration of the Wisconsin ENERGY STAR™ programs into the curriculum, general session, and trade show as well as satellite events such as a new construction awards banquet.

- Use of instructors who have been specifically trained by the Energy Center in adult learning methodologies.
- A trade show with hands-on technology demonstrations to help attendees understand the energy-efficient technologies work.
- Celebration of leadership in energy efficiency—providing recognition through two awards programs, training showcases, and networking.

Given the conference's design intent, the Energy Center decided in 2005 to study the financial return of the conference from the perspective of two key stakeholders and conference sponsors: Wisconsin's ENERGY STAR programs and the Energy Center. The Energy Center addressed two key research questions.

1. Did the conference have an impact on job-site practices or product selection?
2. Were the recognition and community-building activities creating more motivation to maintain builders' commitment to energy efficiency?

In addition, the Energy Center was interested in learning how attendees viewed conference sponsors in order to better design sponsorship recognition activities and to help sponsors assess the value of the conference as a marketing effort.

The 2005 conference was attended by 632 people—most of whom were builders or contractors. It included a trade show with more than fifty exhibits. Educational programming included two general sessions, as well as more than fifty skills-based breakout sessions. Networking and recognition events included two receptions, two awards ceremonies, and break and meal functions in the exhibit hall.

Rationale for ROI Study

The conference is in the midst of a multi-year transition from 100% public funding to a diverse funding portfolio of sponsorships, registration fees, and exhibits. With information about how the conference influences builders' purchasing decisions, Energy Center staff would be in a better position to demonstrate the value of sponsorship and exhibiting at the conference.

Finally, as a mission-driven organization, the Energy Center was interested in discovering whether this large-scale effort, consuming so many organizational resources, had any real impact on energy savings.

Evaluation Methodology

Evaluators were familiar with Kirkpatrick's four levels of training evaluation, on which the Phillips ROI Methodology is based. One previous evaluation in the industry had conducted a benefits/costs analysis on a training program. Isolation techniques, as used within the Phillips Methodology, are standard data-analysis steps used in energy efficiency evaluations to avoid false attribution of energy savings and to ensure a conservative approach to measuring public benefits. However, an ROI calculation had not been used in the energy efficiency industry for a training event. Evaluators combined standard evaluation practices in a comprehensive manner to identify the ROI for this event. Then, they mapped their process to the Phillips ROI Methodology, which provided an interesting case study in the relationship between typical evaluation practices and the Phillips ROI Methodology. The Phillips ROI Methodology follows fundamental evaluation practices, recognizing the assumptions built into statistical analysis. Therefore, the approach reduces the chance of overstating results through the use of conservative standards. The Phillips ROI Methodology does allow for sampling, but does not encourage practitioners to extrapolate this sample group data to the larger population of an entire meeting attendee group, particularly with regard to business impact results. The Energy Center evaluation staff used the extrapolation technique according to the standards of the evaluation profession and the regulated energy industry.

The Energy Center has a long history of program evaluation. Standard procedures within the organization create a "firewall" between the evaluation staff and the event staff. The two teams work together to ensure that data collection instruments accurately reflect the event objectives. Survey instruments are designed by evaluation staff (all of whom have professional backgrounds in program evaluation, statistical analysis, and survey design). Data collection beyond Level 1 and all analyses are conducted by evaluation staff. Event staff review evaluation results only after analysis is complete and approved by the evaluation staff. This objectivity—and the inability of the event staff to influence evaluation results—is seen by the Energy Center as critical to ensuring quality programming.

Evaluation Planning

Energy Center managers and evaluators perceived the ROI study to present a number of potential risks and rewards. Questions included:

- What if the conference—though popular, with a growing attendance—turns out to be producing no significant energy savings?
- What if evaluators cannot isolate the effects of the conference from other Wisconsin ENERGY STAR activities, thereby appearing to have no impact?
- Can the constrained conference budget absorb the costs of the ROI evaluation?
- Since the energy industry is not accustomed to measuring the results of training, will the sponsors and program administrators believe results, provided they are positive?
- Even if attendees attribute changes in their construction practices to the conference, will this have an impact on their interaction with conference sponsors?

To determine whether the risks would be worth the reward, evaluators and senior conference staff met for an afternoon to conduct a "back of the envelope" analysis. Staff reviewed six years of attendee satisfaction data, anecdotal feedback from attendees about their perceptions of the ENERGY STAR program, the conference, and other industry events, estimates of possible energy practices, and the expected savings. Staff determined that a positive ROI was probable, and that the risk involved was modest.

Meeting Objectives

Reaction Objectives

The conference management team has a number of performance objectives around each discipline (registration, exhibits, sponsorship, sessions, logistics, etc.), but for purposes of this case study the following key indicators are targeted:

- Overall Score: Achieve the Energy Center benchmark score of a 4.3 on a 5-point scale for overall attendee satisfaction.
- Customer Service: Achieve 90% or better agreement with the statement: "conference organizers treated me like a valued customer."
- Session Scores: The majority of session scores should equal or beat the organizational benchmark of 4.3, and less than 10% of sessions should fall below a score of 4.0.

Learning Objectives

With more than 600 attendees, more than fifty individual training sessions, and networking and recognition events, it is impractical to measure individual learning for each session with a pre- and post-test. Since learning had not been measured for this conference in the past, evaluators were most interested to discover what concepts attendees would self-report having learned after the event.

Sponsor recall was also a critical factor in determining whether sponsors would be able to attribute a marketing benefit from supporting the conference. A learning objective was that attendees would be able to recall the names of some of the key platinum sponsors who had made the largest investments in the conference.

Application Objectives

For the Application and Business Results levels, conference organizers and evaluators did not pre-determine a measurable goal as there was no baseline data available. However, organizers have used the 2005 study as a baseline to establish application and results goals for the 2006 and 2007 conferences.

Two key objectives have been at the core of the conference since its inception:

- At the conference, building professionals learn new ideas or practices that they implement when building homes, thereby changing the energy consumption of the homes' future occupants.

- Extensive visibility for the Wisconsin ENERGY STAR programs causes more builders and remodelers to join the programs (or to join them sooner) and to modify their building practices to meet program requirements. This changes the energy consumption by their homes' occupants.

These two objectives were established as the easiest to measure. In addition, the conference organizers operated under these more intangible hypotheses:

- The conference's sessions on business practices causes builders to become more successful on the business side of their operation. More successful builders means more homes in the Wisconsin ENERGY STAR program, thereby producing more energy savings.
- Because so many energy efficient construction practices also improve the safety, durability, and comfort of homes, behavior change around energy leads to an improvement of the housing stock in Wisconsin.

These hypotheses are not necessarily unquantifiable, but the lack of established and accepted practices for quantifying some of these outcomes (in the energy industry), and challenges in attribution, would make it more difficult to produce results that energy evaluators would find defensible.

Impact Objectives

Because the Energy Center and the major conference sponsors are mission-driven organizations, the primary objective for the conference was that homes constructed by the conference attendees save energy.

Secondary business impact objectives for the conference included:

- Sponsors—whether publicly funded programs or product manufacturers—experience an increase in program participation or product sales as a result of changes in building practice by attendees.
- Sponsors increase their investment in the conference, strengthening the conference financial position and diversifying its funding sources.

Evaluators determined that obtaining actual sales results from sponsors and exhibitors would be too difficult—and would be perceived by these conference investors as intrusive. However, evaluators altered the typical attendee satisfaction survey at the end of the conference to include a number of questions about attendee demographics and buying preferences that would be shared with exhibitors and sponsors. This was intended to help them draw their own conclusions about the value of their investments in the conference.

ROI Objective

The Wisconsin ENERGY STAR programs are held to a 1:1 benefits/costs standard (0% ROI or break-even). No specific ROI goal was established for the conference because benefits/costs or ROI measures are not traditionally used or considered as part of the evaluation of an event's success in the energy industry. However, evaluators and conference organizers hoped that the conference would yield results at least equal to the standard for non-event program activities.

Data Collection

Table 1 shows the Data Collection Plan at each level of measurement. On-site questionnaires were used to measure satisfaction and planned action. An overall evaluation questionnaire, as well as separate questionnaires for each breakout session and for exhibitors and instructors, provided a rich source of satisfaction and demographic information.

A carefully-designed survey instrument was used for the post-event data collection. Some thought was given to the delivery method of this survey instrument (e-mail, phone interview, etc.), and evaluators determined that since electronic communication was not preferred by the target audience of builders, a phone survey would produce a higher response rate.

Table 1. Completed Data Collection Plan

Level	Objective(s)	Measures/Data	Data Collection Method	Data Sources	Timing	Responsibilities

1	**Reaction/Satisfaction**
	• Overall score
	  Customer Service
	  Session scores
		4.3 on a 5 point scale for overall satisfaction
		
		90% or better on "treated like a valued customer" question
		
		Majority sessions ≥ 4.3; less than 10% fall below 4.0
			Questionnaire	Attendees	Lunch second day of conference	Conference staff

2	**Learning** • Voluntarily recall a sponsor name	No baseline, no goal.	Post-event interview	Attendees in target demographic	10 months following conference	Evaluation staff
3	**Application/Implementation** • Change a building practice or practices	No baseline, no goal.	Post-event interview	Attendees in target demographic	10 months following conference	Evaluation staff
4	**Impact** • Energy savings • Monetary value of energy savings	No baseline, no goal	Internal experts Questionnaire	Internal Experts Industry Standard Values Attendees	10 months following conference Lunch second day of conference	Evaluation staff Conference staff
5	**ROI** • Achieve a 0% (break even) ROI					

The most important objectives depended upon behavior change by conference attendees. The Energy Center collected data about behavior change by designing and implementing structured interviews with a sample of conference attendees to elicit information about how the conference might have changed the construction practices of attendees.

The sample was drawn from conference registration data. Table 2 shows the estimate of the number of various companies represented at the training, as well as the number of each type included in the sample, and the number of interviews completed. Evaluators sampled randomly from the firms represented, providing they met the following criteria:

• Wisconsin-based organization
• Identifiable type of business (based on conference staff knowledge of the firm or clear identification of the business type from the company's name)
• Telephone number in the conference registration database
• Either a builder, remodeler, subcontractor, or participant in the Wisconsin ENERGY STAR programs

Table 2. Conference Attendance and Sampling

Type of Business	Estimated Number in Attendance	Number Sampled	Number Interviewed
Builders	80	24	16
Remodelers	12	2	4[1]
Subcontractors	40	11	4
Consultants	32	13	7
Other	7	0	3[2]
uncertain type	31	excluded	0
No telephone number	8	excluded	0
out-of-state	38	excluded	0
secondary audience	97	excluded	0

[1] The number of interviews with remodelers exceeds the sampled number of such businesses because some firms categorized as builders were self-identified as remodelers during the interviews.
[2] Evaluators did not classify any businesses as "other," but interview responses caused the classification of three respondents as "other" subsequently.

In all, evaluation staff completed structured telephone interviews with thirty-four out of fifty attending residential building firms sampled. These survey completions represented 20% of all builders who attended, 33% of all remodelers, and 10% of all subcontractors. Results presented here are based primarily on self-reports from twenty-four of the thirty-four attending businesses interviewed (the builders, remodelers, and subcontractors among the interviewees). The analysis was supplemented with helpful background information from day-of-event evaluations, an analysis of conference session content, and review of attendee responses for reasonableness.

The structured interviews—which were guided by a computer-aided telephone interviewing system—first identified the aspects of home construction in which the interviewee was involved (e.g., framing, insulation, HVAC specification). Evaluators created nine residential-construction related categories (plus a miscellaneous category for respondents who might not fit elsewhere on the list). The system then cycled the interview through a series of questions for each of the categories, into which the respondent self-identified. The first question asked, "Did you learn or hear about anything new at the conference that prompted you to do something different in...?" If the respondent answered affirmatively, the system prompted the interviewer to ask "What are you doing differently?" and "How is this different from what you did before?" The open-ended responses were recorded. The system also prompted to find out the fraction of homes to which the stated change applied. (Earlier in the interview the evaluator obtained an estimate of annual homes built or remodeled per year by the respondent's firm.)

The instrument consisted of 175 open- and closed-ended questions. Skip patterns directed respondents only to those questions appropriate for them and included some questions twice with wording differences to better fit different types of respondents. The survey took between five and ten minutes for most respondents to complete.

The survey questions were divided into the following modules:

- **Role in Residential Buildings** – Identified the role the builder plays in the residential construction market, as well as specific aspects of a house the builder "touches" in his everyday work. Responses in this section directed the builder to relevant questions in subsequent sections and omitted irrelevant questions.

- **Conference Basics** – Determined how long this builder had been attending this conference, reason for attendance, sponsor recall and importance, participation in sponsoring programs, and whether the conference affected the builder's participation in the Wisconsin ENERGY STAR program. The role of the conference helped in determining the likelihood that self-reported behavior change was actually attributable to the conference.

- **Specific Learning and Behavior Change** – Unaided recall of things learned at this year's conference and implemented as a result, followed by semi-aided questions based on each aspect of a house that the builder "touches" in the course of normal work. Follow-up questions addressed the share of projects for which the builder follows any new process and how this process differs from what was done previously. These responses formed the starting point for energy impact estimates.

- *General Conference Influence* – Rating of programs' (for participants) and conference's influence on the comfort, safety, durability, and energy efficiency of the homes the builder "touches;" follow-up question on how the conference contributed to energy efficiency if rated highly, but not yet addressed in prior responses. This sequence of questions provided one more opportunity to identify behavior change not mentioned earlier, as well as data needed to test the credibility of builder's attribution of behavior change to the conference. (If respondents had identified significant changes in practices earlier in the survey, we expected them to give high ratings to the conference's influence on energy-efficiency in this section.)
- *Firmographics* – Number of homes built, remodeled, or worked on annually by each respondent and share of these homes that are included in Wisconsin ENERGY STAR programs. This information helped to inform the energy impact estimates.

The instrument was published as an on-line survey, but was implemented as a telephone survey. An Energy Center staff person called the sampled attendees to explain the project and request participation in the survey. Then, she delivered the survey via telephone and entered responses. The online survey included the questions she read verbatim, instructions for the interviewer such as possible probes, where relevant, and responses for both closed-ended and some pre-coded open ended questions. Where subsequent questions depended on earlier responses, the online survey instrument automatically displayed the questions that were to be asked next, thereby mimicking the computer-aided telephone interview systems used by survey firms.

Altogether, the twenty-four interview respondents included in the analysis self-reported twenty-nine changes in practices that they attributed to conference attendance. Nine of sixteen interviewed builders reported at least one change in practice, as did three of four interviewed remodeling contractors and three of four subcontractors.

ROI Analysis

Analysis included estimating a range of annual energy savings, as well as extrapolating results to reflect life-time savings. Included in the analysis was triangulation to isolate the effects of the meeting on energy savings and convert those savings to money in preparation for the ROI calculation.

Energy Savings Impact Analysis

Evaluators estimated a range of annual energy savings for each reported change in practice. Depending on the nature of the response, some of these were more speculative than others. Practice changes with more readily quantifiable impacts included changing from 16-inch to 24-inch stud spacing and specifying electrically-efficient furnaces more frequently. These measures are discrete and have savings that can be reasonably estimated from existing studies or engineering calculations.

On the more speculative end were statements such as "I'm doing a better job of air sealing." For speculative statements of practices that would be likely to reduce energy usage, evaluators estimated a likely range using a combination of professional judgment by internal experts and industry standard values—and erring on the side of being conservative.

For other, speculative reported changes in behavior, it was not clear whether any energy savings would result. ("Using different kinds of insulation" was one example.) Evaluators did not include these in the impact results. There were also a couple of cases in which a reported change in practice could increase energy consumption. Therefore, evaluators included these as negative savings.

Internal experts estimated most of the reported changes to have a small impact in a given home, but a few attendees reported larger changes (see Table 3).

Table 3. Sample Measures Attributed to Conference and Energy Savings Assigned

Measure Reported	Number of Respondents	Range of Energy Savings per year per home)
Small Measures		
increased efforts on air sealing	8	2 to 25 therms[1]
changed framing technique	4	0 to 30 therms
insulation changes	5	-30 to 25 therms
increased ENERGY STAR lighting	3	50 to 375 kWh
Large Measures		
specifying geothermal for some homes	2	625 to 725 therms -9000 to -5000 kWh
increased specification of electronically commutated motors in furnaces	2	700 to 1400 kWh

[1]Therms and kilowatt hours are the measures typically used in billing gas and electric usage.

Extrapolation of Results

The last step of the process was to estimate the total impact of the conference in terms of energy savings. This involved several additional sub-steps:

1. Extrapolate the annual savings to the lifetime of the measures. Because energy savings from construction practices can last as long as the home, internal experts are able to estimate with some certainty how long savings from a measure will persist. This approach differs from the Phillips ROI Methodology that typically recommends using only the first year of results in the analysis. However, looking at energy savings over the life of a building is the standard practice in the energy industry.
2. Estimate the persistence of change in a builder's practice over time (explained below).
3. Extrapolate the interview sample to the conference as a whole.

Evaluators implemented all these within a probabilistic analysis known as Monte Carlo analysis. Monte Carlo analysis is a statistical technique in which an outcome based on numerous variables that each have a range of potential values is determined by computing the outcome numerous times using the full range of possible inputs in different combinations. Inputs are usually determined based on random assignment of possible values related to a given probability distribution. The outcome is not a single value, but a range of possible values. Given the considerable uncertainty involved in several steps of the analysis, evaluators did not want to ascribe a false level of precision to the results.

Evaluators used three ranges for measure lifetimes, all of which are determined by internal experts and industry standards:

- Twenty to forty years for practice changes that affect the building shell and therefore are relatively permanent (one example is framing techniques).
- Fifteen to twenty-five years for changes involving equipment such as furnaces that have an expected lifetime in this range.
- Two to seven years for lighting-related changes. This may be conservative because the conference prompted attendees to specify hard-wired fluorescent fixtures that will continue to be fluorescent even after the initial bulbs burn out.

Determining how long a builder will continue to implement a given change in practice, or how long it would be before the builder would have changed practices without the conference, is perhaps the most speculative aspect of the analysis. This duration of practice is called *persistence*, and is important when calculating energy savings over time so that results are not overly optimistic.

Internal experts determined that the net duration in practice changes would in many cases be fairly short. However, it was possible that a young builder could pick up something from the conference that would have a long net persistence. Evaluators assigned a probability curve that reflects the high likelihood of a short persistence, but that acknowledges the possibility of a much longer persistence, as shown in Figure 1. In the Monte Carlo analysis, each practice change is randomly assigned a persistence according to this distribution. This results in most practice changes being assigned a duration of less than ten years, but still allows for the possibility of an occasional long-lasting change.

Figure 1. Estimated Persistence of Practice Changes

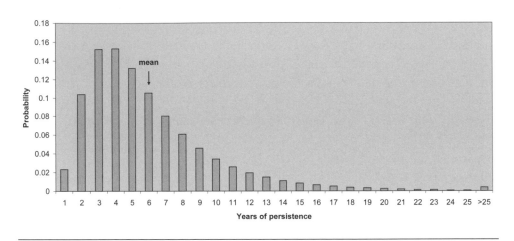

For a given change in practice, the total impacts were then calculated as:

Estimated annual energy savings per home		Attendee reported homes per year		Attendee reported fraction affected by change in practice		Estimated duration of change in practice		Measure life		Total Savings
	x		x		x		x		=	

Each input in this equation has an estimated uncertainty associated with it. To address this uncertainty, the Monte Carlo analysis includes a random fluctuation (within the assigned uncertainty range) in the values of the inputs for each reported change in practice.

As a final step, evaluators extrapolated from the interview sample (twenty-four respondents reported results from a sample of fifty) to the full population of builders, remodelers, and subcontractors who attended the conference (171 estimated). Extrapolating from a sample to the full population is standard procedure for surveys because it allows more efficient use of survey resources. Response from a representative sample provides results that more closely mirror a population than a low response rate for surveys attempted with that entire population. A low response rate can hide systematic bias among those who chose to complete the survey and those who did not.

In this particular project, evaluators linked the extrapolation to the Monte Carlo analysis. Evaluators randomly assigned an interview respondent—including those who reported no changes—to represent each firm in the un-interviewed population of attendees for each Monte Carlo iteration, then aggregated results across the population. More than 5,000 Monte Carlo iterations were run. The net result of this approach was to both extrapolate the interview sample to the full population and also incorporate the uncertainty in the interview sampling process. It requires assuming that the sample of interviewees is reasonably representative of the population of firms, a guess that appears tenable based on internal expert analysis and six years of conference records.

Isolation Method

For this ROI analysis, isolation entailed distinguishing between behavior change reported by conference attendees that was a direct result of the conference, and that which would have occurred anyway. In making this distinction, evaluators collected various self-reports from attendees and triangulated the results by comparing the conference-induced behavior change each data point implied.

The initial and primary isolation was built into the way evaluators collected the data on changed practices by attendees. Attendees were not asked to tell evaluators what they were doing differently, but what they were doing differently *for the first time* after hearing about it at the conference. The wording of this question provided the primary filter to weed out new practices that may have been caused by other factors.

The secondary filters—and sources of information to allow triangulation—were attendee responses to other survey questions designed to determine the conference's effectiveness. These questions included:

- "How does the Better Buildings, Better Business conference fit into the hierarchy of benefits you get from the ENERGY STAR programs (presented as a percentage of total program benefit)?"
- "What share of the training or learning you received from the ENERGY STAR program this year happened at the Better Buildings, Better Business conference?"

A third filter was inherently built into the analysis by having an evaluator who was knowledgeable about residential construction practices assign the input values for the Monte Carlo analysis. This combination put the evaluator in a position to identify overstated or suspicious claims, thereby enabling him to downgrade any such self-reports.

Because changed practices might be adopted by the same attendees at a future date, even without the influence of the conference, the process "isolated" the conference effects over time as explained above.

Conversion Method

Evaluators used an industry standard to estimate that Wisconsin utility avoided costs of four to eight cents per kilowatt-hour and $0.60 to $1.40 per therm, and a discount rate of 5 to 15%. Because these inputs were included in the Monte Carlo analysis as ranges, the results presented later also reflect uncertainty in avoided costs and discount factor.

Results

Results were reported for all levels of evaluation.

Reaction Results

Table 4 shows the satisfaction results from the 2005 conference. The overall attendee satisfaction score objective was 4.3 and was achieved. The customer service objective was achieved for attendees overall and for exhibitors, but not for instructors. Since only 46% of sessions received a 4.3 or better and 19% of sessions received less than a 4.0, session scores fell short of the objective.

Table 4. Reaction Results

Objective	Result
Overall Score: Achieve the Energy Center benchmark score of a 4.3 on a 5-point scale for overall attendee satisfaction.	4.3
Customer Service: Achieve 90% or better agreement with the statement: "conference organizers treated me like a valued customer."	Overall attendees: 92% Exhibitors: 93% Instructors: 85%
Session Scores: The majority of session scores should equal or beat the organizational benchmark of 4.3, and less than 10% of sessions should fall below a score of 4.0	46% of sessions received 4.3 or better 19% of sessions received less than a 4.0

Learning Results

Organizers wanted to find what platinum sponsors they voluntarily recalled. Platinum sponsors included the organizations as shown in Table 5 (with specific utility company names kept confidential), with the percentage of surveyed attendees who volunteered specific sponsor names when asked, "Can you remember any of the sponsors of the conference?" Thirty-four percent of respondents were able to recall Focus on Energy as a conference sponsor; yet, only 3% of respondents recalled that the Energy Center of Wisconsin was a sponsor.

Table 5. Attendee Recall of Sponsors

Conference Sponsor	Percent of Responses
Focus on Energy[1]	34%
Utility A	31%
Home Performance with ENERGY STAR	17%
Wisconsin ENERGY STAR HOMES	14%
Utility B	6%
Energy Center of Wisconsin	3%

[1]Focus on Energy is the umbrella brand for the Wisconsin ENERGY STAR programs as well as many other initiatives.

Application Results

Table 3, as previously shown, captures the changes in practice reported by the twenty-four attendees providing data indicating change—including changes with little and significant energy impacts.

However, attending builders were not any more likely to join either of the sponsoring Wisconsin ENERGY STAR programs than non-attending builders, suggesting that the conference had little or no discernable effect on attendee decisions to become a program participating builder. If the conference had an immediate effect on program participation, one would expect attendees who joined the program to do so closer to the conference's February date than non-attendees who joined the program in the same year. In fact, the average date that either group joined the program in 2005 was June, with non-attendees joining a fraction of a month earlier.

Impact Results

Across the group of interviewed builders, remodelers, and subcontractors, these measures suggest a blended average first-year energy impact of 100 to 230 therms and 230 to 700 kilowatt-hours per firm (the average number of homes affected per firm is between 32 and 44). As a result, this model suggests a total first-year energy impact of the conference of 13,000 to 31,000 therms and 30,000 to 93,000 kilowatt-hours by Wisconsin-based attendees.

ROI Results

Although the estimated energy savings for any one house are small, the aggregate impact of the conference involves extrapolating across:
- An average estimated measure life of more than twenty years

- An average estimated persistence of the practice of six years
- The multiple homes built or remodeled by each firm (which ranged from 1 to 200 across the interview respondents)

Using the monetary values of utility avoided costs of four to eight cents per kilowatt-hour and $0.60 to $1.40 per therm, and a discount rate of 5 to 15%. This results in a value of saved energy of somewhere between $400,000 and $2,000,000 (representing the 90% confidence range from the Monte Carlo analysis), compared to an overall conference cost of about $380,000. The Energy Center calculated conference costs included:

- All fully-loaded labor costs (conference staff track hours spent working on the conference throughout the year). This includes staff time to conduct planning, fundraising, exhibit marketing, conference marketing, registration, conference Executive Committee coordination, and meeting planning, in addition to on-site attendance and support of all Energy Center staff. This figure also included evaluator staff time to conduct the ROI data collection and analysis.
- Outside contractors, such as outsourced contract negotiation and exhibit management, expo company, audio-visual production, printing, mail house, and other event production contractors.
- Facility room rental, food and beverage, and staff and instructor sleeping rooms.
- Instructor honoraria and travel expenses.
- Volunteer and staff recognition events.

The monetary value of the energy savings represents a benefits/costs ratio range of somewhere between about 1.1 and 5.3, or a return on investment of about 5 to 425%. The Monte Carlo model suggests a 97% probability that the present value of the future energy savings exceeds the conference costs.

Determining the return on investment for individual sponsors poses some challenges because benefits could be allocated to the sponsors in different ways and there is no direct linkage between sponsorship dollars and reported behavior changes. For example, the Wisconsin ENERGY STAR programs are the only conference sponsors currently being evaluated based on energy savings. If one were to assign all energy savings to these sponsors, the program's ROI for its sponsorship would be 740 to 3,900%. The sponsor's contribution was $25,000. On the other hand, if one assigned energy savings proportionately to all sponsors, the ROI would be 5 to 425%. Neither of these extremes feels particularly satisfying. The low set of numbers would leave much energy savings without allocations to anyone because the other sponsors would be unlikely to seek credit for it. The higher set of numbers implies causality where it probably did not exist. How these savings should be allocated is still an unresolved question.

Intangible Results

A number of important intangible benefits arose from the ROI study. These include:

- The overall positive impression attendees, sponsors, and exhibitors had of the conference organizer's commitment to quality, due to the level of effort given evaluation activities.
- Usefulness of many types of evaluation data to conference organizers in continuously improving the conference. The ROI impact study, with the 2006 on-site data, encouraged conference staff to use positive results in fundraising and exhibit sales efforts and to communicate positive results and changes in conference programming back to attendees and other stakeholders.
- In a mission-driven organization, conference staff found that the ability to quantify actual energy savings from their efforts is highly motivating.
- Platinum sponsors whose attendee recall was high promoted the conference to their upper management and stepped up their marketing efforts to promote the conference to their customers.
- Two platinum sponsors who did not achieve high attendee recall in the 2005 study increased their level of effort to create visibility at the conference.
- Some product manufacturers increased their sponsorship commitments because they appreciated the amount of demographic and purchasing information provided by the conference staff.
- Developing a baseline for use in setting performance goals for future conferences has had a positive impact on the performance results of the 2006 conference and the planning for the 2007 conference. All of the reaction scores improved from 2005 to 2006.
- The conference motivates and prepares more people to be Wisconsin ENERGY STAR program consultants, increases the number of consultants "selling" the program, and thereby causes more homes to be run through the programs, which results in some incremental energy savings.
- Attendance growth due to brand recognition and increased participation gives the conference more market influence, which contributes to sustainability and future growth.

Credibility of Results

This study was a relatively low-cost (compared to other energy savings impact evaluations) internal impact assessment of an Energy Center conference. The wide ranges of impact estimates—while acceptable for Energy Center purposes because they clearly suggest an overall positive return on investment—may prove problematic for evaluators who need to report annual impact estimates under regulatory scrutiny with a much narrower range of possible impacts. For a regulatory review, the Energy Center suggests the following adjustments and enhancements to reduce the uncertainties in this kind of study.

- *Gather more detail about the behavior change implemented*

Energy Center trained administrative staff to conduct the telephone interviews using a highly structured computer-aided survey instrument. The interviewer did a thorough job, but was not able to ask some follow-up questions that a building expert could devise during an interview. Budget permitting, future interviews could include a follow-up process where a technical expert contacts the respondent about ambiguous or vague descriptions of behavior change.

- *Ask about implementation caused by multiple interventions*

The survey was clearly about the conference, and many of the attendees have long-term relationships with Energy Center staff and intense loyalty to the conference. This holds the potential for socially desired response bias. Evaluators were aware of this risk and attempted to account for it when assigning energy savings, especially when responses to other questions seemed inconsistent with strong impacts from the conference. One way to reduce respondents' overstatement of causality is to ask questions in the context of multiple program measures (i.e., ask the extent to which various potential causes contributed to an implementation of a new idea).

- *Move beyond self-reports*

This study relied exclusively on self-reports by participants and a dose of conservative skepticism built into the analysis to determine what was implemented as a result of the conference and how effectively it might have been installed or implemented. Having an experienced residential building researcher estimate the energy savings was a critical part of this study. However, in the long run—and given more financial resources—it would enhance the credibility of results to move beyond self-reports and include some verification. This could include site inspections, blower door tests, and perhaps even billing data analysis or metering studies if reported changes are substantial enough to warrant employing these impact evaluation tools. All these verification methods require a substantially higher investment in staff costs, so it would be important to weigh these costs against the objectives of the study.

- *Track Persistence*

Lack of empirical information forced the Energy Center to rely on an educated estimate about the persistence of the conference-induced behavior change and assign a wide uncertainty around that estimate. In the case of a training-induced behavior change, persistence is a function of the number of years before a training attendee (1) will give up the newly learned practice, (2) will cease the activity in which he or she applies the practice (e.g., stops building houses), or (3) would have adopted the practice for another reason. More data on any of these issues would allow a more educated estimate of persistence. Again, this approach is more accurate—and much more expensive.

Communication Strategy

Before the study went underway, conference organizers planned to share the results through a formal report to the conference Executive Committee, the platinum sponsors, and the management team of the Energy Center of Wisconsin. However, the methodology and a number of the results inspired an expansion of the communication strategy.

Methodology

The energy efficiency community has struggled for years to measure the energy impacts of training and meetings in an effort to justify program funding allocations. This effort at quantifying such impacts—while explicitly addressing uncertainty—piqued the interest of evaluators and program designers in the wider energy efficiency community. This interest led the Energy Center to publish a paper on the study at an industry conference, and the organization is now exploring ways to incorporate this approach to quantifying the benefits of training for its own events and as a service to energy efficiency organizations. A white paper is planned to highlight the Energy Center's commitment to quantifying the impacts of education and training.

Conference organizers also decided that the high return on investment—as well as the societal benefit of the energy savings—demonstrated strong alignment with the Energy Center mission. This prompted a presentation to the Energy Center Board of Directors about the study as a whole, its methodology and results. Some Board members who viewed the presentation decided to sponsor for the first time, and other increased their level of commitment to the conference.

Sponsor Recall

The voluntary recall of the Wisconsin ENERGY STAR sponsorship by attendees, combined with the positive ROI results, prompted evaluators and conference organizers to present the findings at a general meeting of Wisconsin ENERGY STAR program planners—a much larger audience than intended in the original communications plan.

Another platinum sponsor, Utility A, was recalled by attendees more often than conference organizers expected, as was the technology, geothermal, promoted by by Utility A at the conference. This led conference organizers to present the findings to the Utility A program staff, tailoring a presentation to Utility A brand and technology recall and making recommendations for future investments in the conference.

The low number of Energy Center sponsorship mentions by attendees caused conference organizers to communicate this issue with Energy Center management and conference staff, and resulted in an immediate change in branding strategy for the 2006 conference.

Event Marketing

A number of results proved to be interesting to existing sponsors and exhibitors, including:
- Overall energy savings produced by the conference as a societal benefit
- Purchasing behavior reported by attendees
- Demographic information about attendees
- Sponsor recall by attendees
- Exhibitor satisfaction

Conference organizers knew before the study that this information would be useful. After the results were published, the communications plan expanded to include highlights of this data in the sales and marketing messaging to sponsors and exhibitors.

Lessons Learned

A variety of lessons were learned throughout the evaluation process.

Measuring Enhances Reputation

As the Energy Center staff worked through the ROI study planning and execution, one noteworthy development was that the larger conference community of sponsors, exhibitors, and attendees had a favorable response to the effort of measuring results. Because this type of measurement is unusual for a mission-driven, publicly-attended meeting of a community of practice, it was perceived by stakeholders as a commitment to quality and an investment in better performance in the future. The Energy Center's reputation for quality, accountability, and innovation were enhanced.

Mission Accomplished

The Energy Center is a mission-driven organization that has grown out of a highly regulated industry attempting to quantify most activities. The energy efficiency culture rewards expertise and encourages skepticism. The Energy Center's ability to quantify its progress on fulfilling its mission in a meaningful way was important to a staff motivated by mission. The study helped to position the conference as a serious effort within the energy efficiency community.

Meaning Can Be Found in Behavior Change

The positive ROI created a favorable impression of the conference. However, conference organizers, sponsors, exhibitors, program planners, and instructors were most interested in the specific details around the behavior changes that attendees reported. From both an event marketing and a program design perspective, these specific details were more meaningful than a positive ROI in informing improvements to the overall conference strategy.

Changes in practice details—including what was not changing—allowed conference organizers to alter curriculum to drive specific behavior changes in the 2006 conference, to assess which exhibitors and sponsors were likely to receive the greatest benefit from the conference, and to recommend content and tactics to exhibitors and sponsors in positioning their products to support the changes in practice emphasized by the conference. This also allowed conference organizers to position themselves as assisting in generating more positive results for exhibitors and sponsors.

Sustaining Measurement Practice Is Important

The ROI analysis cost the Energy Center approximately $20,000 in evaluation staff time, which represented a significant investment for a conference in which funding was constrained. The majority of the staff expense was involved in quantifying the energy savings in a way that maximized the credibility of the study. While the Energy Center would not make this investment every year of the conference, the information about attendee behavior change and their perceptions of sponsors is so important to program design and fundraising for the conference that a post-event interview process has been incorporated as standard practice for the event. This will allow the Energy Center to perform trendline analysis and keep a bead on market place changes to inform conference planning and enhance the Energy Center's value to sponsors and exhibitors.

Questions for Discussion

1. Was the cost of the energy savings analysis and the ROI calculation justified within the context of a constrained budget for this conference? Why or why not?

2. What analytical resources was the Energy Center able to bring to the table that were not typical of many meeting departments? Why were these additional resources necessary?
3. Why is it necessary to look at a longer period than one year to accurately assess the results of this conference?
4. How credible are the business impact and ROI results, given the number of responses compared to the size of the population? How might credibility of results be improved?
5. What conference fundraising and exhibit sales strategies could be developed using the ROI study results? How can the Energy Center incorporate these results into its marketing of the conference?

About the Author

Marge Anderson is an Associate Director at the Energy Center of Wisconsin. She leads the organization's Building Performance practice and directs the Energy Center's cross-cutting functions in education and outreach. The Energy Center is twice a recipient of the Award of Excellence in Continuing Education from the American Institute of Architects (a quality award modeled after the Baldridge quality awards) and is a recipient of the Exemplar Award from the International Association of Education and Training (an award which recognizes impact). Ms. Anderson is an active volunteer leader for Meeting Professionals International and currently serves on its International Board of Directors. Marge can be contacted at 608.238.8276, extension 132, or manderson@ecw.org.

Ingo Bensch is a Senior Project Manager at the Energy Center of Wisconsin. He conducts research and evaluations that guide energy-efficiency and training efforts in all sectors. His projects include market assessment for a high-performance building program, evaluations of a daylighting program and a green building project, and market research in renewable energy. He also oversees an extensive evaluation process for all Energy Center education and training events and conducted an evaluation of a statewide energy education program for primary and secondary school teachers. Previously, Mr. Bensch was a program evaluator and supervisor for the Wisconsin Legislative Audit Bureau.

Scott Pigg is a Senior Project Manager at the Energy Center of Wisconsin and is a nationally-recognized expert in energy efficiency program market research, evaluation, and emerging technology research. Mr. Pigg was the Energy Center's lead for both the baseline study for Wisconsin's public benefits program, which established early metrics in terms of market saturation of various appliances and energy efficiency opportunities. He was also the lead on a study to investigate the achievable potential for energy efficiency and customer-sited renewable energy in

Wisconsin, which was called the "tipping point for energy efficiency in Wisconsin" by Wisconsin State Senator Robert Cowles.

Editor's Notes

As shown, this study was supported and undertaken by an organization committed to and well-versed in evaluation and statistical measurements. While the level of statistical analysis used in this case was expected and required by the energy industry, it might not be easily undertaken by other organizations without these resources. Therefore, other means of data analysis could be considered, provided they are deemed credible by the key evaluation stakeholders.

The lessons learned and recommendations derived from the data should be inspirational to others considering pursuit of higher levels of evaluation. Organizations like this are blazing a trail for the larger non-profit world and meetings industry in general.

Case Study
Measuring the ROI in The Annual Franchise Conference International Franchise Company

By Michael V. Hamilton, President, Synchronicity, Inc.

This case was prepared to serve as a basis for discussion rather than an illustration of either effective or ineffective administrative and management practices. All names, dates, places, and organizations have been disguised at the request of the author or organization.

Abstract

In today's business environment, management seeks hard data to compare the benefits and costs of all business operations, including meetings and events. Senior management from International Franchise Company (IFC) expressed an interest in evaluating its Annual Franchise Conference to better understand how the meeting linked to corporate objectives and delivered on attendee expectations. Specifically, IFC wanted to determine if the meeting contributed to the growth and development of its franchise units. Meeting the expectations of attendees was also important to IFC. Franchise owners are considered primary stakeholders of the meeting and contribute significantly to the financial underwriting of the conference. The case study details how to handle a negative ROI value.

Background

IFC's Annual Franchise Conference (the conference) was developed to provide franchise units with a forum for developing excellence through education, networking, and recognition. In March 2005, IFC was host to 110 franchise owners, key employees, and spouses, along with twenty-five IFC management and staff. The conference agenda reflected the importance of the franchise network in the context of the company's launch of its new brand. Conference content explored touch points where the new brand intersected with the customer experience. Education and networking sessions were designed to develop the knowledge and skills needed to use new branding materials as strategic tools driving the marketing and sales process.

Why ROI?

IFC management undertook this ROI study with four key objectives in mind:

1. To improve the meeting by using data to deliver more fully on attendee expectations.
2. To improve the meeting by using data to enhance the relevance of session content, elevate speaker skills, and expand attendee knowledge and skills development.
3. To determine the extent of knowledge and skills transfer from the meeting to the job, while also identifying barriers and enablers that inhibit or support application.
4. To measure the business impact of the meeting, including ROI, and its contribution to IFC's strategic objectives.

Evaluation Methodology

The Phillips ROI Methodology was employed for this evaluation. The result of this approach to measurement is a balanced set of measures: employee reaction to and satisfaction with the meeting, learning acquired during the meeting, application of skills and knowledge learned at the meeting, impact on specific business measures due to the application of learning acquired at the meeting, return on investment (ROI) in the meeting, and intangible benefits.

Evaluation Planning

A comprehensive evaluation plan was developed to meet each of the objectives of this study. Target audience, response rate, ease of administration, and cost factors were all considered to ensure that adequate, quality input was obtained for all levels of evaluation. Objectives for Levels 1 and 2 were developed with those directly responsible for the development, facilitation, and coordination of the meeting, along with input from a representative sample of the franchise network. Objectives developed at this level were mirrored in the expectations set for attendees in pre-meeting marketing and communications. Objectives at Levels 3, 4, and 5 were developed with additional input from IFC's senior management team, including the Director of the Franchise Network and the Director of Brand and Marketing. The challenge for the evaluation team was to develop specific application and implementation objectives (Level 3), business impact objectives (Level 4), and an ROI objective (Level 5) that would represent significant benefits for both IFC and the individual franchise owners. A specific success measure was set to determine the extent to which each objective had been met.

Data Collection and Analysis

With objectives and success measures in place, the evaluation team focused on data collection issues, including increasing response rates and collection methods. Questionnaires were considered the ideal solution from administrative, budget, and attendee response perspectives with both paper and electronic forms used at different levels of evaluation. Attendees were considered the go-to source for data at Levels 1 through 3. Management's performance records were designated the source for the Level 4, Business Impact, data.

The timing of data collection for this evaluation included on-site and post-meeting options. On-site paper questionnaires were used to collect data for Levels 1 and 2. Questionnaires were administered at the end of each breakout and general session and a comprehensive questionnaire was administered at the completion of the final, general session. The most critical timing issue involved data collection for Level 3, Application, and Level 4, Business Impact. These questionnaires were administered at three months and six months after the meeting, respectively. In the case of a few measures, such as the new customer presentation, some attendees would not yet have begun to use the learning gained at the meeting within the three-month period. However, it was decided that collecting data at this point was still preferable to waiting for six-months or a full year because at that point participants might have completely disconnected from the meeting experience. Moreover, it was hoped that requesting feedback from participants at three-months might serve to reinforce the key learning points from the meeting at a crucial time interval.

A summary of data collection plans for each level of evaluation can be seen in Table 1.

Table 1. Data Collection Plan

LEVEL	OBJECTIVES	SUCCESS MEASURES	DESIRED RESPONSE RATE	DATA COLLECTION METHOD/INSTRUMENT	DATA SOURCES	TIMING	DATA COLLECTION BY
1 — REACTIONS/ SATISFACTION & PLANNED ACTIONS	Is the respondent a Franchise Owner, Franchise Employee, or a IFC Employee	N/A	100% of attendees	Paper Questionnaires Forms #1 - #11: Four General Sessions and Seven Breakouts	Program attendees	End of each breakout session and at end of two general sessions	Synchronicity
	How was the presenter's delivery How was the presenter's delivery with the attendees and choice/order of content/activities perceived by the attendees?	4.3 or higher mean score on each session					
	Were the learner outcomes understandable and achieved?	4.3 or higher mean score on each session					
	What level of knowledge/skill did the attendees have before and after each session?	N/A					
	To what degree was the content relevant to attendees' current job and future professional opportunities?	4.3 or higher mean score on each session					
	What will deter attendees from using the knowledge/skills?	N/A		Paper questionnaire; Form #12 Overall Conference Evaluation		End of final general session	
	Obtain input/suggestions for improving program through pre-work and/or special pre/post conference training sessions.	N/A					
	To what degree is the amount, format, and value of networking opportunities between franchisor and franchisee appropriate?	4.3 or higher mean score on each session					
	To what degree is the amount, format, and value of achievement recognition appropriate?	4.3 or higher mean score on each session					

LEVEL	OBJECTIVES	SUCCESS MEASURES	DESIRED RESPONSE RATE	DATA COLLECTION METHOD/INSTRUMENT	DATA SOURCES	TIMING	DATA COLLECTION BY
1 — REACTIONS / SATISFACTION & PLANNED ACTIONS	Obtain a positive reaction to the overall program, faculty, networking opportunities, pre-reading materials, on-line communities, staff, registration, host property, special events, food/beverage, mentors, etc.	4.3 or higher mean score on each session (Attendee care evaluation score)	100% of attendees	Paper questionnaire: Form #12 Overall Conference Evaluation	Program attendees	End of final general session	Synchronicity
	Would the attendee recommend the program to others?	4.3 or higher mean score would recommend					
	Determine which factors caused persons to attend the program.	N/A					
	Determine the perceived value of the program to-date.	4.3 or higher mean score of these questions					
	Extent that program was a good investment for their organization/employer.	4.3 mean score on a 5 point scale					
	Extent that program was a good investment for them personally.	4.3 mean score on a 5 point scale					
	Determine which business measures will most likely be positively influenced due to program attendance.	N/A					
	How much did the attendee and the attendee's company/organization spend on the application fee, the registration fee, housing, travel, food/beverage and incidentals?	N/A					

LEVEL	OBJECTIVES	SUCCESS MEASURES	DESIRED RESPONSE RATE	DATA COLLECTION METHOD/ INSTRUMENT	DATA SOURCES	TIMING	DATA COLLECTION BY
1	How many hours did attendees spend preparing for the program (submitting application, registering, pre-reading, case study team work, etc.)? What percentage of these hours were done on their employer's or own companies' work time? What percentage of these hours were done on their personal time?	N/A					
	How many hours did attendees spend traveling to and from the program site? What percentage of these hours were done on their employer's or own companies' work time? What percentage of these hours were done on their personal time?	N/A		Paper questionnaire: Form #12 Overall Conference Evaluation	Program attendees	End of final general session	Synchronicity
	How many hours did attendees spend on conference pre-work? What percentage of these hours were done on their employer's or own companies' work time? What percentage of these hours were done on their personal time?	N/A	100% of attendees				
	What is the hourly rate paid to attendees by their employer? What currency is this amount expressed in?	N/A					
	What percentage of their hourly rate is awarded in the form of benefits from their employer?	N/A					
	Identify planned actions	Each attendee develops an action plan for two measures that can be positively changed/influenced as a result of the program		Paper Questionnaire: Form #13, two-part Action Plan			

LEVEL	OBJECTIVES	SUCCESS MEASURES	DESIRED RESPONSE RATE	DATA COLLECTION METHOD/ INSTRUMENT	DATA SOURCES	TIMING	DATA COLLECTION BY
22 2 LEARNING	Understanding of modular marketing kit	4.3 or higher mean score from respondents who expressed confidence in their expressed confidence in their ability to identify and explain importance of 10 key branding touch points	100% of attendees	Paper questionnaire: Form #12 Overall Conference Evaluation		End of final general session	Synchronicity
	Grasp of new presentation format	4.3 or higher mean score from respondents who expressed or understood understood relationships between specific target audiences and appropriate brand stories					
	Grasp of new presentation format	4.3 or higher mean score from respondents who know why, when, and how to use a presentation during the sales process			Program attendees		
3 APPLICATION	Implement new modular marketing kit	4.3 or higher mean score from respondents who usually or always: • Target specific audiences • Identify individual prospects within those audiences • Utilize marketing spreadsheet to select appropriate brand stories • Utilize detailed discovery process during initial client interview	95% of attendees	On-line questionnaire: Form #14 for Franchise Owners and Employees; Form #15 for IFC Employees		3 months after conference	

LEVEL	OBJECTIVES	SUCCESS MEASURES	DESIRED RESPONSE RATE	DATA COLLECTION METHOD/ INSTRUMENT	DATA SOURCES	TIMING	DATA COLLECTION BY
	Implement new modular marketing kit	4.3 or higher mean score from respondents who have used the modular marketing kit process to make presentations to: • Targeted prospects • Targeted new prospects					
3 APPLICATION	Implement new sales presentation	4.3 or higher mean score of respondents from the Presentation Beta test group have used the new presentation three or more times	95% of attendees	On-line questionnaire: Form #14 for Franchise Owners and Employees; Form #15 for IFC Employees	Program attendees	3 months after conference	Synchronically
	Implement brand identity in all customer facing activities	In customer engagements, 4.3 or higher mean score from respondents who usually or always. • Address IFC benefits relative to employee recruitment, retention and productivity • Address IFC benefits relative to IAQ and workspace related issues • Address IFC benefits relative to sustainability and other environment related issues. • Address IFC benefits relative to textile care • Address IFC benefits relative to the Network of Knowledge					

LEVEL	OBJECTIVES	SUCCESS MEASURES	DESIRED RESPONSE RATE	DATA COLLECTION METHOD/INSTRUMENT	DATA SOURCES	TIMING	DATA COLLECTION BY
3 APPLICATION	Implement brand identity across all franchise collateral	More than 50% of respondents have mostly or completely incorporated the new IFC brand identity in: • Vans • Signage • Uniforms • Equipment • Collateral	95% of attendees	On-line questionnaire: Form #14 for Franchise Owners and Employees; Form #15 for IFC Employees	Program attendees	3 months after conference	Synchronicity
	What percentage of your time utilizes knowledge earned during The The conference sessions	4.3 or higher mean score from respondents					
	To what degree has content been relevant to the attendee's current job? (Level 1 measure)	4.3 or higher mean score from respondents					
	Identify barriers and enablers to applying learned skills and knowledge	N/A	75% of attendees				
4 BUSINESS IMPACT	• Pipeline Activity	Average 10% increase per franchise in pipeline activity over prior year, same period		On-line questionnaire: Form #16 for Franchise Owners and Employees; Form #17 for IFC Employees		6 months after conference	
	• Sales Cycle	Average 33% reduction in sales cycle from 6 months to 4 months	95% (70% minimum requirement)				
	• Sales	Average 18% increase per franchise in sales over prior year, same period					
5 ROI	Measure ROI of business impacts AND benefits to cost ratio for franchisees and for IFC	25% IFC 25% Franchise Owners					

Results: Reaction and Learning

The impact study produced an overwhelming amount of data. For purposes of this case study, only data that relates to the development of the ROI evaluation has been included.

The data collection process at the meeting yielded excellent response rates, with 100% of attendees completing individual session evaluations. Because of a misunderstanding in communications, the comprehensive, end-of-meeting questionnaire netted only about an 85% response rate. Nonetheless, Level 1 and 2 responses were generally positive and provided valuable insight for the planning of future meetings. A summary of results from the final conference questionnaire can be seen in Tables 2 and 3.

Table 2. Summary of End-of-Conference Reaction

	Mean Score	Participants Satisfied	Participants Dissatisfied
Conference Format:			
• Satisfied with the current conference length	4.46	93.06%	1.39%
• Satisfied with current balance of networking, education recognition and social activities	4.40	87.50%	1.39%
• Find value in the networking opportunities	4.72	97.22%	1.39%
• The awards reception provides a satisfactory level of recognition for franchise achievements	4.36	86.11%	2.78%
• The awards reception motivates/inspires me to improve performance	4.32	80.56%	6.95%
Conference Content			
• Satisfied with the selection of speakers	4.34	83.33%	1.39%
• Satisfied with selection of topics	4.10	80.55%	5.56%
• Would like more in-depth sessions	3.39	47.23%	19.44%
• Would attend pre- or post conference training sessions	3.76	66.67%	12.50%
Conference Operations			
• Smooth registration process (pre-conference)	4.37	86.11%	1.39%
• Smooth registration process (on-site)	4.61	91.67%	0%
• Facilities conducive to learning and networking	4.44	93.06%	0%
• Useful welcome packet	4.21	83.33%	2.78%
• Clear directional signage	4.32	87.50%	0%
• Satisfactory room accommodations	4.35	86.11%	0%
• Satisfactory food and beverage service	3.96	70.83%	9.72%
Overall experience			
• The program met my needs	4.45	81.95%	0%
• The program was a good investment for my organization/employer	4.41	73.61%	2.78%
• The program was a good investment for me personally	4.39	76.39%	2.78%

Table 3. Summary of Learning Responses to End-of-Conference Questionnaire

	Mean Score	Agree	Disagree
In Educational sessions, I learned new knowledge/skills regarding:			
• Employee excellence	3.99	69.45%	5.56%
• Sales and marketing excellence	4.16	79.16%	2.78%
• Operations/technical excellence	3.86	61.11%	6.95%
In networking situations, I learned new knowledge/skills regarding:			
• Employee excellence	4.03	75.00%	4.17%
• Sales and marketing excellence	4.14	75.00%	2.78%
• Operations/technical excellence	4.04	73.61%	6.95%
Overall, the new knowledge skills I have learned:			
• Are important to my position/job	4.31	81.94%	2.78%
• Can effectively apply to my daily work	4.27	80.55%	1.39%

Results: Application and Implementation

Fifty-five individuals, or only 56% of the franchise partners and employees attending the conference, responded to the Level 3 follow-up questionnaire. That rate is significantly lower than the target response rate of 95%, despite multiple attempts to elicit stronger feedback rates by the evaluation team, executive management, and a franchise peer board. Franchise owners responded at a rate of 75%, while franchise employees responded at a rate of 46%. Many factors can impact the response rate of a follow-up questionnaire. In this case, five factors appeared to be primary drivers of the low response rate.

- Franchise owners and their workers are not employees of IFC and do not have direct accountability to IFC management. As a result, they could not be required or mandated to participate in the study.
- Members of the franchise peer group indicated that franchise employees tended to view this study as the responsibility of their management, the franchise partners. As a result, franchise employees were not as likely to respond to the survey. This, in part, explained the especially low turnout on the employee side.
- IFC experienced significant change in its executive management team immediately following the conference. Two senior managers, both champions of this impact study, left the company, severely limiting the evaluation team's ability to drive participation.
- From the data collected, it appears three months did not allow a significant number of franchises adequate time to implement learning acquired at the

conference.

- Because the franchise owners were viewed as having a vested interest in the outcome of this study, it was determined not to offer an incentive to participants. In retrospect, a small but meaningful incentive might have increased participation among the franchise employees. However, it is more likely that in this study, the other four factors listed made the greater impact on response rates at Level 3.

The full set of Level 3 responses can be seen in Table 4.

Table 4. Summary of Application Responses

	Mean Score	Usually or Always Apply	Seldom or Never Apply
Regarding the new marketing kit and my marketing/sales process, I:			
• Target specific audiences	4.12	71.00%	3.60%
• Identify individual prospects within those audiences	4.28	78.20%	0%
• Utilize the marketing spreadsheet to select appropriate brand stories for Individual prospects	3.25	34.60%	20.00%
• Engage in detailed discovery to learn more about individual prospects	4.10	91.00%	3.60%
• Use the marketing kit process to make presentations to new prospects	3.30	36.40%	29.10%
• Using the marketing kit process to make presentations to targeted prospects	2.86	27.20%	36.30%
Regarding the new customer presentation, I:			
• Used the new presentation since participating the Beta Test Program	3.00	33.30%	53.30%
• Used the new presentation and did not participate the Beta Test Program	2.26	17.50%	60.5%
Regarding branding and customer engagements:			
• In customer discussion, addressed IFC benefits relative to employee recruitment, retention, and productivity	3.42	47.40%	19.90%
• In customer discussions, addressed IFC benefits relative to indoor air quality and other workspace-related issues	4.35	78.30%	3.60%
• In customer discussions, addressed IFC benefits relative to sustainability and other environment related issues	4.00	65.50%	7.30%
• In customer discussions, addressed IFC benefits relative to textile care	4.17	72.80%	5.40%
• In customer discussions, addressed IFC benefits relative to our Network of Knowledge	3.42	42.30%	22.10%

Table 4. Summary of Application Responses (continued)

	Mean Score	Usually or Always Apply	Seldom or Never Apply
Regarding the overall application of knowledge from the annual conference:			
• What percent of your total work time did you spend on tasks that require the knowledge/skills learned at the annual conference?	3.41	12.70%	40.10%
• On a scale of 0% (not at all) to 100% (critical), how critical is applying what you learned at the annual conference to your job success	5.76	47.30%	21.90%
Regarding the marketing kit and my marketing/sales process:			
• I have incorporated the new brand identity in franchise			
• Vans	3.28	68.00%	0%
• Signage	2.86	48.00%	4.00%
• Uniforms	3.47	57.00%	9.00%
• Equipment	2.65	47.00%	4.00%
• Collateral	4.08	84.00%	4.00%
• Stationery	3.79	72.00%	8.00%
• I have separated IFC from my other businesses	4.32	76.60%	8.00%

Results: Business Impact

Data for the Level 4 evaluation (Impact) was originally to be obtained from both franchise partners and employee responses to a six-month, post-conference follow-up questionnaire. Resulting response rates were even poorer than those received at Level 3. The questionnaire was re-issued solely to franchise partners, with additional management and peer group entreaties. Unfortunately, the response rate continued to remain low. Only seven of thirty-five franchise owners responded or 20% of all franchise owners who attended the conference. Consequently, the business impact data for this study is significantly understated.

In the Level 4 follow-up questionnaire, franchise owners were first asked to provide data regarding sales revenue, pipeline activity, and length of sales cycle. Of the seven respondents, only one franchise had data for all three measures. Accordingly, the decision was made to eliminate pipeline and sales cycle measures from the study and focus solely on sales revenue.

Results: Isolating for the Effect of the Conference

The isolation technique utilized for this study was the attendee or performer's estimate of impact. It is worth noting that when asked what other factors might have contributed to the business improvement, four of the seven respondents, or 57%, noted that much of the revenue increase in this period was due to contracts signed in the six-month period prior to, or before, the conference took place. This suggests that perhaps another reason for the poor response rate could be that franchises did not yet have any results directly attributable to the conference. Perhaps the study should have been delayed for one year or longer.

At the same time, two respondents cited targeting the right customers and extending the new brand as other factors contributing to their improvement. Ironically, both those factors relate directly to the learning objectives and focus of the conference content.

Results: Data Conversion

The monetary business impact figure still needed to be adjusted with two significant calculations before a benefit could be attributed to the conference.

- First, standard profit margins were used to downwardly adjust the monetary benefit to reflect only that portion of the revenue that represented company profit. Factoring in the standard profit margin accomplished this step and discounted for job costs, sales and marketing expenses, and general overhead. In the case of IFC, the standard profit margin from franchise operations is 13% of revenue (6% from royalty fees and 7% from product purchases). In the case of the franchise network, the standard profit margin for franchise operations is 60%. This adjustment is shown in Table 5.
- A final adjustment involved the use of annual values. Since the conference represented a short-term intervention, the ROI Methodology requires that only the first year of benefits be used in calculating the ROI. Because the data collected in this study represented only a six-month value, the benefit was multiplied by a factor of two, converting it to an annual value. Table 5 shows the annualized converted data from each respondent. The aggregate converted data is $50,688.09 for IFC and $233,945.02 for the franchise network.

Table 5. Business Impact Isolated and Converted

BUSINESS IMPACT	Respondent #1	Respondent #2	Respondent #3	Respondent #4	Respondent #5	Respondent #6	Respondent #7
Sales figures for the six month period between March 1, 2004 - September 1, 2004 as measured by "gross revenues"	$267,426.00	$352,846.00	$240,000.00	$305,539.58	$142,576.00	$364,010.00	$1,700,000.00
Sales figures for the six month period between March 1, 2005 - September 1, 2005 as measured by "gross revenues"	$366,512.00	$368,114.00	$276,000.00	$419,633.71	$261,354.00	$376,110.00	$2,800,000.00
Business Improvement	**$99,086.00**	**$15,268.00**	**$36,000.00**	**$114,094.13**	**$118,778.00**	**$12,100.00**	**$1,100,000.00**
ISOLATION TECHNIQUE (From the Participants)							
Percent of improvement attributed to the conference	25.00%	0.00%	50.00%	0.00%	10.00%	0.00%	20.00%
Confidence estimate (0-100%)	75.00%	100.00%	50.00%	100.00%	20.00%	100.00%	75.00%
Isolation Factor Adjusted Amount	18.75%	0.00%	25.00%	0.00%	2.00%	0.00%	15.00%
Business improvement isolated for effect	**$18,578.63**	**$0.00**	**$9,000.00**	**$0.00**	**$2,375.56**	**$0.00**	**$165,000.00**
DATA CONVERSION							
Standard profit margin - 13%	13.00%	13.00%	13.00%	13.00%	13.00%	13.00%	13.00%
Data converted for monetary value	$2,415.22	$0.00	$1,170.00	$0.00	$308.82	$0.00	$21,450.00
Annualized converted data	**$4,830.44**	**$0.00**	**$2,340.00**	**$0.00**	**$617.65**	**$0.00**	**$42,900.00**
RESPONSE AGGREGATE	**$50,688.09**						
Level 4 Business Impact Isolated for Effect and Converted - Franchise Network							
DATA CONVERSION							
Standard profit margin - 60%	60.00%	60.00%	60.00%	60.00%	60.00%	60.00%	60.00%
Data converted for monetary value	$11,147.18	$0.00	$5,400.00	$0.00	$1,425.34	$0.00	$99,000.00
Annualized converted data	**$22,294.35**	**$0.00**	**$10,800.00**	**$0.00**	**$2,850.67**	**$0.00**	**$198,000.00**
RESPONSE AGGREGATE	**$233,945.02**						

Meeting Costs

Separate cost profiles were developed for IFC and for the franchise network to develop distinct ROI streams later in the analysis. Using a fully-loaded costs approach, consideration was given to the time participants spent at the meeting and the cost of time spent preparing for and traveling to and from the meeting. The determination of this cost was based upon the participant's annual salary plus bonuses and benefits, and was assessed with a series of questions on the final page of the comprehensive, end-of-meeting survey that also collected Level 1 and Level 2 data.

From that data, a worksheet was created that summarized the total cost per registrant to attend the conference. Tables 6 and 7 show the total cost for franchise attendees and IFC employee attendees, respectively, broken down according to registration fees, travel and incidental expenses, and the cost of time based on salary plus benefits.

Table 6. Summary of Participant Costs, Franchise Network

Attendee Type	Registration Fee	Participant's T&E Costs to Costs to Attend (not including registration	Value of Time	Total Costs to Attend
Aggregate Franchise Partners Costs	$39,750.00	$114,885.00	$190,702.00	$345,337.00
Aggregate Franchise Employees Costs	$12,750.00	$65,508.00	$52,107.80	$130,365.80
Aggregate Spouse Costs	$2,500.00			$2,500.00
TOTAL FRANCHISE ATTENDEE COSTS	$55,000.00	$180,393.00	$242,809.80	$478,202.80

Table 7. Summary of Participant Costs, IFC Employees

Attendee Type	Registration Fee	Participant's T&E Costs to Attend (not including registration)	Value of Time	Total Costs to Attend
Aggregate IFC Staff Costs	0.00	$28,600.00	$55,200.00	$83,800.00
TOTAL IFC STAFF COSTS	0.00	$28,600.00	$55,200.00	$83,800.00

A fully-loaded cost profile also includes all direct expenses of the meeting. Table 8 lists IFC's direct expenses for the conference under the category headings of Program Costs, Contribution from Budget, and Evaluation Costs. Program Costs included all the direct expenses incurred by the meeting from the venue, third party producers and organizers, awards, and miscellaneous including the cost of conducting the front-end needs assessment, designing the meeting, and project managing the development of the meeting.

Table 8. Direct Expenses – IFC

Program Costs	
Creative Services	29,245.00
Recognition	8,450.00
Speaker Costs	9,500.00
Production	13,150.00
Food, Beverage & Entertainment	48,000.00
Registration	7,380.00
Hotel/Master Bill	5,000.00
Miscellaneous	2,000.00
Conference Management	20,600.00
Subtotal	**$143,325.00**

Contribution from Budget	
Contribution from Operations budget	38,500.00
Subtotal	**$38,500.00**

Evaluation Costs	
ROI Impact Study	30,000.00
Subtotal	**$30,000.00**

The franchise network bore a direct expense of its own. A percentage of franchise revenue funds, an IFC promotional budget, and a portion of that budget is used each year to help fund the conference. The portion of the budget that was used for the conference became a direct expense to the franchise network, listed as Franchise Overhead. These expenses were $32,000.

To create a distinct cost profile for each organization, the participant costs were then combined with the direct expenses to produce two separate, fully-loaded cost models. Tables 9 and 10 show the result.

Table 9. Fully Loaded Costs – IFC

Attendee Costs	
Cost of time (IFC staff only)	55,200.00
Travel expenses (IFC staff only)	28,600.00
Subtotal	**$83,800.00**

Program Costs	
Creative Services	29,245.00
Recognition	8,450.00
Speaker Costs	9,500.00
Production	13,150.00
Food, Beverage & Entertainment	48,000.00
Registration	7,380.00
Hotel/Master Bill	5,000.00
Miscellaneous	2,000.00
Conference Management	20,600.00
Subtotal	**$143,325.00**

Contribution from Budget	
Contribution from Operations budget	38,500.00

Evaluation Costs	
ROI Impact Study	30,000.00
TOTAL	**$295,625.00**

Table 10. Fully-Loaded Costs – Franchise Network

Attendee Costs	
Cost of time (Franchise personnel only)	242,809.80
Travel expenses (Franchise personnel only)	180,393.00
Registration Fees	55,000.00
Subtotal	**$478,202.80**

"Overhead" Costs	
Franchise dollars from Promotional Fund used for the conference	32,000.00
TOTAL	**$510,202.80**

ROI

For the franchise network, the business impacts discussed above under Level 4, Business Impacts, represented its entire benefit, based on existing data. However, the conference generated two additional revenue streams for the IFC that must be included in the ROI calculation. The first of these revenue streams is the $55,000 in fees generated by the conference registration process. Similarly, an infusion of $32,000 from the franchise promotional fund also must be counted as revenue in the IFC ROI calculation.

Table 11 shows the full benefit picture for IFC and the full benefit picture for the Franchise Owners Network.

Table 11. Total Conference Benefits IFC and Franchise Network

IFC	
Level 4 Business Impact isolated for effect, adjusted for profit margin, and annualized	$ 50,688.09
Registration fees	55,000.00
Contribution from franchise promotional fund	32,000.00
TOTAL	**$137,688.09**
Franchise Network	
Level 4 Business Impact isolated for effect, adjusted for profit margin, and annualized	$233,945.02
TOTAL	**$233,945.02**

Calculating the net benefit is now a simple matter of subtracting the fully-loaded costs from the total benefits discussed above.

For IFC

$$\text{ROI (\%)} = \frac{\$137,688.09 - 295,625.00}{\$295,625.00} \times 100 = -53\%$$

For The Franchise Network

$$\text{ROI (\%)} = \frac{\$233,945.02 - 510,202.80}{\$510,202.80} \times 100 = -54\%$$

Not surprisingly, the calculation resulted in a negative evaluation for both groups. Lack of response at Level 4 created a data gap that negatively impacted the results of this study. To maintain the highest possible level of credibility, the Phillips ROI Methodology takes an ultra-conservative approach and mandates an assumption of zero business impact for all non-responders. With only four franchise partners reporting positive business impact and an assumption of zero results for the other 31 franchise partners, this study was virtually assured to produce a negative ROI value. Indeed, given the available data, no other conclusion can be confidently and credibly drawn.

Other Scenarios

While the amount of Level 4 data collected was small, the numbers were significant enough to suggest that it might be an interesting exercise to use the data collected to *speculate* about other potential outcomes, generating "what-if" scenarios. For instance, because of the low response rate to the Level 4 questionnaire, we only considered a total business improvement of $1,495,326.13 for the study. And yet, we know from IFC corporate records that the aggregate franchise business improvement in sales between the two periods from March 1, 2004 through September 1, 2004 and March 1, 2005 through September 1, 2005 was actually $2,305,000 business improvement in sales figures. That data alone is enough to create a positive ROI for the Franchise Network.

As in the earlier ROI calculation, the business improvement of $2,305,000 first needs to be isolated for effect, then downwardly adjusted by a margin rate of 60%, and finally multiplied by two to annualize the results. Using a conservative isolation factor assumption of 20% (meaning that 20% of the business improvement was due to the application of knowledge and skills gained at the conference), the Franchise Network realizes a positive ROI of 8%. If we increase the isolation factor to 25% (the highest rate mentioned by any of the respondents to the Level 4 questionnaire), the Franchise Network realizes a positive ROI of 35.5%.

Because IFC's profit margin is considerably lower than the franchise profit margin, it would appear that a 50% isolation factor would have to apply before IFC could break even. But there are other factors to consider. Remember that the ROI Methodology uses only first-year benefits because the intervention (the meeting) is of a short-term nature. However, the sales contracts that franchises negotiate are almost always long-term, multi-year affairs. Making the conservative assumption that the contracts are for a two-year period would mean the ROI calculation for IFC must include two years of benefits and not just an annual benefit. With this change in the calculation, IFC breaks even at a conservative isolation factor of 17.5% and shows a positive 11% ROI at an isolation factor of 20%. Higher isolation rates (unlikely) or longer term contracts (very likely) would push the ROI even higher.

Finally, it must also be remembered that due to a lack of franchise record-keeping, the study abandoned its original intent to evaluate the impact of the conference on pipeline activity and sales cycle. Had these measures been included in the business impact data collection as planned, the resulting ROI might have been higher.

Intangibles

The same follow-up questionnaire used to collect data for Level 4 business impacts was also designed to gather information regarding intangible values associated with the conference. The low response rate to that questionnaire again made it difficult to draw firm conclusions from the data. Nonetheless, it is interesting to consider the responses offered. Table 12 summarizes the results from the seven respondents when asked about the influence of the conference on intangibles.

Table 12. Intangibles

	Mean Score	Agree	Disagree
To what extent did the conference also influence			
• Employee morale	3.00	57.14%	28.57%
• Enhancement of job skills	2.86	42.85%	42.86%
• Job satisfaction	2.57	28.57%	42.86%
• Customer satisfaction	2.71	28.57%	28.57%
• Operational efficiencies	2.28	0.00%	42.86%
• Time savings	2.00	28.57%	71.43%
• Cost savings	1.57	0.00%	71.43%

Lessons Learned

In hindsight, the conference planning team and the evaluation team both could have benefited from soliciting additional input from the franchise network during the planning stages. Input from the network most likely would have revealed that most franchises were not collecting data on pipeline activity and sales cycle. Network input certainly would have revealed that most franchises would not have sufficient impact data to share at six months.

Recommendations and Use of Results

Interestingly, this impact study influenced the conference before any attendee completed a questionnaire and before any results were tabulated. The process of working through evaluation planning, including the work of setting measurable objectives, resulted in direct changes to the conference format and content during the design and planning stages: all *before* the conference actually took place.

While the study did not reach its goals of evaluating the application or the impact of knowledge learned at the conference, it generated a list of fourteen supportable conclusions and eight recommendations for management to consider. Most of the recommendations were implemented in the design and format of the conference in the following year. Recommendations were based largely upon the results of Level 1 and Level 2 data and primarily addressed conference format, educational content, and marketing. As a result of this study, IFC has committed to evaluate all future conferences at Levels 1 and 2 as part of a continuous improvement program.

References

Phillips, J.J. *Return on Investment in Training and Performance Improvement Programs*, 2nd Edition. (Burlington, MA: Butterworth-Heinemann, 2003).

Questions for Discussion

1. What could have been done to increase response rates to the questionnaires?
2. Discuss the role of an executive champion in a Level 5, ROI, impact study. What could the evaluation team have done to fill the gap when the champions for this study left the company?
3. Would additional input from attendees have helped improve the meeting and/or the impact study?
4. Consider the decision to develop one ROI stream for IFC and another for the franchise network? How meaningful is the latter?
5. What do you make of the author's attempt to develop "what-if" scenarios based on the limited Level 3 and Level 4 data collected? Does it impact the

credibility of the study? What value does it provide for the stakeholder groups?

About the Author

Mike Hamilton is president of Synchronicity, Inc., a creative agency specializing in meetings, trade shows, and face-to-face events. He has more than twenty-five years of industry experience, including nearly every aspect of creative production and concept development, writing, producing, staging, and especially, measurement and evaluation. Mr. Hamilton is certified by the ROI Institute in the Phillips ROI Methodology and is a well-known speaker and evangelist for evaluation in the events industry. He can be contacted by phone at 815.464.1252 or by email at mike@GetSynchronicity.com .

Editor's Notes

This case study is an excellent example of an ROI process and strategy used to evaluate a meeting from multiple ROI perspectives: the meeting organizer and the meeting attendee. It underscores the need for high response rates to data collection tools, such as questionnaires, or the resulting ROI from the meeting could be negative. The case also points out the importance of balancing the need for timely results against allowing sufficient time for meeting attendees to apply the knowledge and skills learned from the meeting and subsequent business results to occur before collecting data. The detail in the data collection plan is helpful, as is the ability to impact other scenarios on ROI.

Chapter 9
Intangible Benefits

The results of meetings and events include both tangible and intangible measures. Intangible measures are the benefits (or detriments) directly linked to a meeting that cannot or should not be converted to monetary values. By definition, from the guiding principles of the ROI Methodology, an intangible benefit is a measure that is purposely not converted to money (i.e., if a conversion cannot be accomplished with minimum resources and with credibility, it is left as an intangible). Table 9-1 lists common examples of these measures. Some measures make the list because of the difficulty in measuring them; others because of the difficulty in converting them to money. Others are on the list for both reasons.

Table 9-1. Common Intangibles

• Accountability	• Intellectual Capital
• Alliances	• Innovation and Creativity
• Attention	• Job Satisfaction
• Awards	• Leadership
• Branding	• Loyalty
• Capability	• Networking
• Capacity	• Organizational Commitment
• Clarity	• Partnering
• Communication	• Poverty
• Corporate Social Responsibility	• Reputation
• Employee Attitudes	• Stress
• Customer Service (Customer Satisfaction)	• Team Effectiveness
• Engagement	• Timeliness
• Human Life	• Sustainability
• Image	• Work/Life Balance

Wearing the intangible label does not mean these items cannot be measured or converted to monetary values. In one study or another, each item has been monitored successfully and monetarily quantified. However, in a typical meeting evaluation, these variables are considered intangible benefits because of the difficulty in measuring the variable or the difficulty in converting the data to monetary values.

While the concept is not new, intangibles are becoming increasingly important. Intangibles drive funding, they drive the economy, and organizations are built on them. In every direction, we see that intangibles are not only increasingly important, but critical to organizations.

The good news to report in this chapter, building on Chapter 8, is that more data previously regarded as intangible, are now converted to monetary values. Because of this, classic intangibles are now accepted as tangible measures, and their value is more easily understood. Consider, for example, customer satisfaction. Just a decade ago, few organizations had a clue as to the monetary value of customer satisfaction. Now, more firms have taken the extra step to link customer satisfaction directly to revenues, profits, and other measures. Companies are clearly seeing the tremendous value that can be derived from intangibles. As this chapter will illustrate, more data is being accumulated to show the monetary value, moving some intangible measures into the tangible category.

Some meetings and events are implemented because of the intangibles. For example, the need to have greater collaboration, partnering, communication, teamwork, or customer service will drive meetings and events. In the public sector, meetings are driven by the need to reduce poverty, to employ disadvantaged citizens, and to save lives. From the outset, the intangibles are the important drivers and become the most important measures.

Measuring the Intangibles

Although intangibles may not be perceived as high in value as tangible measures, they are critical to the overall evaluation process. In some meetings, intangibles are more important than monetary measures. Therefore, these measures should be monitored and reported as part of the ROI evaluation. In practice, every meeting, regardless of its nature, scope, and content, will produce intangible measures. The challenge is to identify them effectively and report them appropriately.

Often, we explore the issue of measuring the difficult to measure. Responses to this exploration usually occur in the form of comments instead of questions. "You cannot measure it," is a typical response. We disagree. We think anything can be measured. What the frustrated observer suggests is that it is not something you can count, examine, and see in quantities, such as items produced. In reality, a quantitative value can be assigned or developed for any intangible. If it exists, it can be measured.

Several approaches are available for measuring intangibles. Some typical intangibles can be counted such as an employee complaint. Unfortunately, most intangibles are based on attitudes and perceptions and must be measured in some way. One approach is to list the intangible measure and have the participants indicate the extent to which the meeting has influenced the measure, using a five-point scale. Table 9-2 lists six intangible items from a national sales meeting. The respon-

Table 9-2. An Example of Measuring Intangibles

Indicate the extent to which you think your application of the information, knowledge, skills, and contacts learned in the meeting had a positive influence on the following business measures.
Please check the appropriate response beside each measure.

Business Measure	Not Applicable	Applies But No Influence	Some Influence	Moderate Influence	Significant Influence	Very Significant Influence
Customer satisfaction	☐	☐	☐	☐	☐	☐
Stress	☐	☐	☐	☐	☐	☐
Communication	☐	☐	☐	☐	☐	☐
Brand awareness	☐	☐	☐	☐	☐	☐
Response time	☐	☐	☐	☐	☐	☐
Teamwork	☐	☐	☐	☐	☐	☐

dent is asked to indicate the meeting's influence on each measure. Scales can be created in many ingenious ways. When repeated, used, refined, and modified, these often become industry standards.

Another approach to measuring the intangible is to connect it to a tangible, which is easier to value. This was described in the previous chapter. As shown in Figure 9-1, most hard-to-value measures are linked to an easy-to-value measure. Although this link can be developed through logical deductions and conclusions, having empirical evidence through a correlation analysis is the best approach. However, a detailed analysis would have to be conducted to ensure that a causal relationship exists. Just because a correlation is apparent does not mean that one caused the other. Additional analysis and supporting data could pinpoint the actual causal effect.

Figure 9-1. The Link Between Hard-to-Value and Easy-to-Value Items

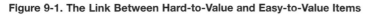

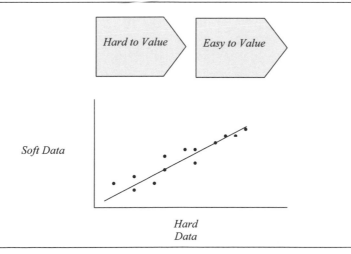

Through the difficulties of measuring intangibles, remembering that these are usually combined with a variety of tangibles to reflect performance is helpful. Also, intangibles are often associated with non-profit, non-government, or public sector organizations.

Converting to Money

Converting hard-to-value measures to money is challenging, to say the least. There are examples of this in many other books. (Phillips and Phillips, 2007) The interest in the monetary contribution is expanding. The client who often funds or supports a particular meeting sometimes seeks monetary values, among other measures. "Show me the money!" is a familiar request from many stakeholders.

The approaches of conversion to monetary value were detailed in Chapter 8. The specific methods used represent approaches that may be used to convert intangibles to monetary values. These will not be repeated here. However, showing the path most commonly used to capture values for intangibles is helpful. Figure 9-2 shows the typical approach of converting intangibles to monetary values.

Figure 9-2. Converting to Money

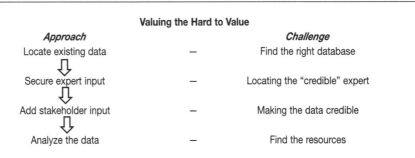

The first issue is to locate the data or to measure it in some way, making sure that it is accurate, reliable, and reflects the concept. Next, an expert may be able to place a monetary value on the item based on experience, knowledge, credentials, and previous track record. Stakeholders may provide their input, although the input should be factored for bias. Some stakeholders are biased in one way or the other—they want the value to be smaller or larger, depending on their particular motives. These may have to be adjusted or thrown out all together, based on the biased approaches. Finally, the data are analyzed using the conservative processes described in Chapter 8, often adjusting for the error in the process. If the conversion cannot be accomplished with minimum resources and with credibility, it is left as an intangible.

Identifying Intangibles

Intangible measures can be taken from different sources and at different times in the meeting lifecycle, as depicted in Figure 9-3. They can be uncovered early in the process, during the initial discussion of the need for the meeting. For example, employee satisfaction, an intangible measure, is identified as a measure that will be influenced by the meeting. It will be monitored with no plans to convert it to a monetary value. From the beginning, this measure is destined to be a non-monetary, intangible benefit reported along with the ROI results.

Figure 9-3. Identifying Intangible Measures During the Meeting Lifecycle

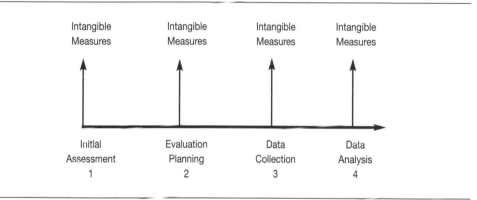

A second opportunity to identify intangible benefits is in the planning process, when the evaluation plan is developed. The planning team can usually identify the intangible measures expected to be influenced by the meeting. For example, a team-building meeting in a large multinational company was planned, and an ROI analysis was desired. The meeting planner and other staff members identified potential intangible measures that were perceived to be influenced by the meeting, including collaboration, communication, and teamwork.

A third opportunity to identify intangible measures presents itself during data collection. Although the measure is not anticipated in the initial meeting design, it may surface on a questionnaire, in an interview, or during a focus group. Questions are often asked about other improvements linked to the meeting, and participants frequently provide several intangible measures for which no plans are available to assign a value. For example, in the evaluation of a customer service meeting, participants were asked what specifically had improved about their work area and relationships with customers as a result of the meeting. Participants provided more than a dozen intangible measures attributed to the meeting.

During data analysis and reporting, the fourth opportunity to identify intangible measures occurs when attempting to convert data to monetary values. If the conversion loses credibility, the measure should be reported as an intangible benefit. For example, in a sales training meeting, customer satisfaction was identified early in the process as a measure of the meeting's success. A conversion to monetary values was attempted, but lacked accuracy and credibility. Therefore, customer satisfaction was reported as an intangible benefit.

Analyzing Intangibles

For each intangible measure identified, some evidence of its connection to the meeting must be shown. However, in many cases, no specific analysis is planned beyond tabulating responses. Early attempts to quantify intangible data sometimes results in aborting the entire process, and no further data analysis is conducted. In some cases, isolating the effects of the meeting may be undertaken using one or more of the methods outlined in Chapter 7. This step is necessary when clients need to know the specific amount of change that has occurred in the intangible measure as a result of the meeting. In most situations, however, the direct link to the meeting can be obtained by asking a specific question, "To what extent has this meeting influenced this measure?" A five-point scale could be used for responses.

Intangible data often reflect improvement. However, neither the precise amount of improvement nor the amount of improvement directly related to a meeting is usually necessary. Since the value of this data is not included in the ROI calculation, intangible measures are not normally used to justify the continuation of an existing meeting. A detailed analysis is not required. Intangible benefits are often viewed as additional evidence of the meeting's success and are presented as supportive, qualitative data.

Final Thoughts

Get the picture? Intangible measures are crucial to reflecting the success of a meeting or event. While they may not carry the weight of measures expressed in monetary terms, they are nevertheless an important part of the overall evaluation. Intangible measures should be identified, explored, examined, and monitored for changes linked to meetings. Collectively, they add a unique dimension to the evaluation report since most, if not all, meetings involve intangible variables.

Notes

Phillips, J. J. and P. P. Phillips. *Show Me the Money* (San Francisco, CA: Berrett-Koehler, 2007).

Chapter 10
Reporting Results

With results in hand, what's next? Should the results be used to improve the meeting, change the design, show the contribution, justify new meetings, gain additional support, or build goodwill? How should the data be presented? The worst course of action is to do nothing. Communicating results is as important as achieving results. This chapter provides useful information to help present evaluation data to the various audiences using both oral and written reporting methods.

Key Issues about Communicating Results

Communicating results is critical to the accountability of meetings and events. Evaluation data means nothing unless the findings are communicated promptly to the appropriate audiences so they will be aware of the results and can take action. Here are a few important reasons why communication is necessary:

1. Communication is necessary to make improvements in meetings and events.
2. Communication is necessary to explain contributions of meetings and events.
3. Communication is a politically sensitive issue.
4. Different audiences need different information.
5. Communication must be timely.
6. Communication should be targeted to specific audiences.
7. Media should be carefully selected and tailored to the audience.
8. Communication should be unbiased and modest.
9. Communication must be consistent—representing both positive and negative information.
10. Testimonials are more effective coming from respected individuals.
11. The audience's opinion of the meeting will influence the communication strategy.

These general principles are important to the overall success of the communication effort. They should serve as a checklist for the meeting planner when disseminating results. The process of communicating results must be systematic, timely, well-planned, and represent the components occurring in the sequence shown in

Figure 10-1. These steps are briefly described here.

Figure 10-1. Communication Model

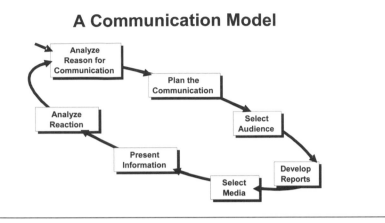

A Communication Model

The Reasons for Communication

The reasons for communicating results depend on the specific meeting, the setting, and the unique needs. Some of the most common are:

- Securing approval for the meeting and allocating resources of time and money.
- Gaining support for the meeting and its objectives.
- Securing agreement on the issues, solutions, and resources.
- Building credibility for the meeting planning team.
- Reinforcing the need for the content in the meeting.
- Driving action for the improvement of the meeting.
- Preparing participants to provide data for the evaluation.
- Showing the complete results of the meeting.
- Underscoring the importance of measuring results.
- Explaining the techniques used to measure results.
- Motivating prospective participants to be involved in the meeting.
- Demonstrating accountability for expenditures.
- Marketing future meetings and events.

Because there may be other reasons for communicating results, the list should be tailored to each meeting.

Plan the Communications

Any successful activity must be carefully planned to produce the maximum results. This is a critical part of communicating the results. Communications planning is important to ensure that each audience receives the proper information at the right time and that appropriate actions are taken. Several issues are important when planning the communication of results:

- What will be communicated?
- When will the data be communicated?
- How will the information be communicated?
- Where will the information be communicated?
- Who will communicate the information?
- Who is the target audience?
- What are the specific actions required or desired?

When an evaluation plan is approved, the simple communication plan is usually developed. This should detail how specific information is developed and communicated to various groups and the expected actions. In addition, this plan details the timeframes for communication, and the appropriate groups to receive the information. The planner, key clients, and stakeholders need to agree on the extent of detail in the plan. To communicate appropriately with target audiences, four specific documents are usually produced when the evaluation is taken to the impact and ROI levels. The first report is an impact study showing the approach, assumptions, methodology, and results using all seven data categories. In addition, barriers and enablers are included in the study, along with conclusions and recommendations. The second report should be a five-to-eight page executive summary of the key points. The third report is a one-page overview of the results for those individuals who understand this method. The fourth report is a brief, two-page narrative of the process and results written as a story. These documents should be presented to the different groups based on their needs. A suggested approach is:

Audience	Document
Participants	Brief narrative
Managers of participants (optional)	Brief narrative
Senior executives	Complete study, executive summary, one page summary
Meeting and events staff	Complete study, one page summary
Client	Complete study, executive summary, one page summary

Key stakeholders who understand the methodology	One page summary
Prospective participants	Brief narrative

If this is the first ROI study conducted with a client, a face-to-face meeting should be administered with key executives. The purpose is to ensure that executives understand the methodology, the conservative assumptions, and each level of data. The barriers, enablers, conclusions, and recommendations are an important part of the meeting. Later, after two or three studies have been conducted, this group will receive only a one-page summary of key data items. A similar meeting should be conducted with the meetings and events staff, where the complete impact study is described and used as a learning tool.

The Audience for Communications

When approaching a particular audience, the following questions should be asked about each potential group:
- Are they interested in the meeting?
- Do they really want to receive the information?
- Has a commitment to include them in the communications been made?
- Is the timing right for this audience?
- Are they familiar with the meeting?
- How do they prefer to have results communicated?
- Do they know the meeting planner? The meetings and events staff?
- Are they likely to find the results threatening?
- Which medium will be most convincing to this group?

For each target audience, three actions are needed. To the greatest extent possible, the meeting planner should know and understand the target audience. Also, the planner should find out what information is needed, and why. Each group may be different. Some want detailed information, while others prefer a brief report. Finally, the meeting planner should try to understand audience bias. Some audiences will quickly support the results, whereas others may not support them. Most will be neutral. The team should be empathetic and try to understand differing views.

The potential target audiences to receive information about meeting results are varied in terms of job levels and responsibilities. Determining which groups will receive a particular piece of communication deserves careful thought, as problems can arise when one group receives inappropriate information or when another is omitted altogether. A sound basis for proper audience selection is to analyze the reason for the communication, as discussed earlier. Table 10-1 shows common target audiences and the basis for selecting each one.

Table 10-1. Common Target Audiences

Reason for Communication	Primary Target Audiences
To secure approval for the results	Top executives
To gain support for the meeting	Client, managers, team leaders
To secure agreement with the issues	Participants, meeting and events team
To build credibility for the meeting and events team	Top executives
To drive action for improvement	Meetings and events team
To prepare participants for the meeting	Participants
To enhance results and quality of future feedback	Participants
To show the complete results of the meeting	All stakeholders, client
To underscore the importance of measuring results	Client, meetings and events team
To explain techniques used to measure results	Client, meetings and events team
To create desire for a participant to be involved	Prospective participants
To demonstrate accountability for expenditures	Top executives
To market meetings and events	Prospective clients, executives, participants

Information Development

The type of evaluation report depends on the extent of detailed information presented to the various target audiences. Brief summaries of results with appropriate charts may be sufficient for some communication efforts. In other situations, particularly with significant meetings requiring extensive funding, the amount of detail in the evaluation report is more crucial. A complete and comprehensive impact study report may be necessary. This report can then be used as the basis of more streamlined information for specific audiences and various media. The report may contain the sections detailed in Table 10-2.

Table 10-2. Format of an Impact Study Report

- General Information
  - Background
  - Objectives of study
- Methodology for Impact Study
  - Levels of evaluation
  - ROI process
  - Collecting data
  - Isolating the effects of the meeting
  - Converting data to monetary values
- Data Analysis Issues
- Results: General Information
  - Response profile
  - Success with objectives
- Results: Reaction and Perceived Value
  - Data sources
  - Data summary
  - Key issues
- Results: Learning
  - Data sources
  - Data summary
  - Key issues
- Results: Application and Implementation
  - Data sources
  - Data summary
  - Key issues
- Results: Impact and consequences
  - General comments
  - Linkage with business measures
  - Key issues
- Cost of Meeting
- Results: ROI and Its Meaning
- Barriers and Enablers
  - Barriers
  - Enablers
- Conclusions and Recommendations
  - Conclusions
  - Recommendations
- Exhibits

While this report is an effective, professional way to present ROI data, several cautions need to be followed. Since this document reports the success of a meeting involving a group of participants, complete credit for the success must go to the participants (and sometimes their immediate leaders). Their performance generated the success. Another important caution is to avoid boasting about results.

Huge claims of success can quickly turn off an audience and interfere with the delivery of the desired message.

The methodology should be clearly explained, along with assumptions made in the analysis. The audience should easily see how the values were developed and how the specific steps were followed to make the process more conservative, credible, and accurate. Detailed statistical analyses should be placed in the appendix.

Communication Media Selection

Many options are available to communicate meeting results. In addition to the impact study report, the most frequently used media are meetings, interim and progress reports, a variety of publications, and case studies. Table 10-3 shows the variety of options.

Table 10-3. A Variety of Options for Communicating Results

Meetings	Detailed Reports	Brief Reports	Electronic Reporting	Mass Publications
Executives	Impact study	Executive summary	Web site	Announcements
Managers	Case study (internal)	Slide overview	E-mail	Bulletins
Stakeholders	Case study (external)	One-page summary	Blogs	Newsletters
Meeting and Events Team	Major articles	Brochure	Video	Brief articles

If used properly, meetings are fertile opportunities for communicating results. All organizations have a variety of meetings, and some may provide the proper context for reporting meeting results. Regular meetings with management groups are common. A discussion of a meeting and event and the subsequent results can be integrated into the regular meeting format. A few organizations have initiated periodic meetings for all key stakeholders, in which the meeting planner reviews progress and discusses the next steps. A few highlights of the meeting results can be helpful to build interest, commitment, and support for the continuation of the meeting.

To reach a wide audience, the meeting planner can use internal, routine publications. Whether a newsletter, magazine, newspaper, or electronic file, these types of media usually reach all employees or stakeholders. The information can be effective if communicated appropriately. The scope should be limited to general interest articles, announcements, and interviews. For most meetings, results are achieved weeks or even months after the meeting is conducted. Participants need reinforcement from many sources. If results are communicated to a general audience, additional pressure may exist to continue the meeting or similar ones in the future.

Internal and external Web pages on the Internet, company-wide intranets, and e-mail are excellent vehicles for releasing results, promoting ideas, and informing participants and other target groups. E-mail, in particular, provides a virtually instantaneous means with which to communicate and solicit responses from large numbers of people. For major meeting evaluation, some organizations create blogs to present results and secure reaction, feedback, and suggestions.

A brochure might be appropriate for meetings conducted on a continuing basis, where participants have produced excellent results. Also, a brochure may be appropriate when the audience is large and continuously changing. The brochure should be attractive and present a complete description of the meeting, with a major section devoted to the results obtained with previous participants, if available. Measurable results and reactions from participants, or even direct quotes from individuals, could add spice to an otherwise dull brochure.

Case studies represent an effective way to communicate the results of a meeting. A typical case study describes the situation, provides appropriate background information (including the events that led to the meeting), presents the techniques and strategies used to develop the study, and highlights the key issues in the evaluation. Case studies tell an interesting story of how the meeting was conducted and how the evaluation was developed, including the problems and concerns identified along the way.

Case studies have value for both internal and external use. As shown in Table 10-4, the internal use is to build understanding, capability and support. Case studies are impressive to hand to a potential client and convincing for others who are seeking data about the success of meetings and events. Externally, case studies can be used to bring exposure and recognition to the meetings and events team and help the organization brand its overall meetings and events function. Professionals in this industry are eager to read actual studies. A variety of publication outlets are available for case studies—not only in meetings and events publications, but also in general publications.

Table 10-4. Internal and External Use of Case Studies

Case Study Internal Use	Case Study External Publication
Communicate results	Provide recognition to participants
Teach others	Improve image of function
Build a history	Enhance brand of function
Serve as a template	Enhance image of organization
Make an impression	

The Presentation of Results to Senior Management

Perhaps one of the most challenging and stressful communications is presenting an impact study to the senior management team, who funded the meeting or study. The challenge is convincing this highly skeptical and critical group that outstanding results have been achieved (assuming they have) in a reasonable timeframe, addressing the salient points, and making sure they understand the process. Two particular issues can create challenges. First, if the results are impressive, it may be difficult to convince the executives about the validity of the data. On the other extreme, if the data are negative, it may be challenging to ensure that executives do not overreact and look for someone to blame. Several guidelines can help ensure that this process is planned and executed properly.

Plan a face-to-face meeting with senior team members unfamiliar with the ROI Methodology for the first one or two major impact studies. The good news is they will probably attend the meeting because they have not seen ROI data developed for this type of meeting and may be skeptical. The bad news is that it takes a lot of time, usually one hour, for this presentation. After a group has had a face-to-face meeting with a couple of presentations, an executive one-page summary may suffice. At this point, they understand the process, so a shortened version may be appropriate. After the target audience is familiar with the process, a brief version may be necessary, which will involve a one- to two-page summary with charts and graphs showing the six types of measures.

When making the initial presentation, the results should not be distributed prior to, or even during, the presentation. It should be saved until the end of the session. This allows enough time to present the process and results and for the audience to react to them before they see the ROI calculation. Present the ROI Methodology step by step, showing how the data were collected, when they were collected, who provided the data, how the effect of the meeting was isolated from other influences, and how data were converted to monetary values. The various assumptions, adjustments, and conservative approaches are presented along with the total cost of the meeting so that the target audience will begin to buy into the process of developing the ROI.

When the data are actually presented, the results are shown one level at a time, starting with Level 0, moving through Level 5, and ending with the intangibles. This allows the audience to see the inputs and indicators, reaction, learning, application and implementation, business impact, and ROI. After some discussion on the meaning of the ROI, the intangible measures are presented. Allocate time for each level as appropriate for the audience. This helps overcome the potentially emotional reactions to a particularly positive or negative ROI.

Collectively, these steps will help prepare for and present one of the most critical meetings in the ROI process. Figure 10-2 shows the approach to this important meeting with the client and senior executives. Improving communications with this group requires developing an overall strategy and a defined purpose.

Figure 10-2. Presenting the Impact Study to Executive Sponsors

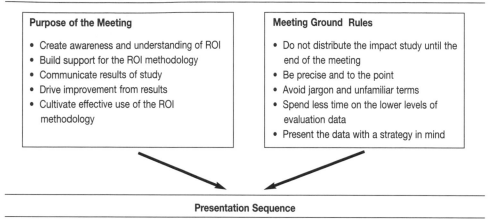

Purpose of the Meeting

- Create awareness and understanding of ROI
- Build support for the ROI methodology
- Communicate results of study
- Drive improvement from results
- Cultivate effective use of the ROI methodology

Meeting Ground Rules

- Do not distribute the impact study until the end of the meeting
- Be precise and to the point
- Avoid jargon and unfamiliar terms
- Spend less time on the lower levels of evaluation data
- Present the data with a strategy in mind

Presentation Sequence

1. Describe the meeting and explain why it is being evaluated
2. Present the methodology process
3. Present the input and indicators
4. Present the reaction and learning data
5. Present the application data
6. List the barriers and enablers to success
7. Present the business impact
8. Show the costs
9. Present the ROI
10. Show the intangibles
11. Review the credibility of the data
12. Summarize the conclusions
13. Present the recommendations

Reactions to Communication

The best indicator of how effectively the results of a meeting have been communicated is the level of commitment and support from clients, executives, and sponsors. The allocation of requested resources and strong commitment from top management are tangible evidence of management's positive perception of the meeting results. In addition to this reaction, a few techniques can measure the effectiveness of the communication efforts.

Whenever results are communicated, the reaction of the target audiences can be monitored. These reactions may include non-verbal gestures, oral remarks, written comments, or indirect actions that reveal how the communication was received. Usually, when results are presented in a meeting, the presenter will have some indication of how the results were received by the group. The interest and attitudes of the audience can usually be quickly evaluated. Comments about the results—formal or informal—should also be noted and tabulated.

Final Thoughts

Communication of results is the final step in the evaluation of meetings and events. This is a crucial step in the overall evaluation process. If this step is not taken seriously, the full impact of the results will not be realized and the study may be a waste of time. The chapter began with general principles and steps for communicating results, which can serve as a guide for any significant communication effort. The various target audiences were discussed and, because of its importance, emphasis was placed on the executive group. A suggested format for a detailed evaluation report was also provided. Much of the chapter included a presentation of the most commonly used media for communicating results, including meetings, client publications, and electronic media.

Special Offer from The ROI Institute

Space limitation allows only a small number of case studies to be published in this book. However, additional cases are available to download at www.roiinstiute.net under the meetings and events tab.

Also, the ROI Process Model, an indispensable tool for implementing and presenting ROI in your organization, is available at no charge. This 11"x 25" multicolor foldout shows the ROI Methodology flow model and the key issues surrounding the implementation of the ROI Methodology. This easy to understand overview of the ROI process has proven invaluable to countless professionals when implementing the ROI Methodology. Please return this page or email your information to the address below to receive your free foldout (a $6.00 value). Please check your areas of interest in ROI.

Please send me the ROI Process Model described in the book. I am interested in learning more about the following ROI materials and services:

☐ Workshops and briefing on ROI   ☐ Books and support materials on ROI
☐ Certification in the ROI Methodology   ☐ ROI software
☐ ROI consulting services   ☐ ROI Network information
☐ ROI benchmarking   ☐ ROI research

Name _____

Title _____

Organization _____

Address _____

_____

Phone _____

E-mail Address _____

Functional area of interest:

☐ Corporate Meeting   ☐ Government Meeting   ☐ Meeting Management
   Professional   Professional   Professional
☐ Association/Non-Profit   ☐ Supplier Meeting   ☐ Other (Please specify)
   Meeting Professional   Professional

Return this form to: The ROI Institute
                        P.O. Box 380637
                        Birmingham, AL 35238-0637
Or e-mail information to info@roiinstitute.net
Please allow four to six weeks for delivery.